THE 1%

Conquer Your Consulting Case Interview

Unlock the secrets behind modern case and fit interviews and join the one percent that breaks into McKinsey, BCG, Bain, and other top firms

DR. FLORIAN SMERITSCHNIG

Written by a former McKinsey consultant and interview expert who conducted more than 1,000 consulting interviews with the best track record in the industry

**Strategy
Case.com**

Table of Contents

Acknowledgments ix
About the author ix

PART 1   INTRODUCTION:
MAXIMIZE THE VALUE OF THIS BOOK 1

[1]   Is this book for you? 3
      My mission and goal for you 3
      What this book covers (and what it doesn't cover) 5
      Who is this book for? 7

[2]   Extract the most value 8
      How to work with this book 8
      How the book is structured 8

PART 2   INTRODUCTION TO CONSULTING INTERVIEWS:
FIGURE OUT WHAT YOU ARE UP AGAINST 9

[3]   Learn about the process and differences 12
      How is the consulting interview process structured? 12
      How has interviewing changed since the COVID-19 pandemic? 16
      What are the differences across firms? 17
      What are the differences across roles? 19

[4]   Set up a preparation plan 22
      How to think about structuring your preparation 22
      What is the best interview preparation plan? 24

PART 3   INTRODUCTION TO CASE INTERVIEWS:
WHAT'S THIS SPECIFIC INTERVIEW FORMAT ALL ABOUT? . .33

[5]   Get the basics on the setup, the skills, and the scoring 35
      What is a case interview? 35
      What skills are assessed in a case interview? 37
      How is a case interview scored? 43
      What is the role of professional interviewers and how do they behave? 44

[6]   Learn about the different formats of case interviews 47
      What types of case interviews are there? 47
      Who drives the case interview (candidate or interviewer)? 50
      What is the difference between a first and final round (partner) case interview? . 53

PART 4 THE PARTS OF A CASE INTERVIEW: DEVELOP YOUR BASIC CASE INTERVIEW SKILLS 57

[7] Learn how to deal with the case brief 59

[8] Draft the perfect frameworks, issue trees, and brainstorming answers 62
What is a framework in a case interview? 63
Why do you need to structure your approach? 64
Are there different types of frameworks? 65
What characterizes a strong case interview framework? 68
Should you learn case interview frameworks by heart? 73
How can a first principles approach help you create frameworks and not get
stuck? 74
How to create a strong framework: example 85
How to create a strong brainstorming answer: example 86
What is the best step-by-step approach for structuring and brainstorming? . . . 88
How can you train your structuring skills? 90

[9] Interpret exhibits the right way 91
What is the role of charts and data tables in consulting case interviews? 91
What types of charts are common in case interviews? 92
What are data tables and how are they used in case interviews? 100
How do you interpret exhibits in case interviews with a step-by-step approach? 101
What are the typical insights in an exhibit? 103
How to solve a typical exhibit interpretation: example 105
How can you avoid common pitfalls in exhibit interpretations? 108
How can you train exhibit interpretation? 109

[10] Ace all case interview math problems 111
Why do candidates struggle with consulting math? 111
What is the purpose of case interview math? 112
How should you approach case math questions with a tested step-by-step
approach? 113
What should you do when you get stuck on the approach? 118
How to solve a typical case math problem: example 119
What are typical math problems and key formulas? 121
What are the important math concepts and the most common shortcuts? . . . 126
What comprises a winning case math mindset? 135
How can you train your case math skills? 144

[11] Deliver the perfect recommendations 146
Why do you need to think about a recommendation? 146
How can you set up the perfect top-down recommendation? 146

PART 5 BRINGING IT ALL TOGETHER: BECOME AN EFFECTIVE PROBLEM SOLVER 149

[12] Develop a hypothesis-driven mindset to move through the case 151
How can hypotheses and synthesizing help you move through a case? 151
What should you do if you get stuck and don't know how to move forward? . 159

[13] Communicate like a management consultant 162
What features characterize the perfect case communication? 162
Why and how should you overcommunicate? 163
What are the key communication phrases for each part of the case? 164

[14] **Develop the right meta habits** **171**
How much time should you take to think and solve the case? 171
How should you write your case interview notes? 174
How can you avoid and recover from mistakes? 176

PART 6   UNIQUE CASE FORMATS: HOW TO ACE INTERVIEWER-LED
AND WRITTEN CASE INTERVIEWS **179**

[15] **Ace written case interviews** **181**
What is a written case interview? 181
How do you approach a written case interview? 181

[16] **Ace the McKinsey Problem Solving Interview** **186**
What is the McKinsey Problem Solving Interview? 186
What skills are assessed by McKinsey? 187
What is the format of the McKinsey case? 188
What are the standardized McKinsey case interview questions? 189
How should you prepare for a McKinsey case interview? 193

PART 7   REAL CASE EXAMPLES:
WORK ON YOUR FIRST FULL CASES **195**

[17] **Candidate-led case: Public Sector Education** **197**

[18] **Interviewer-led (McKinsey) case: Public Sector Education** **210**

PART 8   KILLER PREPARATION STRATEGIES:
MAXIMIZE THE IMPACT OF YOUR EFFORTS **221**

[19] **Employ the most effective preparation strategies** **223**
Why should you stay away from memorizing case interview frameworks? . . 223
How can you practice alone? 224
How can you practice with peers? 229
Should you hire a case coach and how can you work with a coach? 232
How should you measure your progress with case preparation notes? 236

[20] **Learn these business and problem-solving concepts** **238**
What are simple business definitions that you need to know? 238
What are more advanced business concepts and analytical tools? 244

PART 9   INTRODUCTION TO FIT INTERVIEWS:
BECOME A WELL-ROUNDED CANDIDATE **253**

[21] **Understand the importance of the personal fit** **255**

[22] **Understand what you need to demonstrate in a personal fit interview** **256**
What is the airport test? 256
What is the skills and development potential test? 256
What is the client-readiness check? 257

PART 10 TYPES OF FIT INTERVIEW QUESTIONS: PREPARE THE MOST IMPACTFUL ANSWERS. 259

[23] Do not fumble the introduction (icebreakers). 261

[24] Know your resume 262
How can you introduce yourself and your resume? 262
What are some more specific resume questions and how
can you answer them? 263

[25] Make sure that you "fit" 265
How can you demonstrate your cultural fit? 265
How should you answer more specific fit questions? 268

[26] Demonstrate your skills, industry, or functional expertise 274
What are general consulting skills questions?. 274
What are IT-related questions?. 275
What are industry and functional knowledge questions? 276
What are technical questions?. 276
What is the McKinsey Technical Experience Interview?. 277

[27] Tell personal stories 279
What are personal stories that matter?. 280
What are the characteristics of a good story?. 286

[28] Ask the interviewer the right questions at the end 288
Why should you make the most of this opportunity? 288
What questions could you ask the interviewer? 289

PART 11 STORYTELLING WITH THE SCORE FRAMEWORK: GIVE YOUR MOST IMPACTFUL ANSWERS 291

[29] Tease your story with a brief summary 293

[30] Dive into your story using the SCORE framework. 294

PART 12 THE MCKINSEY PERSONAL EXPERIENCE INTERVIEW: PREPARE DEEP AND IMPACTFUL STORIES. 299

[31] Understand how McKinsey employs the PEI 301

[32] Tell the perfect stories. 303
What are the right stories for the PEI? 303
What makes a PEI story stand out? 306
How should you select your own personal stories? 308
How detailed should your stories be? 308
Should you create stories that can be used for every dimension? 309

[33] Set up and communicate your stories the right way 310
How should you introduce your PEI story? 310
How should you discuss your story in the most impactful way? 311
How should you practice your answers? 315

[34] What is the McKinsey values and purpose interview?. 317

PART 13 HABITS, MINDSET, AND APPEARANCE:
WIN THE GAME BEFORE YOU GET THERE 319

[35] Work on the right mindset 321
     What are the character traits of successful applicants? 321
     How can you connect with the interviewer?. 323
     How can you deal with a stress interview? 324

[36] Dress to impress 325
     How should you dress for your interviews?. 325
     What else is important for your appearance? 326
     What else should you bring for the interviews? 327

PART 14 FURTHER RESOURCES AND FINAL WORDS:
PRACTICE WHAT YOU HAVE LEARNED 329

[37] Further preparation materials. 331
     StrategyCase.com and personal coaching offering. 331
     Free practice case interview resources 332

[38] Final words and contact details. 335

Acknowledgments

I want to give my sincere gratitude to everyone who has helped me develop the ideas of this book directly and indirectly. This goes out to my mentors and colleagues at McKinsey, who shaped my perspective on problem-solving, mentorship, and personal development. My dear coachees and clients over the last couple of years: Thank you for making this such an enjoyable and fruitful endeavor of mutual learning, collaboration, and success. I hope you strive in your careers as you did in your interviews!

I also want to give credit to my clients, friends, and colleagues, who beta-read earlier versions of this book and provided valuable input and advice. The list is too long to name every one of you (and some might want to stay private), but you know who you are, and I owe you! I want to thank my editor Melissa for her input and final touches, Kateryna and Mariano, who designed this book, and Albert, who helped me with publishing.

Finally, I want to thank my loving partner Anna, who has helped me through some difficult times that coincided with working on this.

I dedicate this book to my parents Andrea and Alfred, who have always shown unwavering support for everything I do.

About the author

Florian was a consultant with McKinsey for five years. He holds a Doctorate Degree from the Vienna University of Economics and Business and a master's degree from the Hong Kong University of Science and Technology. Over the last two years, he has personally run more than 1,000 coaching sessions and directly coached more than 150 people to get an offer from McKinsey on top of many offers for BCG, Bain, tier-2 consulting firms, as well as boutique and in-house consulting firms. In addition, he has helped more than 10,000 applicants with consulting applications and interviews via StrategyCase.com. To learn more, see his profile on www.preplounge. com/en/profile.php?id=337437, visit StrategyCase.com, or add him on LinkedIn.

Congratulations! You are one of the first readers of this new book. To thank you for your trust and support, I would like to offer you a free gift.

The Ultimate Case Interview Industry Cheat Sheets

- ☑ Deep dive analysis on all relevant industries covered in case interviews (including more obscure and creative verticals)
- ☑ 27 up-to-date industry deep dives with information on financials, business models, key challenges, and future outlooks
- ☑ Applicable for all firms: McKinsey, BCG, Bain, tier-2 firms, boutique consulting firms, and in-house consultancies
- ☑ Become an industry insider and surprise your interviewer with your insights when creating frameworks, answering brainstorming questions, interpreting charts and math results

Please visit StrategyCase.com/The-1-Percent-Free-Gift and enter your e-mail address to get access to your gift.

PART 1

Introduction:
Maximize the Value
of This Book

[1] Is this book for you?

My mission and goal for you

"Help me to help you to make you successful."

These were the words of a McKinsey partner on my first engagement when we grabbed a coffee together.

It struck me as an elegant approach to business and life in general, highlighting how mutual collaboration and support can achieve the highest outcomes for individuals. Since then, this attitude has stuck with me during my work at McKinsey and beyond. It was my north star for creating StrategyCase.com, helping thousands of people get their dream job in top-tier consulting.

This is also the guiding principle behind this book. Here I've condensed my knowledge from 10 years of interactions within the top-tier consulting industry, living and breathing all aspects of it. I've viewed the industry from different perspectives: first as an applicant during the internship recruitment cycle with most top-tier firms, then as an intern with (AT) Kearney, later on as an applicant for full-time positions with — again — most firms, and eventually as a consultant with McKinsey and Company.

During my internship applications, I went through many interview failures and some successes. I adjusted my approach, and a year and a half later, I successfully managed to get my dream job at McKinsey and Company. There I learned what it takes to be a top-tier consultant, how to properly recruit new talent, and to develop younger colleagues as well as clients to reach their highest potential. In total, I have sat on the interviewee side through more than 65 case and personal fit interviews, both for internships as well as full-time roles.

Since I left the firm, I've worked as an independent advisor and VC as well as a consultant application and interview coach, where **I have conducted more than 1,000 coaching sessions and interviews over the last two years alone**, that is on average more than one meeting per day, including weekends. As a comparison, a typical consulting interviewer only manages around 20 to 30 interviews in their whole career.

I've developed a highly updated, focused, and global perspective on top-tier consulting recruiting and interviews and gained a unique perspective on the global consulting recruiting landscape, especially on the changes that came into effect due to the pandemic. This was achieved through interviewing and working with candidates for all firms, roles, and from more than 70 countries. In this process, I directly helped secure hundreds of offers for my clients, most notably more than 150 with McKinsey, not only the toughest consulting firm to get into but the toughest firm globally to get a job with, according to Forbes.

The people I've coached to obtain offers come from all backgrounds and walks of life, for all geographies and all kinds of positions. I've worked with interns with little work experience to graduate and post-MBA hires up to experienced professionals with more than 15 years of work experience who become direct-entry partners. My clients have ranged from regular students to Olympic athletes, members of a royal family in the Middle East, and even high-ranking U.S. political figures. I've answered thousands of questions in personal conversations, direct messages, emails, forums, and on platforms such as PrepLounge and Quora, as well as giving university lectures on different topics related to consulting applications and interviews. I know both what is needed to get into consulting firms and what is on applicants' minds when they start their recruiting journey.

With this book, I want to share my insights and learnings from my personal interview and consulting journey, both from failures and successes, as well as from my personal work with hundreds of clients, helping them receive top-tier offers. Due to the way the book has come together, and the depth of insights presented, I believe this is **the most comprehensive source on top-tier consulting interviews you can find.** The book you read has been battle-tested before launch, going through multiple iterations and feedback cycles with more than 50 of my recent clients as well as friends who are consultants, recruiters, and interviewers from across the globe. They have provided their feedback, input, and their personal experience.

Let me take you by the hand to help you navigate the competitive and complex topic of top-tier consulting interviews and *help me to help you to make you successful.*

What this book covers (and what it doesn't cover)

Yet another case interview book, you might be thinking. **Ninety-nine percent of consulting applicants fail yet recommend the same resources that failed them in the first place.** You are not going to succeed by following what everyone else is doing. Rest assured that this book tackles consulting interviews from a completely different angle than the two classic books on the topic and other prominent case interview resources. It is written from an up-to-date practitioner's perspective, which is reflected mainly in three key differences.

First, the book provides you with a practical approach to solving cases that develops and relies on the right skills. My goal is to improve your metacognitive skills (what to do at each point during the case), your problem-solving skills (how to approach the problem and each individual question that relates to it), and your communication skills (how to convey your answers most effectively).

The current offer for consulting interview books does not serve customers well. *Case in Point* by Cosentino is not practical. *Case Interview Secrets* by Cheng is outdated. While the authors of both books deserve praise and recognition for being pioneers in the development of consulting application and case interview learning materials, the value of their books is limited. Cosentino is a career advisor who has never worked for a consulting firm, while Victor Cheng worked at McKinsey for two years before the turn of the century. What both their methods have in common is that they focus on memorizing frameworks for business problems, which worked 15 years ago. But firms have adjusted their interviews, putting more emphasis on creative cases that test the inherent problem-solving skills of applicants, not their ability to memorize and replicate ideas. A completely new approach to solving case interviews is needed, which I provide.

Second, most materials put great emphasis on problem structuring and frameworks and give much less attention to other elements of the case. While it is essential to start your case with a strong framework, it is equally important to learn how to move through the case by using effective hypotheses, interpreting charts the right way, and performing swift and accurate quantitative analyses, all while communicating precisely. This book covers not just the beginning but all elements of the case interview in great depth and shows you how to move from A to Z in the most effective manner. I discuss preparation strategies and exercises to support your skill-building and performance improvement in all areas, hence not only telling you what to do but also how to excel at it.

Third, most consulting interview resources focus on case interviews, which are the most daunting element in a typical consulting recruiting journey. Yet, the fit interview, which covers questions about your motivation, personality, skills, and achievements, is as important as the case interview. Too many times, I have seen candidates invest all their effort in case preparation, neglecting the fit part and then failing since they have neither prepared the right answers nor practiced their delivery. Both the case and the fit have equal bearing on the hiring decision, and a strong case performance cannot outweigh a weak fit, and vice versa. That is why I cover ninety-five percent of all potential consulting fit interview questions in this book and show you how to think about strong answers and effective delivery to impress your interviewers.

In a nutshell, why is this book different? It is a one-stop-shop solution covering every aspect of consulting interviews, including:

- ☑ case interviews, personal fit interviews, and McKinsey's Personal Experience Interview
- ☑ candidate-led and interviewer-led formats
- ☑ business cases, market sizing cases, written case interviews and brainteasers
- ☑ pre-screening calls and first-round interviews through to final-round interviews
- ☑ structuring, chart interpretation, quantitative reasoning, and hypothesis generation
- ☑ synthesizing and moving through the case to recommendations
- ☑ note-taking, case communication and dealing with mistakes
- ☑ preparing with peers, alone, or with professional coaches
- ☑ and many more things.

The book is up-to-date and provides actionable, accurate, and effective advice. It highlights the changes that consulting recruiting has gone through over the last couple of years since the start of the 2020s and clears up the misconceptions, half-truths, and outright lies I've seen online. The book revolves around an effective methodology, the right behaviors, actions, and mindset to become an efficient problem solver and storyteller. I focus on building self-sufficiency and independence, offering you the right plan and tools to tackle the interview journey.

This book **does not cover** any step that comes before the interviews, such as building your resume, researching the different consulting firms, networking, drafting the perfect application documents, and acing aptitude and recruitment tests.

Who is this book for?

Few industries are as competitive to break into as top-tier consulting. In firms such as McKinsey, BCG, and Bain only one percent of applicants make it through the process. You must show a consistent outperformance across multiple interviews to receive an offer. That is why you need a strong preparation guide that helps you tackle the issues from all angles.

This book is for everyone preparing for consulting interviews, e.g., undergraduates, graduates, MBA graduates, interns, full-time hires, experienced and professional hires, PhDs, business majors, non-business majors, generalist consultants, specialized consultants, support staff, and researchers. It's appropriate for case interview beginners, advanced case interviewees, and experienced case solvers. The mismatch between the current state of preparation materials and my experience with my own clients from all walks of life, as well as their feedback, encouraged me to write this book. Hence, I believe that regardless of your background and experience, if you wish to ace consulting case and fit interviews, you can benefit from it.

[2] Extract the most value

How to work with this book

The book covers all steps of the consulting interview journey. If you are early on in your journey, it makes sense to start from the beginning. If you are already well advanced in your preparation or have little time, I recommend you briefly glance over the initial chapters, then focus on the chapters you are most interested in. Every section of this book is written in a way that no prior knowledge is needed to understand and master the concepts. That way, you can start reading this book at any chapter to extract the information and value you need at that specific moment.

How the book is structured

I introduce the interview process, differences across roles and firms, and preparation plans and timelines. I dive deeper into case interviews and discuss the types, scoring, and skills. I dissect each element of a case to show you what to expect and how to tackle it. We then go from good to great by combining theory and practice so that you can deliver a performance that will secure your offers. I discuss preparation exercises and the most important business concepts. I then show you ninety-five percent of all potential fit questions with strong answers and storytelling techniques to get the highest scores for your structure, content, and delivery. I end the book by discussing key performance drivers and logistics. I share my final thoughts and links to further practice and preparation materials.

PART 2

Introduction to Consulting Interviews: Figure Out What You Are Up Against

Congratulations! If you are holding this book in your hands, you likely made it past the resume screening stage, and potential other assessments, and have now been invited to your first round of consulting interviews. You already fared better than roughly seventy-five percent of all applicants so far. For every 100 applicants, 75 are rejected at the screening stage. Another 20 do not make it past the first-round interviews. Roughly fifty to seventy-five percent of those that pass round one get the offer. In case you are still working on your resume, cover letter, networking, and aptitude tests, please visit StrategyCase.com/Consulting-Applications for further guidance and help.

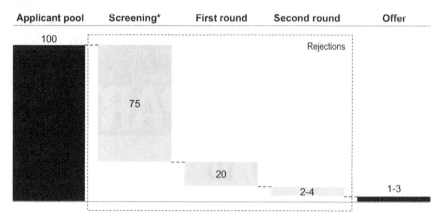

* Includes application documents and aptitude test screening

■ Breakdown of the typical consulting application funnel and rejections at top-tier firms

While there are some variations depending on the size of the company and the particular office, as well as the role, the application and interview process is fairly standardized among most management consulting firms. For the top-tier firms, the table above represents an accurate overview of the funnel and the associated rejection rates.

In any case, you should get a breakdown of the process and its duration for your target office before sending your application. Such information is available on the company website or directly from recruiters, current employees you have networked with, as well as from friends who have already gone through the process. When applying to multiple firms, keep in mind that the full hiring process can sometimes drag out. I've worked with clients who were in the funnel for six months before completing all steps and receiving the offer. At the minimum, you should budget for one month, more realistically two months from the moment you submit your application.

To make sure you are on top of the process and know what awaits you, let's cover some basics first before diving deeper into both parts of the interview. More concretely, in this section, I answer five questions:

- ☑ How is the consulting interview process structured and what are its stages?
- ☑ What are the differences across firms and their interviews?
- ☑ What are the differences when interviewing for an internship, a full-time position, and for an experienced hire position?
- ☑ How can you tailor your preparation plan based on your background, experience, and timeline?
- ☑ How has interviewing changed since the COVID-19 pandemic and what does it mean for you?

[3] Learn about the process and differences

How is the consulting interview process structured?

Once you've made it past the screening stage, your problem-solving and self-marketing skills are put to the test. However, before you can dive into case interview and fit interview preparation, you should know how the interview rounds and the associated assessments are structured.

Consulting interviews are very different from what you know from other industries. Depending on the position, the size of the firm, and the office location, you need to go through one to a maximum of three interview rounds. For senior hires, the number of interviews can be higher depending on the job position, simply because more is at stake for the hiring firm. Interns usually go only through one interview round and potentially a pre-screening call or an aptitude test. Let's look at the different stages:

Phone screening interviews

Some firms or offices employ an additional screening round before the actual on-site interviews. These initial interviews are usually conducted by HR (rarely by a current consultant) via telephone and are fit-based, gauging your motivation and background. They are also often used to discuss interviewing logistics and timelines going forward. Phone interviews at this stage rarely include a business case or business case questions. If they do, it is to filter out candidates who have no idea how case interviews work to avoid scheduling two to three on-site interviews when there is no chance of success. For instance, many McKinsey offices in North America are currently employing a phone screening case interview conducted by the firm's alumni. If a firm conducts a pre-screening fit or case interview, the same principles apply that I discuss in later chapters.

Aptitude and recruitment tests

Some firms employ aptitude tests to evaluate applicants' problem-solving skills, verbal, logical, and numerical reasoning, or personality traits. Most of those tests are conducted virtually, hence you can take them from home. They are either set in the same context and environment as a typical case interview (e.g., the BCG Chatbot Case, the Kearney Recruitment Test), or more creative and a bit more abstract (e.g., the McKinsey Imbellus Solve Game, the Pymetrics Test, the SOVA Test). Aptitude and recruitment tests are used as a gatekeeper to the interviews, or their results are evaluated in combination with your first-round interview performance. The difficulty and passing grades of these tests usually vary substantially across firms. A word of caution: Some firms have you repeat a test in their office once you pass to ensure the performance demonstrated at home was really yours. For specific recruitment tests, check out StrategyCase.com/Consulting-Aptitude-Tests, where I discuss these tests in more detail.

First-round interviews

For larger firms, the first *real* interview round is usually held either at one of the firm's offices or in a hotel. Candidates go through two to three interviews between 50 and 75 minutes each. At the time of publishing in winter 2022/23, most firms still interview remotely via Zoom because of the COVID-19 pandemic. A typical consulting interview usually covers three areas:

1. **Personal fit interview.** Questions in this part of the interview revolve around your background and try to gauge your motivation, personality, achievements, and skills. *Duration: between five and 30 minutes.*
2. **Case interview.** The case interview is the core part of the interview and the most difficult to master. A case interview revolves around a real-world (business) question. The interviewer acts as the client and provides all the information needed for you to analyze a situation and come up with an answer. The key is to structure your approach to the situation, ask the right questions to elicit more information from the interviewer, perform qualitative and quantitative analyses, and eventually deliver a solid recommendation. Most interviewers give you one exhaustive and longer case. The minority discuss

several short cases. McKinsey interviews are in-between. You work on one longer case, yet the interviewer directs you with a series of questions. Smaller firms still employ more creative assessments such as brainteasers. *Duration: between 15 and 60 minutes.*

3. **Questions to the interviewer.** At the end of every interview, you have a chance to ask the interviewer some questions about the firm and their experience. This part of the interview usually has no impact on your evaluation and is an opportunity to learn more about each firm. *Duration: between two and five minutes.*

Final-round interviews

In the final round, you face one to three interviews. In theory, the format is the same as in the first round(s), combining the three sections outlined above. However, in practice, some final-round interviewers follow a much less structured and stringent approach. Interviewers might try to confirm findings from the first round(s) or test you in areas where you appeared weakest. While earlier round interviews are usually conducted by associates and project managers, final-round interviews are conducted by junior partners, partners, and even senior partners in some cases. For senior lateral hires, all interviews might be conducted by senior leaders.

The final interview

The last interview is often conducted by a senior partner, who might conduct another formal interview and can still veto a hiring. However, in most cases, they just want you to sign the contract. Elite firms invest a substantial amount in recruiting, and it is rare to find enough candidates that make it through the whole process. After you have delivered four or more stand-out interview performances, they are willing to go the extra mile to make you sign. If you want to discuss starting dates or any other requests, this is where they are most willing to make concessions and where you have the biggest leverage.

If your performance was strong across multiple rounds but some doubts remain in one specific area, in rare cases, you might be invited for another deciding tie-breaker interview, usually with a partner.

Power rounds

Some firms or offices have streamlined the process to conduct all interviews in one day with what is called a *power round*, a *super day* or a *marathon day*. In the morning you go through all interviews of round one and, if successful, continue in the afternoon with the final round. You might leave the office with an offer or hear about the decision soon after. While such an interview marathon is exhausting with up to six interviews and an aptitude test in one day, it is quite efficient, and you know the hiring decision quickly.

Special formats

Some firms employ specific assessments such as role-playing exercises, mimicking daily issues of consultants (e.g., difficult client conversations), or group discussions about certain issues. These formats are rare and are most commonly employed by tier 3, in-house consulting and boutique consulting firms. Written case interviews are sometimes employed by BCG and Bain, amongst others.

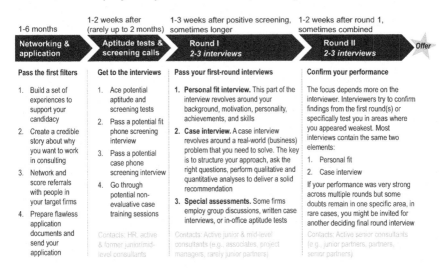

■ Overview of a typical consulting interview process

Bar firm and office specific adaptations to this process, the chart above covers ninety-five percent of what the recruiting funnel of all top-tier consulting firms looks like.

How has interviewing changed since the COVID-19 pandemic?

Consulting firms are still dealing with the pandemic at the time of publishing and there are currently two major differences that candidates face when interviewing:

1. For most positions, interviews are held remotely via Zoom. Some firms have started to interview again in the office, usually only for the final round. HR will inform you about the logistics surrounding your interviews. The way cases are conducted virtually is almost the same as within the office. The main differences are threefold. First, it is a bit harder to create a personal relationship with the interviewers. Second, there is a higher risk of misunderstandings and miscommunication due to missing non-verbal cues and connectivity issues, and third, charts are presented via screen share rather than on physical printouts.

2. Due to the remote nature of the interviews, it might be that your interview round is spread over multiple days depending on the availability of the interviewers. While previously, all interviews of the same round were usually conducted on a Friday or Monday back-to-back in the office, now it could be that you have one interview on a Monday, one on Thursday, and a third one on Friday, sometimes even at odd times of the day. I have noticed that interviews are rescheduled more often on short notice compared to pre-pandemic times or are scheduled abruptly. The interview schedules are less stable and less predictable.

I doubt that consulting firms will go back fully to their pre-pandemic interview mode, inviting every candidate to the office. For most firms, I expect some sort of hybrid model, conducting the first-round interviews virtually and inviting successful candidates to the final round in the office.

What are the differences across firms?

First, let's have a brief look at the different types of firms, followed by their assessments.

Consulting players overview

The strategy consulting landscape is split into five distinct segments. All things equal, some are easier to break into. As an indication, it is usually harder to get into MBB (McKinsey, BCG, Bain) vs. tier-2 firms vs. boutique firms vs. Big Four vs. in-house consulting firms.

1. MBB: McKinsey, BCG, Bain

McKinsey and Company, the Boston Consulting Group (BCG), and Bain and Company are the three most prestigious strategy consulting firms, usually working with C-level executives of the largest firms as well as public sector clients. These three usually attract the best talent and provide the most exciting projects and exit opportunities. Their presence is global as they cover all industries and functional areas of expertise.

2. Tier-2 firms

Tier-2 consulting firms generally enjoy favorable recognition among clients and potential applicants, yet the prestige, the work, exit opportunities, and salaries rank below MBB in most geographies and areas. The most prominent examples include Strategy&, LEK, Oliver Wyman, Kearney, and Roland Berger. These firms usually have a global presence and vast industry and functional coverage. There are less benefits compared to MBB while the drawbacks of a consulting career are often more pronounced (e.g., longer working hours, more to prove, less support staff).

3. Big Four + Accenture

Big Four refers collectively to the four largest professional services firms in the world, Deloitte, Ernst & Young, KPMG and PricewaterhouseCoopers (PwC). Originally, the Big Four were mostly active in the tax and auditing space, but over the last decades, they have widened their scope to include strategy consulting. Similarly,

Accenture, a global technology consulting firm, expanded into strategy consulting. Work hours and the work-life balance are usually better compared to MBB and tier-2 firms, but there are much fewer benefits.

4. Boutique firms

Boutique consulting firms are usually smaller than the ones described above, but they often specialize with a very strong reputation either in a specific geography or within a specific industry or functional area. Some are founded by former MBB partners. Their scope is usually narrower and more focused. In certain areas, they can compete with MBB. Lifestyle is more variable and can match MBB in terms of hours and pressure; sometimes it is more relaxed.

5. In-house consulting firms

Over the last decades, large corporations became aware of the value that external consultants bring to the table, but they had to deal with the high price tag that is associated with external professional service firms. To benefit from an independent and specialized strategic outside-in perspective and the analytical firepower at a lower cost point, corporations built their own internal consulting divisions. The work-life balance is better compared to that of external advisors, sometimes close to a nine-to-five job.

Different assessment procedures for different firms

What all firms have in common is that their main assessment tools responsible for the hiring decision are the case interviews and the personal fit interviews, hence guiding the focus of this book. This becomes even more relevant when you target solely MBB, tier 2, and Big Four firms. The success rates differ significantly across firms. While in MBB, only one to three percent of qualified applicants receive an offer, in most tier-2 firms that number is around three to five percent. For others, there is more variation. For instance, the hurdles for some prestigious boutique firms are like those for MBB, while other firms in that category have a less stringent hiring process. There is some variation and other assessment tools are employed as well, mainly by smaller firms.

Below I have summarized the various interviewing and assessment tools for different types of firms. Before starting your preparation, perform your research about the different evaluation tools of the firms of your choice.

	MBB	Tier-2	Big 4	Boutique	Inhouse
Aptitude test	✓	?	?	?	?
Phone screening	?	?	?	?	?
Standard interview	✗	✗	?	?	?
Technical interview	?	?	?	?	?
Case interview	✓	✓	✓	✓	✓
Fit interview	✓	✓	✓	✓	✓
Situational interview	?	?	?	?	?
Group discussions	✗	✗	✗	?	?
Success rate of qualified candidates	1-3%	3-5%	3-10%	1-10%	5-10%

✓ All firms ✗ No firm ? Some, do your research

■ Overview of different assessments by different firms

What are the differences across roles?

You can enter the industry at three different stages of your career, which has implications on the process:

1. during your university years: Intern, most of which convert to a full-time offer
2. straight after graduation or within two years of graduating: Full-time graduate hire
3. a few years into your career. Experienced or professional hire.

Most join directly out of university as graduate hires. The core principles to prepare your application and be ready for the interviews are the same across all three. If you are interested in the application process in general (such as resume, cover letter, and networking), refer to StrategyCase.com/Consulting-Applications.

Internship vs. full-time role

The application process and the interviews for full-time and internship roles are very similar. Normally, the screening stage consists of the same elements for both interns and full-timers. Their application documents are screened, and if found suitable, candidates move on to online tests, a phone interview, or directly to the first round of interviews. Interns receive the offer or rejection right after, while full-timers can expect a second round and sometimes a third round if they are on an experienced hire track.

While the evaluation criteria for interns are a bit more relaxed, by no means does this imply that they are allowed to score much worse than full-time hires in the case or the fit interview. At the end of the day, the role and responsibilities of an intern are the same as those of a new full-time hire. What does that mean in practice?

Case interviews. The evaluation dimensions are the same, yet the required performance across all criteria is (slightly) lower for interns, depending on the stage of their education and career; even more so in tier-2 and smaller consultancies. For instance, as an intern you are not expected to provide answers that are as exhaustive or well qualified. Your hypotheses might be weaker, and you might need a bit longer to answer the client's question. It is also acceptable to show less business sense and intuition.

Fit interviews. For the fit part, answers provided by an intern should cover the same content elements, yet interviewers naturally expect them to be embedded in more junior contexts. For instance, if asked about a leadership role, an intern might discuss a situation where they were leading an undergraduate team to work on a presentation for a university course. For a full-time hire, their answers and stories should highlight the more senior background and demonstrate the bigger impact of their actions. For the latter, the story might still revolve around a university project, but the team might have been bigger, the project was longer or more complex, and the outcome was more impactful. Overall, full-time hires are expected to appear more mature and confident.

Professional and experienced hires

Experienced hires join consulting firms after a few years with other companies, usually early or in the middle of their career. Depending on the company and the role, at least three years of previous work experience is usually required. Candidates with a PhD are also considered experienced hires in most firms. Experienced hires can either join as generalists or due to their work experience as specialist consultants for a specific industry or functional area. They go through the same process of case and fit interviews.

Case interview. There is no difference in the way the case interviews are conducted, and experienced hires are expected to perform like graduate hires. However, I have noticed that they usually prepare less for their case interviews since they assume that they are able to solve problems based on their experience and reputation alone. Unfortunately, the case interview is a very specific format and without preparation even the best strategic thinkers fail since they are not used to the flow and the way they are expected to answer and move through the case. Unprepared senior interviewees often face rejections after the first interview round. If the experienced hire is going for a specialized consulting position, the content of the case might be focused in that area.

Fit interview. As for the fit interviews, questions like those for graduate hires are asked, but it is much more important to demonstrate seniority and experience throughout the interview. Expect more targeted questions on specific experiences and skills. On top of that, pay special attention in your preparation to questions on why you want to switch careers and employers at this stage. The content of your answers should be akin to what interns or graduate applicants discuss, but your answers should be set in a more senior and mature environment, and the impact of your actions needs to be several magnitudes bigger. For instance, instead of leading a team of three students on a school project, you led a team of eight working on a C-level initiative.

Now that you know what you are up against, let's have a look at how you should structure your preparation.

Set up a preparation plan

How to think about structuring your preparation

Consulting interviews are – to a certain degree – a learned skill. Preparation time and effort strongly correlate with candidates' performance – no surprises here. The key question now is how long you should prepare for your interviews with top-tier firms so that your skills are up to par with what is expected from a successful candidate.

There is no one-size-fits-all answer. Your starting position is determined by your background, problem-solving experience, and willingness to learn. Once you arrive at the live interviews, you need to be at the peak of your preparation and demonstrate strong problem-solving and storytelling skills. So how long does that usually take?

Structuring the preparation process

I recommend clients invest a minimum of two weeks full-time and no longer than three months on the side of other commitments into interview preparation. You need the minimum time to learn and internalize the case habits and thinking, then solve a significant number of cases and drills using your newly learned toolkit to build up speed and accuracy in your analyses, on top of preparing and rehearsing your personal fit answers. If you have significant weaknesses in one area – for instance, working with math problems – I recommend a minimum preparation time of one month. Generally, it is a smart strategy to start preparing before sending out your application documents, as sometimes interview dates can be set two weeks from screening.

I also set a maximum time because the marginal returns of your invested time decrease the longer you practice or – as I have seen – even turn negative after a certain point. Think of it as almost a case preparation burnout, which is especially relevant for applicants who are preparing while working a stressful and demanding full-time job. The appropriate timespan for your preparation also depends on how much time you are able or willing to invest each day. I recommend spending at least a few hours every day preparing for the upcoming interviews if you are short on time and only have three weeks or less. If you have more time, you can benefit from off days or lighter workload days to reset your brain and avoid case fatigue.

Quality over quantity

Time and effort are worth nothing if your preparation is not effective. You could work three months on the wrong skills, internalizing the wrong habits, going only through low-quality cases, practicing only with inexperienced case partners or bad case coaches and, as a result, see no meaningful improvement in your performance.

To avoid a lack of progress, apply an 80/20 approach to focus on the key skills needed to pass the interviews. This is a concept which is often used by consultants. It refers to the fact that you should always work on the 20% of the solution that gives you 80% of the impact; in other words, take the effective and efficient route. The more time you have available after nailing the key requirements, the more you can refine your skills and work on the last 20%. In practical terms this means the following: Consulting firms focus on strength-based feedback. You are not expected to distinguish yourself in every area or dimension that is evaluated, yet you are expected to cover all bases satisfactorily and, on top of that, perform exceptionally well in certain areas.

For the case interviews, it is important that you lift your weaknesses to a level that is acceptable, making sure that you deliver results in each area of the case (e.g., perform math accurately but maybe not as swiftly as possible with the most elegant approach available) and then build on your strengths to turn them into performance spikes that get you the offer (e.g., by creating a particularly broad and deep initial structure for the case). To make this clearer, let's look at three hypothetical candidate scenarios:

☑ **Candidate 1**: This candidate usually gets an offer.
   a. Solid performance across all cases in all areas
   b. No mistakes or one or two minor mistakes or lack of attention
   c. No or very limited interviewer guidance or intervention needed
   d. Performance spikes in certain areas (e.g., extremely fast and accurate math)

☑ **Candidate 2:** This candidate usually does not receive an offer since they did not demonstrate clear spikes. Being good is not good enough.

    a. Solid performance across all cases in all areas

    b. No mistakes or one or two minor mistakes or lack of attention

    c. No or very limited interviewer guidance or intervention needed

    d. No performance spikes

☑ **Candidate 3:** This candidate usually does not receive an offer since their performance was not consistently strong enough across several cases.

    a. Solid performance across most cases in most areas

    b. Several minor mistakes across cases or one major mistake in one case

    c. Some interviewer guidance needed

    d. Performance spikes in certain areas

Consulting firms know that people have different talents and strengths, and they want to see those during the interviews. Just being good in every case is not good enough. You need to demonstrate clear performance spikes and it is easier for you to develop them in areas where you already feel confident and proficient at the start of your preparation. In addition, consulting firms also want new hires they can trust with all different aspects of the work; hence, you should be able to work flawlessly across all parts of the case as well, i.e., showing a solid, not necessarily outstanding, performance.

What is the best interview preparation plan?

Strong candidates usually put in around 100 to 150 hours of interview preparation if they are starting from scratch. Business majors or professional hires usually need 30% to 50% less time as they are more familiar with solving problems in a business context. In general, you should split your time across the following six activities:

1. **Read business publications** such as *McKinsey Insights*, *BCG Insights*, *The Economist*, or *The Financial Times* to become familiar with current hot topics, typical problems, phrases, keywords,

and concepts that are relevant in the business world. This is especially applicable for non-business majors. Depending on how much time you have, I recommend you incorporate five to 20 hours of business reading into your preparation agenda. Reading is a simple task you can do on your commute or at the end of the day to wind down. Additionally, you become familiar with your potential employer's approach to problems if you read their publications and articles. To find the relevant research for your target firm, google *<target firm name> + <research> or <insights> or <publications>*.

2. **Familiarize yourself with basic business concepts and terminology**. This is more relevant for non-business majors, but my experience shows that even candidates with a business background could use a refresher on the basic concepts that are taught at business school. I cover all core business concepts as well as business math formulas and definitions for case interviews later. Familiarize yourself with those and try to understand them from a conceptual perspective and a practical point of view. I recommend you spend around one to five hours on it.

3. **Read through a variety of different cases** if you are new to case interviews to get an understanding of how they work, what the process and typical flow looks like, and what problems you are dealing with. You can find several real case examples throughout this book as well as links to free case resources at the end to provide you with enough reading and practice material. Depending on your experience with case interviews, spend between two to 10 hours on this task. This is again something that can be done on the go or when you are too tired to actively think through cases on your own. By reading cases, you build your repertoire of potential structuring ideas, hypotheses, chart interpretation tricks, as well as approaches and shortcuts to quantitative reasoning parts.

4. **Actively work on cases.** While the first three (passive) ideas build your knowledge base and understanding, the core part of your preparation should be active problem-solving with cases and case components. On your own, you can either conduct case interview drills, working on structuring, chart, and math questions individually, or work through full cases. Your problem-

solving skills are like a muscle. The more (high-quality!) cases you solve, the better you become. I recommend my clients perform at least 30 hours of individual drills, up to 80 hours if they start from scratch or have specific weaknesses.

5. **Go through mock interviews.** The most realistic way to work on your case interview skills is by performing mock interviews with peers and coaches. You want to go through simulated interviews and create as realistic conditions as possible by focusing on quality cases and quality case partners. When practicing with peers, act both as interviewee and as interviewer as the latter gives you a new perspective on the whole process. I usually recommend at least 20 hours of mock interviews, up to 40 if my clients have more time or more pronounced development needs. Going through live interview simulations is exhausting and drains your energy, but it is worthwhile to build up your stamina and resilience.

6. **Work on your personal fit answers.** Craft strong answers to the most common questions, then practice, rehearse and iterate based on feedback you receive from peers or coaches. When practicing alone, record yourself and listen to your answers. At the very least, spend five hours on this part; it can take up to 20 hours if you prepare for multiple firms or craft deep Personal Experience Interview stories for McKinsey and practice them appropriately.

I discuss each of these building blocks in much more detail in **Chapter 19** on skill building and preparation, including instructions on how to perform drills on your own, how to interview someone else, how to select the best coach, etc.

Business publications	Business background	Case reading	Practice drills	Full case practice	Personal fit preparation

• Read business publications such as *The Economist*, *The Financial Times*, *Bloomberg Business News*, etc.
 • Read consulting firm research output such as McKinsey Insights, BCG Insights, etc.
	• Familiarize yourself with simple business concepts and frameworks
	 • Learn about the most common business terminology
	 • Do not waste your time on memorizing frameworks
		• Read through cases to understand how they work
		 • Get a feel for the typical problems that you need to solve
		 • Understand the different elements and identify how to move from the beginning to the end
			• Practice drills focusing on the different elements
			   • Structure
			   • Exhibits
			   • Math
			 • Practice your communication for each element
			 • Practice moving from one part of the case to the next using hypotheses and syntheses
				• Perform full case practice
				   • Alone
				   • With peers
				   • With a case coach
				 • Simulate the interview conditions as closely as possible
				 • Perform interviews back-to-back
					• Draft your answers for personal fit questions
					 • Practice your answers and communication with friends, peers, and coaches

0-20 hours	0-5 hours	2-10 hours	30-80 hours	20-40 hours	10-20 hours

■ Consulting interview preparation building blocks

A key question I receive often is: *"It all seems overwhelming. Where should I start? How can I kick off my consulting interview preparation and make the best use of my time?"*

Let's look at an example process for someone that has one month to prepare.

Focused interview preparation

Take two days to familiarize yourself with the mechanics of the case interview. Learn about the skills and the evaluation before diving into the individual elements and the ways these elements connect. Become familiar with the right habits, preparation, and skill-building techniques. Read the case interview section of this book to get a detailed overview of everything you need to know.

Open a sample casebook (you can find several free resources in **Chapter 37**) and read through 10 cases to get an insight into varied case examples, question types, approaches, potential answers, case progression, and recommendations. When reading through a case, answer each question yourself before going to the sample answers. Get a feel for the process and the thinking that is needed to solve a case as well as an indication of how difficult it is for you to come up with good answers at this point. You want to understand your strengths and weaknesses early on.

Plan your preparation over the next couple of weeks with a calendar, slotting in the different tasks and exercises (e.g., case reading, drills, case practice alone, case practice with peers). I provide a weekly sample plan at the end of this chapter and discuss preparation exercises in more detail in **Chapter 19**.

Now would be the best time to engage a case coach if that is what you plan on doing. At the beginning of your preparation, the return on investment is the highest as they can point you in the right direction, potentially saving you a lot of time. I cover this in **Chapter 19** and advise you how to select the best coach and how to collaborate in the most fruitful way. Alternatively, you could watch mock interview videos, which I provide a link for in **Chapter 37**. If you don't want to work with a coach or pay for your preparation, find strong case buddies and schedule a couple of meetings over the next few days. I discuss how to work with case buddies in **Chapter 19** as well.

Over the next two to four weeks, dive into drills on your own as well as case practice with peers and coaches. Use the instructions and the free resources described later in the book to work on full cases as well as separate structuring, charts, and math exercises. When working on your own, do not only write down your answers, but also practice the right communication habits and phrases. Record yourself and listen to it. Shift your focus to areas you are struggling with to build your baseline performance. For instance, if you are struggling with approaching math problems, spend 40% to 50% of your preparation time dissecting math problems and drills. On top of that, read business publications and written cases to build up your business sense and intuition.

Build your preparation around quality instead of quantity. Going over 100+ cases does not mean much if you are not applying the right habits to score high or are working with low quality case books or inexperienced case partners. For peak performance, get the best of everything and work with the best to make your dream become a reality. Find strong case partners on websites such as PrepLounge.com. Case partners should be preparing for the same firm as you, ideally have a business background, or might even be experienced hires with a consulting background. Strong case partners might also have a skill profile with opposite strengths and weaknesses compared to you; that way, you can both learn from each other. Do not always practice with the same people but with a diverse group of case partners. Besides university casebooks, sprinkle in recruiting cases provided by most firms on their website to get a feel for the specific case format that individual firms employ. You can find relevant links in **Chapter 37**.

Create an error log for the different elements of the case (structuring, chart interpretation, case math, moving through the case, etc.). Write down every element and question of a case you were struggling with, including a potential answer. Pay attention to that error log as it tells you where to put the most effort. Are there any questions types you are struggling with more? Are their specific industries or functional areas you do not understand? For charts, do you struggle with interpreting scatter plots? For math, do you struggle specifically with percentages? You get the idea.

Continue with live cases, drills, and business sense development by focusing on the areas that are most important for your progress. As you progress, focus on your weaknesses! For instance, if you are bad at structuring problems, practice structuring drills. If you struggle with math, practice basic pen-and-paper calculations or the creation of solutions paths. You need to lift those weaknesses to an acceptable level. This covers the baseline.

Develop your strengths! Make sure to consistently outperform in areas that you perceive as strengths. This is what gets you the offer. The preparation process is iterative, and you should constantly improve your performance and increase your confidence. If this is not the case, step back, be honest with yourself, and try to understand why you're not improving. Adjust your schedule and preparation plan accordingly.

Get structured and relevant feedback from strong practice partners. The better the mock interviewer, the more realistic the case practice. Similarly, the more detailed and accurate the feedback, the quicker you progress toward your goal of understanding and acing case interviews. If you are on a tighter deadline or want to make quick progress, consider substituting peer group practice with professional mock interviewers. Practice with high-quality partners only to avoid learning and repeating faulty habits and behaviors. Finally, take all the feedback you get from case partners with a grain of salt. They are not experts and might mean well, but their insights could be based on wrong information or a tip they read from an untrustworthy source. Scrutinize the feedback together with your case partners to mutually improve. Build up stamina as you progress and increase the number of mock case interviews in a single day, ideally in quick succession to simulate the stress and exhaustion of the real interview day experience.

Attend a few interviews or recruitment days with second- and third-tier consulting firms to get real experience and exposure. You should do this once you feel confident and have performed well in several subsequent mock interviews. Besides the valuable learning opportunity, you might get fallback options if your desired offer with another firm does not materialize. Apply and schedule these interviews well in advance to avoid overlaps, which can involve a bit of planning. Consulting interview days are mostly on Fridays or in some larger offices on Fridays and Mondays, hence, you can — at a maximum — attend two interview days per week. With COVID and remote interviewing, this has become a bit more flexible.

Give yourself a break for one or two days every now and then. Use weekends to refresh your mind. Be careful not to neglect other responsibilities or interests. Do not stop exercising or go all crazy about the upcoming interviews. I see this a lot and it is not conducive to good performance. Make sure to get enough playtime during your preparation. These periods improve your performance over time and make sure the learned habits stick and you do not burn out in the process.

Do not forget the personal fit interview. As the interview date comes closer, allocate some time to draft your answers for the fit questions based on the personal fit interview chapters of this book. Practice those stories with friends and family, peers, and professional coaches. Let them ask you difficult questions. Iterate your answers until they are polished, structured, and concise.

Rest one or two days before big interviews. One, ideally two days before your interviews should be spent on anything but cases. You want to approach the interviews with a fresh and relaxed mind. Rather focus on things that help you relax, e.g., meeting friends and family, going outside, doing some sports, meditating, reading a fiction book. If you feel guilty about not doing anything on the day before the interview, you might rehearse your fit or PEI answers for one or two hours. Other than that, relax. You want to be hungry and eager to solve cases when it is time for the live interviews.

By diligently sticking to a plan like the one outlined above, your preparation should put you in a position to ace every case challenge without running the risk of over-preparation or burnout. To illustrate this, I have created a sample plan with 30 to 35 hours in a typical week for someone who devotes most of their time to interview preparation to get up to speed within one month.

If you have two months to prepare, you could shorten or space your preparation blocks out more, hence resulting in a lower workload per week with more time to focus on your weaknesses and build on your strengths. This would also be relevant if you are working full-time while preparing. In such cases, you could invest 12 hours per weekend and five to 10 hours during the week to get to a similar level of preparedness.

I have not included any aptitude test preparation in this plan. For some firms, add 10 to 20 hours to your preparation to specifically focus on aptitude and recruitment tests. The skills needed for those tests often match with the skills needed for the interviews, so the preparation is complementary.

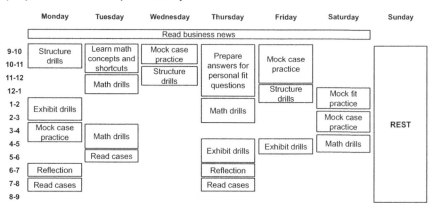

■ Illustrative week plan for a candidate who prepares full-time within one month

Make the preparation plan work for you and not against you. Think about what the best times are for you to learn new content, whether you would rather work in the morning, afternoon, or evening. Don't forget rest days to avoid burnout or case fatigue, especially if you are working full-time.

Reflect on your efforts at least twice a week to change course if needed. Be honest with yourself and your progress. Is it as expected or is it lagging? Change the content of your preparation or increase the time spent each week until you are satisfied and back on track. Keep an open mind and adjust your plan to stay effective. You know that you are ready when you can solve every mock case and practice drill without too much trouble and stress and have prepared answers for every personal fit question that I cover in **Part 10**.

Lastly, if the interviews are approaching quickly, and you do not feel ready and are not under any pressure to get the offer as soon as possible, reschedule your interviews. For most firms and most offices, this is possible. Two more weeks of preparation can make the difference, and I always recommend my clients reschedule if either of us feels they are not ready.

PART 3

Introduction to Case Interviews: What's This Specific Interview Format All About?

[5] Get the basics on the setup, the skills, and the scoring

For most candidates, the case interview is the biggest hurdle. As a former McKinsey consultant and interview expert, I've specialized in helping my candidates to tackle this part of the recruiting journey effectively. I've found that a lot of the information, specifically on the case interviews, is wrong, outdated, or assumed to be the same across all firms and presented by "experts" who have never seen a consulting firm's office from the inside. Consequently, the advice can be detrimental to your recruiting success. In this chapter, I'll help you understand the intricacies of the case interview as a first step in your preparation by answering the following questions:

- ☑ What is a consulting case interview?
- ☑ What skills are assessed, and how are you scored?
- ☑ What is the role of the interviewer, and what is on their mind?

What is a case interview?

The case interview is employed by all top-tier consulting firms to test the analytical capabilities and communication skills of applicants. It simulates a client situation, where you are tasked to solve a specific (business) problem (e.g., *"Why are our revenues decreasing?"*) or implement a client request or answer a client question (e.g., *"We want to become more customer friendly"*). You need to figure out how your client can achieve a certain goal or solve a problem by influencing the right levers. Typical cases might start in the following way:

> *"Over the last year, our client, a Caribbean tour operator has seen a significant decrease in bookings. The CEO wants us to find out what happened and increase the bookings again back to baseline levels from three years ago."*

Here, the goal is to increase bookings back to baseline levels.

> *"Our client, a leading guitar brand, has asked us whether or not they should open up a new factory in Indonesia for a new line of entry-level guitars."*

Here, the goal is to provide a recommendation about opening a new guitar factory.

> *"We are working with the government of a small developing country to create a strategy that would spread education to children between the ages six to 14 in remote villages. We need to devise a ramp-up plan for the next 24 months to make this a reality."*

Here, the goal is to come up with a plan for educating children in remote villages.

As you can see, these situations and problems and the associated goals are varied and diverse, and usually taken from a real-life client engagement of your interviewer. Yet, while every case brief is unique, you would follow the same logic and approach when solving the case. You always need to figure out what levers you should move and how to reach a desired outcome. To solve a case successfully, there are a couple of tasks that are interdependent and partially iterative in nature. You need to:

- ☑ understand a client request and operationalize the goal(s)
- ☑ create an analytical framework to investigate the situation
- ☑ use hypotheses to elicit more qualitative and quantitative information from your interviewer by going through your framework, asking targeted questions
- ☑ analyze, interpret, and contextualize the information collected through the discussions, charts, graphs, and data tables, as well as quantitative problems
- ☑ synthesize your findings and relate them back to the initial case brief
- ☑ identify the root cause(s) of the problem, and find the most suitable approach and the right levers to pull
- ☑ provide recommendation(s) to satisfy your client's request.

The interview is a dialogue between you and the interviewer, where you need to structure your approach, propose concrete ideas and analyses, gather information, spot insights on data tables and charts, solve quantitative tasks, and provide recommendations, all while communicating in a professional, structured, and calm way.

The case interview is difficult since it involves several different skills that you need to demonstrate, not just in one part of a case but consistently across all parts within one case and across multiple interviews in succession. Candidates usually go through three to six case interviews before receiving an offer. Consistency is key as you need to convince all interviewers by solving their respective cases. Not an easy feat! Let's have a look at the different skills at play and how they are evaluated.

What skills are assessed in a case interview?

While during the screening stage, consulting firms check your resume to establish that you might have the potential to be a good candidate, during the interviews, they want to put that potential to the test to see if you can develop into a world-class consultant.

Once hired, you are put in front of the client, where you represent the prestigious legacy of your firm from day one. Hence, the skillset you need to display in a case interview is the same as that required in the daily life of a management consultant. The case interviews are essentially a trial-run to gauge how well you would be able to solve problems and communicate later on.

Before you start your preparation, it is important to understand what aspects the interviewer scores your performance on. Knowing what interviewers look for, you can tailor your approach, interpret feedback, and work toward mastery of each area. Below are the seven key dimensions you need to focus on, including examples of how you can display mastery in each. In later chapters, I show you how these skills translate to real case examples, and how you can employ and hone them most effectively.

Problem-solving

- ☑ Do you understand what the overarching problem and client request is about?
- ☑ Can you identify and operationalize the goal(s) of the client?

☑ Can you deconstruct the problem or situation into its parts, structuring a MECE (mutually exclusive, collectively exhaustive) issue tree (framework), covering all aspects without overlaps?

☑ Do you understand the most important components/drivers/ levers in this situation?

Application in a case interview: To provide a recommendation at the end of the case interview, you need to work on one or multiple problems or tasks for the fictitious client. Great candidates clarify the situation, operationalize the goal(s) of the client, then set up their analysis by splitting the problem into multiple components, the most common tool to achieve that being the *issue tree* (see **Chapter 8**).

A good problem deconstruction is the anchor that keeps you focused and on track while moving through the case and investigating the situation. Once you have received the question you are trying to solve during the case, you need to create your issue tree with each branch of the tree representing a part of the problem or situation you would like to investigate. These parts are drivers or levers you can influence to change the outcome for your client. Your approach should be MECE, meaning that it should cover all aspects of the problem or situation without overlaps.

Creativity

☑ Do you think about a situation holistically, offering broad, deep, and insightful perspectives, adding new ways of thinking on top of more commonsense ideas?

☑ Are you able to look at the situation from different perspectives?

☑ Can you draft a range of concrete ideas and rich descriptions that qualify why your mentioned areas are important to investigate?

☑ Are you able to come up with creative ideas, solutions, and recommendations?

Application in a case interview: One way to rise to the top of a bunch of case interview candidates is to demonstrate a spike in creativity. When thinking about the situation and your issue tree, go as broad and as deep as possible. Try to come up with creative angles/top-level ideas to the problem that cover it exhaustively (the breadth), and draft rich descriptions with concrete ideas that support each top level (the depth). Refrain from using memorized frameworks like 90% of other applicants.

Remember: Creativity is nothing without structure. Keep your creative thoughts contained in a MECE structure as described above. Additionally, once you have identified the root cause of the problem or the gist of the situation or are simply asked to brainstorm ideas and solutions, come up with creative insights on top of more common ideas you might have. For instance, remembering our guitar manufacturer and their new factory example from above, a standard insight would be to consider the cost of the venture. Creative insights would be to consider the impact of a new low-cost line of guitars on brand reputation and the effect of cannibalization on the existing product lineup.

Analytics

- ☑ Can you link the structure with creative thinking to create meaningful and logical analyses on a deep enough level based on sound arguments?
- ☑ Are you using a hypothesis-driven approach to your problem-solving, i.e., have a clear picture of where you think the case solution can be found most likely, hence, tackling high-impact issues first by asking the right questions and always being aware of where to go next, potentially changing course if needed?
- ☑ Can you swiftly interpret and synthesize data, charts, exhibits, and statements made by the interviewer in the context of your hypotheses?
- ☑ Do you see interdependencies in different parts of the problem, your analyses, and proposed solutions and understand how the key drivers/levers of the problem or situation interact with each other?

Application in a case interview: Analytical rigor links structure and creative thinking, guiding you as you move through your issue tree to investigate the situation. Employ a hypothesis-driven approach to your problem-solving, i.e., have a clear picture of where you think the solution of the case is buried. This way, you can qualify and justify why certain areas are important to investigate, tackle likely high-impact issues first, lead the interviewer, and ask the right questions to elicit relevant information quickly. After going through a branch of your issue tree, synthesize your findings and discuss how they relate to your status quo in the case, then move to the next branch if needed until you find the key pieces of information that help you solve the case. Move vertically, then horizontally. When receiving new information such as data from exhibits, interpret it with your hypotheses in mind. You should never boil the ocean, i.e., try to analyze everything there is, but follow a concrete and logical course of action and analysis, focusing on areas where you believe the most impact lies (80/20).

Demonstrate that you can move the case forward on your own by synthesizing and discussing the next potential analyses or implementation measures for your ideas. Show that you are adaptable when new information pops up that might make you change course. Keep in mind how the different parts of the situation interact with and relate to each other. Employing these habits significantly increases your chances to figure out the root cause(s) of the problem or understand the key drivers of the situation quickly, which helps you to devise a sound recommendation, even if you do not have the perfect information.

Quantitative reasoning

- ☑ Do you understand how a certain number/outcome of a calculation could help you move forward, and can you interpret quantitative outcomes in the context of the case?
- ☑ Are you able to structure quantitative problems, drafting the correct approach to calculate the desired outcome variable(s)?
- ☑ Are you able to comfortably perform calculations and manipulate large numbers, relying on simple pen-and-paper math and mental math?
- ☑ Can you move swiftly and accurately through math questions, spotting traps and using shortcuts or are you prone to making repeated smaller or larger mistakes?

Application in a case interview: There are four steps that expert case solvers ace when cracking math problems. First, they understand what specific quantitative analysis could help their understanding of the problem or enable them to provide a recommendation and how. Second, they set up the correct analysis and approach to calculate a desired outcome variable. It's necessary to think about the information required to answer the question, set up the right equations, ask for more data if needed, all while paying attention to potential traps or shortcuts. Even simple computations often include a twist. Third, they swiftly and accurately perform calculations, relying on pen-and-paper math. Calculations usually revolve around simple arithmetic. Fourth, strong candidates present their answer to the interviewer, interpret it in the context of the case, then move on from there.

Communication

- ☑ Do you communicate in a concise, effective, structured and top-down manner?
- ☑ Are you using logical and coherent sentences, professional language, and business vocabulary?
- ☑ Do your statements add value to your analysis, or do you ramble?
- ☑ Are you leading the conversation or merely getting dragged along by the interviewer?

Application in a case interview: Strong candidates communicate like consultants, which is essential for three reasons. First, you need to guide the interviewer through your issue tree and thinking, second, elicit the right information, and third, convince the interviewer about your ideas and recommendations. For all three, you need to communicate top-down, starting with the key point, then providing supporting arguments for it. You want to ensure that your statements are to the point, coherent and demonstrate good command of business language. Time is limited so avoid endless rambling about topics or going in circles, repeating what you have already said.

Ensure you share your thoughts and considerations with the interviewer. They need to understand how you reach a certain conclusion or insight. For instance, when discussing your drafted analysis, tell the interviewer what you would like to investigate as well as why you think that's a good idea.

Lastly, lead the conversation. Remember to be in the driver's seat all the time.

Maturity and presence

- ☑ Are you confident and present in the room/on the video call and demonstrate case leadership?
- ☑ Are you comfortable with silence while taking time to think and asking clarification questions or asking for guidance?
- ☑ Do you come across as friendly and professional with a pleasant countenance and gesticulation?
- ☑ Are you professionally dressed and does your appearance match the setting?

Application in a case interview: Consulting firms are looking for mature leaders. Interviewers want to see that they can put you in front of senior clients, where you represent the legacy of the firm and the credibility of your team. They want to make sure that you are self-standing, cool under pressure, engaged and confident in difficult discussions and situations as well as act and dress professionally. In addition, interviewers want to hire candidates that are genuinely engaging, nice, and pleasant to be around since they might soon spend 16 hours a day with you in the same (small) team room for several weeks in a row.

Business sense and intuition

- ☑ Can you get up to speed with a new industry, client, and situation quickly?
- ☑ Are you asking the right questions that help you understand and move forward?
- ☑ Can you make sense of new information quickly and interpret it properly in the current context?
- ☑ Can you provide suitable, actionable, sensible, and relevant recommendations for the situation at hand?

Application in a case interview: Business sense is sort of an enabler for *Analytics* (discussed above). While you are certainly not expected to know details about a certain industry or a specific context of the case, you need to be able to demonstrate business sense and intuition, which is mostly just common sense. You should be able to quickly understand a new situation – even just by asking targeted questions about how a specific business works, what the main cost drivers are, how the business makes money, etc. When receiving new information or insights during the case, you need to be able to make sense of it in the context of the business and relate it back to the information you already have as well as the situation at hand.

Interviewers would like to see you quickly gravitate toward and identify the root cause of a problem or the key drivers/levers of a situation (see *Analytics*, above), which is easier if you are quick to navigate uncharted territories. Use your common sense, experience, and knowledge of other industries or contexts to explain certain phenomena in the case, for instance, when working with assumptions or interpretations. Business sense and intuition also drive the quality of your proposed recommendations.

How is a case interview scored?

All consulting firms score case interviews in a similar manner, even though their scale and terminology might differ slightly. After every interview, interviewers fill out a feedback sheet, covering the aspects discussed in the previous section in one way or another. For each section, they rank your performance across a five-point scale:

1. **Insufficient:** Candidate does not display a basic command of the desired skill
2. **Adequate:** Candidate displays an average command of the desired skill
3. **Good:** Candidate displays a solid command of the desired skill
4. **Very Good:** Candidate displays a strong command of the desired skill
5. **Distinctive:** Candidate displays mastery of the desired skill.

Interviewers add a written commentary on their overall impression, highlighting positive, negative, as well as neutral observations.

Two things are crucial for you to get the offer. First, you need to steer clear of the first two categories. Insufficient and adequate ratings usually lead to direct rejection. At a minimum, you need to display a good performance for every skill within an interview as well as across interviews. Second, you need to demonstrate clear performance spikes, i.e., several very good and distinctive ratings across all interviews; the more the better to make the cut and get the offer. The latter provides the interviewer with arguments and reasons to make a hiring recommendation about your performance to fellow interviewers and the firm. You can find a link to the feedback sheet in **Chapter 37** to use during peer case practice.

Candidate name:	Interviewer:	○ Intern ○ Associate ○ BA ○ Manager		
Strategy Case.com	1	2	3	4	5
Problem-solving					
Analytics					
Quantitative					
Creativity					
Communication					
Maturity & presence					
Business sense					
Overall comments:					
Strengths:					
Development needs:					
Date:	○ Hiring recommendation	○ Rejection recommendation		

■ Example of a case interview performance evaluation sheet

What is the role of professional interviewers and how do they behave?

Case interviews are by their very nature a highly structured process. The interviewer takes the role of a fictitious client or your project manager with the goal to jointly move through and solve a (business) case.

Firms try to ensure that the format of the case and the evaluation metrics are standardized across cases and interviewers. Even though each case is different, the types of questions, the case flow, the evaluation metrics, and the difficulty level should be the same to allow for a fair evaluation and comparison of all candidates. That is not always the case and when interviewing with different firms, you will encounter varying interview types and styles depending either on the company, the individual interviewer, or the particular office, as well as different levels of professionalism and structure. The more professional a consulting firm, the less variance there is in the individual interviewers' or offices' style, and the more structured and objective the whole experience is.

You should get detailed information about the process and format of the interviews and logistics well ahead of time. Additionally, you might receive access to training resources beforehand, and sometimes even take part in a case interview coaching call or a virtual coaching session together with other candidates.

On the interview day, you receive your interviewers' profiles. Each has prepared a standardized and tested case in line with the firm's interviewing guidelines. With this calibrated case, they can grade your performance objectively as described above. Of course, personality and personal liking still play a role, but due to the objectivity and structured interview approach that top firms employ, each candidate has the same chances.

In smaller firms, you do not get as much advance information or access to training resources. Additionally, interviewers usually have more leeway in how they conduct the interview and rate your performance. Such firms spend much less on recruiting, and the whole process is simply not as standardized. For instance, I did an interview at a boutique firm, where I had to design and solve my own case at the same time. While interesting and challenging, the process was more chaotic, and every candidate had to solve a different non-calibrated case, making it much harder to evaluate and compare objectively. It might be more difficult to prepare for unstructured case experiences, but firms that employ such formats generally have lower performance expectations.

Find out early how interviews are conducted at your target firm to practice the right way and to tailor your approach accordingly. When you know exactly what to expect and what is expected of you, absent of surprises, the experience feels more natural and you can use your full mental resources to crack the case.

A word of caution: Be aware of the odd unprepared or irritated interviewers that appear from time to time, for instance, because they had to fill in for a colleague at the last minute. They might be in a bad mood, they don't have a lot of time, they are distracted since a client call blew up in their face five minutes ago, etc. Such interviewers are not only unprofessional but a danger to your success, especially if they come up with a case on the spot, which could lead to mutual confusion and an unpleasant experience. I regularly receive horror stories about poor interviewer performances across all firms from my clients. For instance, I have a client whose interview was conducted while the consultant was in a taxi, with the connection constantly cutting out. Another had an interview with a senior partner who muted himself to take work calls during the interview and was highly irritated when talking to the candidate.

If you encounter an unprofessional interviewer or go through an unfortunate experience, contact HR and tell them about it. State politely why the experience made it impossible to perform at your best. In those two recent cases, after they got in touch with HR, both got another chance and the performance of their unpleasant interview was not considered; both ended up with the desired offer. It pays off to push back on bad recruiting experiences and share your frustrations with HR.

Learn about the different formats of case interviews

Before dealing with consulting applications, most candidates have never heard about case interviews. In this chapter, I'll dive deeper into the format and answer the following questions:

- ☑ What are the different types and variations of case interviews?
- ☑ What are the differences between a candidate-led and interviewer-led case interview?
- ☑ What are the differences between first and final round case interviews?

We can classify case interviews based on these three criteria: the type of case, the driver of the case, and the interview round.

First, the type of case. Most top-tier firms employ typical business case interviews, some employ market sizing cases; very few still employ brainteasers. Second, we can differentiate between candidate-led cases and interviewer-led cases. For most firms, case interviews are conducted in a candidate-led format, meaning that you must move through the case autonomously, shaping the direction of your analysis moving from insight to insight to eventually arrive at a conclusion. Most notably, McKinsey employs an interviewer-led format, in which the interviewer takes the lead and guides you through the case, asking a series of questions. Third, case interviews differ based on the status and progress of your application. Most candidates expect more difficult cases in their final round. More often than not, this is not true as all interviews focus on the same skills and use the same evaluation metrics.

What types of case interviews are there?

Consultancies employ three different types of case questions to screen applicants.

Brainteasers

A brainteaser is the umbrella term for odd, usually quite short, questions that test your analytical capabilities. Your goal is to grasp, structure, and creatively solve them. Do not act surprised if the interviewer asks you questions such as *"Why are manhole covers round?"* – you should come up with a structured answer, listing several potential explanations or, *"How many tennis balls can you fit in a Boeing 747?"* – you should come up with a strong analytical answer, demonstrating that you are able to break down the problem into multiple parts and coherently analyze it.

For every brainteaser, come up with a logical approach, reasonable assumptions, and perform quick calculations if needed. Top-tier firms rarely employ these types of questions since they are quite detached from actual business problems and do not allow for objective evaluation metrics and comparison of candidates.

Market sizing and estimation questions

One of the most frequent tasks of consultants on a project is to calculate the size of a market or estimate potentials (e.g., the revenue of a new product, the cost of a new production facility). That's why these types of questions are often used in case interviews. Such questions can be part of a longer business case or asked standalone. Typical questions sound like: *"What is the size of the dairy market in China, in USD revenue per year?"* or *"How many diapers can we sell in Germany each year?"* Sometimes interviewers ask more abstract estimation questions such as, *"How many doors are in the city of Los Angeles?"*, which is essentially a brainteaser.

The key is to create an equation with the main drivers of the number you are trying to estimate. Ask for data or – if not available – come up with estimates on the spot, basing them on reasonable assumptions. Finally, plug in the numbers and perform your calculation; then, interpret the outcome. The process and speed is more important than the correctness of your answer, which should be in the right ballpark. It is appreciated when you take shortcuts and use simple numbers. Avoid the semblance of being precise over being pragmatic. Adding more variables does not make the outcome more accurate but takes more time and increases the risk of mistakes in your approach and calculation. I cover a market sizing example with an appropriate approach and replicable strategy in the case math section in **Chapter 10**.

Business cases (McKinsey: Problem Solving Interview)

Business cases are the most common and the most difficult questions you can encounter in a case interview. Most top-tier firms solely employ business cases in their selection process. You are asked to solve a typical business problem of a fictitious client. To do this properly, you split the problem into its components and identify levers you can work on, ask the right questions to work your way through the case, analyze the facts given to you, and eventually draw proper conclusions. Typical business cases – same as actual consulting engagements – are usually placed in an industry and functional matrix. Industry refers to the type of business, i.e., what product or service the client is selling, and function refers to the area of the business, i.e., what part of the business you are dealing with.

The **typical industries** you might encounter in a case interview are: Aerospace, Agriculture, Automotive, Chemicals, Consumer Goods, Defense, Education, Electronics, Energy (Oil, Gas, Power), Financial Services, Healthcare, Industrial, Infrastructure, Logistics, Materials, Media, Metals and Mining, Paper and Packaging, Pharmaceuticals, Private Equity and Principal Investors, Public and Social Sector, Real Estate, Retail, Semiconductors, Technology, Telecommunication, Transportation, Travel and Tourism. For an overview and deep dive of 27 industries, including business models, financials, challenges, and trends, check out the link to further resources in **Chapter 37**.

The **typical functions** you might have to deal with in a case interview are: Corporate Finance, Digital, Implementation, Manufacturing, Marketing and Sales, Mergers and Acquisitions, Operations, People and Organizational Performance, Recovery and Transformation, Risk and Resilience, Strategy, Sustainability.

Every period has its focal topics. For instance, while digitization has been a hot topic for consulting firms over the last 10 years, sustainability and the pandemic response are the key focal points at the moment. Expect to receive more cases related to these topics.

Based on the industry and the function, case questions might revolve around the following topics (not exhaustive): Business model evaluation, Changes in the market, Competitive or situational response, Growth strategies (organic or inorganic via mergers and acquisitions), Market entry, Operational optimization, Pricing strategies, Product introduction, Profitability (i.e., growing revenue and reducing cost), Strategic positioning, Restructuring, and more creative cases (see the initial framework example about the *machine breakdowns* later in the sections about frameworks and issue trees in **Chapter 8**). Firms are moving away from framework-based, standard business cases to more creative problems that demand candidates think on their feet.

The remainder of this book focuses on actual business cases and market sizing questions, since they make up the majority (more than ninety-nine percent) of case interviews in top-tier firms. If you are interested in brainteaser questions, a quick Google search yields hundreds of practice problems to solve.

Who drives the case interview (candidate or interviewer)?

When it comes down to who is driving the case, there are two types of interviews, interviewer-led and the candidate-led ones. Most firms employ candidate-led case interviews, with the notable exception of McKinsey, which follows an interviewer-led approach. Some firms such as Oliver Wyman or Strategy& sometimes employ elements of both interview formats, while (very!) rarely McKinsey final round interviews might also contain elements of a candidate-led interview.

Both types have certain things in common:

- ☑ The elements of the case are the same. You must structure problems, generate hypotheses, interpret exhibits, and work through some calculations, come up with a recommendation, etc.
- ☑ The skills that are assessed are the same. You need to exhibit strong problem-solving skills, creativity, analytics, good communication, etc.

However, there is one key difference.

In the candidate-led case, you drive the case yourself. It is your responsibility to move down the right path of analyses and elicit the correct information by asking effective questions related to the right items of your issue tree to end up with enough insights to provide a recommendation.

In interviewer-led cases, you take ownership of every question and go into greater detail, while the interviewer guides you from question to question. If you answer each individual question well, McKinsey interviewers often do not ask for a recommendation at all.

Candidate-led cases

Due to the nature of your role as an autonomous investigator, it is much easier to get lost, walk down a wrong branch of the issue tree or waste a ton of time. The initial framework is your analytical lens and tool to identify the key levers that are essential to answer the client's question or solve the client's problem. Maybe you won't even figure out the situation at all since the relevant problem areas were never part of your initial issue tree in the first place. That is why you should formulate a clear hypothesis about the key drivers of the problem before developing the actual framework and then diving deeper. While interviewers try to influence you to move in the right direction (pay attention to their hints!), it is still up to you what elements of the problem you would like to analyze and how. Each answer should lead to a new question, driven by your hypotheses, on your quest to find the root cause of the problem or to understand the situation and the levers you can pull to come up with a recommendation. The upsides are that you have more control over the case and its direction and do not need to create the exhaustive frameworks necessary for a McKinsey case. Your top-level buckets for a candidate-led and interviewer-led case would be the same, yet for a candidate-led case, you discuss areas on a deeper level only if they promise to validate your thinking and hypotheses.

Interviewer-led cases (McKinsey-style)

The interviewer guides you through a series of three to seven connected questions (for McKinsey: structure, exhibit, brainstorming, and math, sometimes a recommendation) that you need to answer, synthesize, and develop recommendations from. The initial framework is your map that should consider all elements of the situation, touching on everything that is relevant, yet not necessarily critical for the solution. You should still answer each question with a hypothesis-driven mindset to demonstrate your spike in this area. However, for McKinsey it is more of a demonstration exercise as there is rarely a single correct answer or single correct hypothesis. Irrespective of your hypothesis, interviewers move the case forward through a series of separate and often unrelated questions.

These types of cases are arguably easier to prepare for and to go through since the risk of getting lost along the way is low. If you struggle with one question, you can start from scratch with the next question. Your initial issue tree cannot derail the outcome of your case entirely. The downsides are that you need to draft a more exhaustive framework with equally deep and balanced ideas, and you have less control over the direction of the case. I talk more about the time you should take to think and talk for both candidate-led and interviewer-led cases in **Chapter 14**.

While in a candidate-led case, the main goal is to reach a sound recommendation after going through your issue tree, asking the right questions, analyzing the right data, etc., your task in an interviewer-led case is to provide sound and self-standing answers to each individual question. Think of the latter as a series of mini cases, where you tackle each question specifically. I believe interviewer-led cases are easier to solve as you only need to worry about one problem at a time (while still remembering the context of the case). As a result, it is also much less about the correct result or solution (except for the numerical part), but much more about your approach, exhaustiveness, and creativity of ideas. It is almost impossible to go off on a tangent and not reach an outcome, whereas in a candidate-led case you always run the risk of investigating completely irrelevant parts of the issue tree, losing time, and coming up with a faulty conclusion or none at all.

While you should practice a common set of skills (structuring and idea generation, math, exhibit interpretation, hypothesis generation, and communication), you need to follow a different game plan for each interview format. Knowing what steps to take and when to take them makes it easier for you to focus on problem-solving, creativity, and your analytics throughout. I prepare clients for both formats and how they study and how they approach cases makes a significant difference in their performance. A one-size-fits-all approach does not work, especially when we are talking about the level of competitiveness and the low offer rates in top-tier firms. You want to be well prepared for each type of case and use the different formats to your advantage.

In fact, case interviews are very formulaic in nature and there is a certain checklist of habits – what to do and when – you should employ to go through in order to maximize your outcomes. This checklist is different between the types of cases. In the later chapters, we go through each building block of a case and then discuss the different game plans for both types of cases for you to internalize and follow going forward.

With your game plans internalized, practice each case format individually and make it clear at the beginning of a practice session with a case buddy what format the case should be. When working with peers, I would recommend that you switch to an interviewer role from time to time as this gives you new insights into similarities and differences between both approaches.

What is the difference between a first and final round (partner) case interview?

My clients commonly ask questions about the differences between the interview rounds. Most have a greater respect for final round interviews as they expect them to be much harder, which is not true. There are more similarities than differences between interview rounds. The differences are the seniority of interviewers, the focus areas, and the structure of the interview.

First round interviews are usually conducted by more junior interviewers such as associates or project managers, final round interviews by more senior staff such as junior partners, partners, and sometimes even senior partners. The belief that this makes final round interviews more difficult can largely be debunked as it is mainly based on perception rather than reality.

The fact that a partner interviews you instead of an associate might play with your nerves and make the situation more stressful, even though the case is just as easy or hard as in the previous rounds. In that sense, your evaluation of the interview is purely based on your interpretation of the situation and not on the actual content. Another reason why you read a lot about more challenging partner interviews is that when the interviews deviate from what people expect, they are more likely to post about it online, hence giving others the impression that such situations are more common than they are.

The logic behind having owners of the firm interview you is to have an additional set of eyes at a senior level on promising applicants who have made it through all filters thus far. Final round interviewers are looking for confirmation of what they have been told about you or dispelling potential doubts raised by previous interviewers. In practice, that could either mean that they are focusing on your perceived strengths, or worse, focusing on your perceived weaknesses from the first round, which might feel more difficult for you. For instance, if the feedback in round one was positive on all aspects but math (e.g., *"I want to see more initiative and shortcuts in drafting the approach for the math questions"*), they might tailor the case to include more quantitative elements in the final round. Consequently, between interview rounds you need to work on the areas that have been identified as potential weaknesses.

You might have a feeling about your weaknesses or have received specific feedback after the first round from interviewers or HR in a follow-up call. In any case, you should always ask for feedback and improvement potential (including concrete examples) to understand your strengths and weaknesses from their perspective. The more detailed the feedback you receive, the more focused your adjusted preparation can be.

The last key difference that is noticeable across all firms is that final round interviews are sometimes less structured and more chaotic than first round interviews. Even though the interview guidelines (format, questions, length, evaluation criteria, conduct, etc.) might be the same, senior interviewers sometimes deviate and run the show based on their own perception and preferences. This could mean that they might:

- ☑ focus on one specific aspect of the interview, the case or the fit (to confirm previous interviewers' perception of your strengths or drilling into weaknesses)
- ☑ focus on specific elements or question types such as structuring and brainstorming, if you are going through a case
- ☑ have you answer a series of unrelated case questions
- ☑ not allow you to take time to think, even if you ask for it
- ☑ make the interview more conversational
- ☑ do two short cases in quick succession
- ☑ make up cases on the spot

- ☑ challenge your answers to see how you would defend your point of view
- ☑ focus on general fit and motivational questions rather than full story questions such as in the McKinsey Personal Experience Interview
- ☑ want to have a normal conversation to get to know you since they are already convinced about your problem-solving skills and fit.

Everything is possible. Whatever the interview may be about and whatever the style of the interviewer, do not panic and stick to the rules and habits I discuss in this book. Being forced to change gears quickly, adjusting to less structured interviews, and going through more stressful situations are just other ways to evaluate your fit with the company and the role. I remember the story of one of my clients who had to go through eight structuring and brainstorming questions in one final-round interview with the interviewing partner constantly challenging his answers. One of my recent clients had the opposite experience, where one of the final-round interviewers, the managing partner of the office, only showed interest in what she did outside of work. While she was eager to demonstrate her case skills and discuss strong fit stories that we prepared, the conversation never got past her musical interests and skills. Both of my clients ended up getting the offer, puzzled about their experience.

Still, keep in mind that at McKinsey, ninety-five percent of final-round interviews are fully standardized. For other firms, that number is a bit lower and correlates more broadly with the relatively less structured nature of their interviews. For the large majority, final round cases should not be more difficult than first round cases.

PART 4

The Parts of a Case Interview:
Develop Your Basic Case Interview Skills

Let's make it more practical by going through the individual parts of a case interview in a step-by-step manner, complementing theory with practical examples. This way I can introduce you to all the intricacies that are hard to describe relying on theory alone and answer the following questions in a broader sense:

- ☑ What are the different elements of a case interview?
- ☑ How should you kick off a case interview and deal with the case brief?
- ☑ How should you approach issue trees and frameworks?
- ☑ How can you interpret charts and data most effectively?
- ☑ What's a good way to approach case math?
- ☑ How can you come up with a recommendation in the end?

[7] Learn how to deal with the case brief

At the beginning of every case interview, your interviewer tells you about a client situation and problem that they are trying to solve. At the end of their brief, they might ask a specific question that you need to answer during the case. For instance, a brief could look like this:

> "Our client is a large German sporting goods manufacturer, one of the top three globally, serving 160 countries mainly with shoes, apparel, and sports equipment. They have seen an increasing demand for more sustainable products from customers, essentially requiring environmentally friendly options. Hence, they have asked us to help them reduce their CO_2 emissions without impacting profit."

There are two things you should do immediately:

1. Play back the brief in your own words.
2. Ask follow-up questions about the situation and the goal.

First, play back all the information you have received in your own words to make sure you have understood what the case is about. Many websites and books recommend playing back only the most important information. I argue against that. You don't know what part of the information is relevant and important. Sometimes, a data point mentioned in an accessory sentence might be crucial for you to understand the problem or to solve the case. Hence, play back every detail you have received. Be aware that sometimes cases have two conflicting goals (such as in our case brief above), so you need to consider interdependencies when working on a solution.

Second, ask clarification questions to learn more about the situation and the goal. You want to make sure you understand the business and the situation in all areas that are relevant for the case. For instance, if you work on reducing CO_2 emissions for the client mentioned above, you should not ask about the client's marketing efforts or pricing strategy, as it has little or no relevance to this case.

Rather, try to understand how the client's value chain operates, how they produce, move goods around, and how they sell those products, all areas where CO_2 is emitted. Your questions should be targeted and not a learned-by-heart list that you ask in every case regardless of the goal and the situation.

Also, if you do not understand a concept or word, now is the time to clarify its meaning. You are not expected to know everything. Even though it is likely common knowledge, a reasonable question for a generalist consultant could be: *"What are CO_2 emissions and where do they come from?"* If you have a background in sustainability or are applying for a specialist position, such questions are less appropriate.

When asking about the goal, you need to operationalize it to get a proper target metric as well as a time frame to implement all measures. Initial case briefs are often vague on purpose so that you need to clarify and operationalize the goal by yourself. You want to understand what the specific goal is and how the client is measuring it. Only if you have a clearly defined goal will you be able to work toward it during the case. For our case brief from above, potential questions could be:

- ☑ *"What metric are they using to measure CO_2 and by how much should we decrease it? By 10% of their current tons of CO_2? More? Less?"*
- ☑ *"How much time do we have to implement the solution?"*

You could also ask, *"Does the client have any other goals?"* A potential answer from the interviewer could be: *"Our client wants to reduce emissions by 25% within three years and 50% within five years."*

Now you have something to work with and work toward. Every measure you discuss during the case should be evaluated in relation to the specific case goal(s), in our case, the reduction of CO_2 and the stability of profits.

The interviewer provides you with additional information as requested. Sometimes, they either do not have any data, which means that it is not relevant for the case or tell you that you will get to that at a later stage (e.g., *"The data has been requested but we have not received it yet"*), which is a promising sign that you should investigate that direction further as the case progresses. There is no theoretical limit on how many questions you can ask at the beginning of a case. However, time spent in this part takes time away from you actively working on the case and solving it. Hence, I recommend that playing back all information and asking targeted questions should be done within the first three minutes. You likely never have immaculate data and all possible information throughout the case, just as consultants never have perfect data to base their decisions on during real engagements.

Now that you have understood what the case is all about and have received the requested clarifications and additional information, it is time to structure your approach.

[8] Draft the perfect frameworks, issue trees, and brainstorming answers

After playing back the prompt and asking clarification questions to understand the situation fully, you need to structure your approach and create a case interview framework, also called the issue tree. Getting the framework right is the first step to successfully acing the case. As with most other aspects of the case interview, it is a skill that needs to be learned, internalized, and practiced for you to perform at your best during the interviews. Hence, make it a priority in your preparation. I'll give you a head start by answering the following questions:

- ☑ What is a case interview framework?
- ☑ Why do you need to structure your approach?
- ☑ What are the different types of frameworks?
- ☑ What are the differences between structuring and brainstorming?
- ☑ What are the characteristics and principles of a good case interview framework?
- ☑ Should you learn case interview frameworks by heart?
- ☑ How can you create frameworks from scratch?
- ☑ What method can help you approach case interview frameworks systematically?
- ☑ What should you do if you get stuck and don't have any ideas?
- ☑ How can you practice your structuring, brainstorming, and idea-generation skills?

In this section the terms framework, issue tree, and structure are used interchangeably.

What is a framework in a case interview?

A case interview framework is used to break the problem you are trying to solve for the client or the situation you are trying to understand down into smaller problems or components. It is the roadmap you establish at the beginning of the interview that guides your problem-solving approach throughout the case and should help you identify the root cause(s) of the client's problem and find levers you can pull to improve the situation, or simply to find answers to the client's question(s).

A case interview framework consists of a top level (several aggregate areas to look at) and multiple sublevels and associated ideas that support each top-level bucket. To illustrate, a common and basic approach you might find often in some case interview examples is the profit framework. This is used when you are tasked to solve an issue regarding your client's profit (e.g., *"Our client's profit has gone down over the last year, and we are not sure why that's the case."*). Revenue and Cost represent the areas that directly influence your client's profit in the most aggregated way, hence, you would put those two ideas at the top of your framework. The top of your framework should be exhaustive to accurately include all areas of the problem. To analyze the problem effectively, you would then need to go deeper and list ideas on the sublevels that influence the main variables at the top. You can do this by creating the branches of your issue tree.

Issue trees

The best-practice approach to structuring a case is to build an issue tree with branches, which are split into several sub-branches. To stick with the profitability example, look at the framework below. Each box represents one area to look at during the case to identify potential issues, root causes, or levers you can pull to resolve the situation. As you go down the issue tree, moving top-down, each area is split into more granular components. As you move up the issue tree, bottom-up, granular ideas are grouped into higher-level, more general and aggregated buckets. Dissecting the situation like this helps you identify the problem and its magnitude (the what), the underlying reasons (the why), to then propose suitable solutions to fix it (the how).

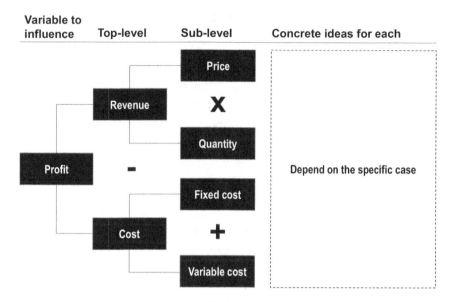

■ Example of a simple profit framework

It doesn't matter whether you draft your framework from left to right or top to bottom. Find a format that works for you and stick to it.

Why do you need to structure your approach?

The initial structure you come up with serves three important purposes:

1. Roadmap

It is the initial roadmap you establish that guides your problem-solving throughout the case. Once you lay out your planned approach, you go through the buckets of your issue tree to find the root cause(s) of the client's issue, then identify and evaluate your ideas to answer your client's question. It serves as the anchor that grounds you as you move through your analyses and investigation. By deconstructing the situation into its parts, you are looking at it as a collection of levers you can move in different directions to influence your outcome.

2. Communication device

It is used as a communication device to guide the interviewer through your thought process and approach. Also, verbally moving through the structure allows you to ask targeted questions about additional information on the buckets of the issue tree.

3. Problem-solving test

Coming up with a proper structure and communicating it well is a test in itself. The interviewer wants to see how you tackle unfamiliar problems and situations and understand their constituent parts. When listening to your approach, they evaluate your thinking, logic, analytical capabilities, problem-solving prowess, as well as communication skills.

Are there different types of frameworks?

There are two types of frameworks that depend on the nature and the progress of the case.

At the beginning of a case, you must deconstruct a problem or situation into its parts to kick-off your analysis. While in a candidate-led case, you need to do this automatically and autonomously, in an interviewer-led format, the interviewer asks you a specific question (e.g., *"How would you approach...?"* or *"What factors would you look at when...?"*). This is what is often called a case interview structure.

Alternatively, you need to come up with a structured list of concrete ideas in a brainstorming-like manner, usually a case element you might encounter midway or toward the end of a case when thinking deeper about potential issues or solutions. Both for a candidate and interviewer-led case you might be asked directly (e.g., *"What initiatives can you think of to...?"* Or *"What problems could lead to the fact that...?"*).

Let's talk about both in more detail.

Case interview structure: Figuring out a problem by creating a structured approach

When figuring out a problem or situation, a case framework is the starting point and anchor of your problem diagnosis by defining the different areas you want to analyze during the progression of the case. Think of it as the roadmap of different analyses related to the different levers you can pull to solve the issue and answer the client's question. At the top level, you need to think about all potential areas you want to look at to fully cover the problem, which refers to the exhaustiveness of your structure. Once you have created your top level, you need to drill deeper into each, creating a hierarchy of sublevels with the most concrete ideas at the bottom to look at in order to figure out what is wrong exactly or what levers you can influence to solve the issue. For each individual branch, you then start collecting more information from the interviewer, which might be provided verbally, in the form of exhibits or through solving quantitative problems.

Let's look at an example based on our CO_2 reduction case. A potential top-level bucket could be *Transportation*:

1. **Top level:** The ideas are clear and logical: *"I want to understand the CO_2 emissions generated by the transportation of our client's products."*

2. **Sublevels:**

   a. Every idea is matched with a precise and concrete analysis about a particular lever you can influence: *"I want to break transportation down into long-haul and short-haul transportation and see the total emissions and individual emissions for both, then compare it to the rest of the value chain or comparable market data to see if transport is a particular problem. For the long haul, I will look at two things. First, our modes of transport to see if we are using the most CO_2-friendly modes of transport, e.g., ships instead of planes, and if we are already using ships, I want to be using the most CO_2-friendly companies. Second, I will look into the size of our shipments, e.g., more consolidated shipments would lead to less CO_2 per unit compared to smaller shipments. For the short haul, I wish to understand two things. First, are our client's transportation routes optimized, and second, what types of trucks are they using, e.g., we could replace the fleet with hybrid or electric vehicles going forward, directly reducing CO_2."*

   b. Every idea and analysis is linked to a clear hypothesis: *"If we identify the total emissions for transportation and compare it to the other emission drivers in the value chain, we will know if we should focus on this area. If we understand the core drivers of emissions related to our transportation, we can then think about ways to reduce it by comparing it to best practices."* The hypothesis helps you to qualify your thinking and justifies your proposed approach.

If you replicate this approach for all other top-level buckets of your framework, you will understand what the problem is and how big it is (the what), before isolating where it is coming from (the why), to then work on solutions (the how).

Brainstorming and idea generation: Coming up with concrete ideas

Some cases might require you brainstorm, sometimes even right from the start. Brainstorming questions are like general structure questions and prompts, just with a narrower focus. Such case questions can be framed positively *(e.g., "What ideas do you have that would decrease flight delays?")*, negatively (e.g., *"What problems could you think of that lead to lower customer satisfaction?"*) or neutrally (e.g., *"What reasons are there that our machines break down at different rates in different locations?"*). Rarely, you might also be asked directly about what type of data is needed or what analyses you would conduct to provide an opinion on a specific topic (e.g., *"What data would you need to understand how much CO_2 our client emits and where would you get the data from?"*). A new type of question I have seen recently is *"Who would you talk to and what would you discuss with them to find out more?"*

Compared to structure questions, idea generation questions are more focused on actual ideas that you can bring to the table. For such questions, you would not create a MECE roadmap of areas you would like to explore with specific analyses, but rather discuss a structured and exhaustive contemplation about a specific topic. For instance, when you are asked about reasons for lower customer satisfaction, you would not discuss analyses such as conducting surveys or tracking customer behavior but rather focus on actual reasons such as long waiting times, bad service experience, etc. In turn, these reasons represent potential levers you can pull to improve the situation for your client. Like for a wider structure question, the top of your issue tree needs to capture the problem in its entirety by being broad and exhaustive, while at the lowest level, you need to pay attention to two things:

1. Every idea is relevant and concrete, hence, is a lever that can be influenced: e.g., *"Long waiting times."*
2. Every idea is well justified and qualified with a hypothesis: e.g., *"Long waiting times have a negative impact on the customer experience, which then leads to lower customer satisfaction ratings."*

Apart from those considerations, what else do you need for a strong framework?

What characterizes a strong case interview framework?

A strong case interview framework follows several content criteria and principles.

Content criteria of strong frameworks

An excellent structure is broad at the top level, goes into great depth on the sublevels, and consists of meaningful and insightful ideas.

Breadth: Does your top level cover the problem exhaustively? Many candidates think that it is important to have a lot of top-level ideas, yet quantity is not an indication of exhaustiveness. For instance, in a profitability case, the two top-level buckets *Revenue* and *Cost* cover the problem fully.

There are many such cases, where two to three top-level buckets are enough and allow you to structure the problem properly. You will rarely need more than four or five ideas to cover any given problem. Top-level buckets should be general and aggregated ideas for two reasons. First, this enables you to generate the necessary depth by creating more concrete ideas below. If your top-level buckets are already concrete, you might not be able to support it with several lower-level ideas. Second, if your top-level ideas are too concrete, you need many ideas to capture the problem fully. You would end up with a long line of top-level ideas, lacking depth, structure, and MECE-ness (for an explanation of this, see below). For our sample structure related to the investigation of CO_2 emissions from above, a meaningful top-level bucket could be *Transportation*. A bad top-level bucket would be *Understanding the composition of our short-haul fleet*.

Depth: How deep do you go into each top-level bucket to come up with relevant and concrete analyses/levers below? How well can you support your top level with the actual ideas that influence it? If you have a general top-level idea such as *Transportation* you need to discuss meaningful areas and analyses that relate to it. Only if you go deep enough can you identify the root cause of a problem or understand the situation fully. The case solution is never visible when looking at averages or aggregate ideas. It could be that on average our client's CO_2 emissions related to transportation are in line with the industry standard. However, by digging deeper you might find that while our client's short-haul transportation is fully optimized, they have not looked at long-haul transportation at all and there is significant improvement potential still.

Aim for three levels of depth to get to meaningful insights, usually through specific areas to look at and related analyses (e.g., Top level: *Transportation*; Sublevel one: a. *Long haul*, b. *Short haul*; Sublevel two, below *Long haul*: i. *Shipment size*, ii. *Shipment weight*, iii. *Transportation and shipping companies*).

Innovation: How meaningful and insightful are your ideas and thoughts? Have you thought about the most commonsense areas as well as some more creative and out-of-the-box areas or ideas to investigate? Tell the interviewer something they have not heard before. For instance, taking our transportation example from above, investigating the delivery truck fleet would be a commonsense idea. Thinking about replacing part of the delivery fleet with drones would be a creative, out-of-the box idea.

Another example: When looking at a simple profitability case, as highlighted earlier with the common top-level ideas *Revenue* and *Cost*, add a creative third bucket such as *Financing* if it would fit the case goal (e.g., you are dealing with a struggling client and need to ensure short-term survival; in that case, *Financing* would not directly contribute to the operating profit but could help alleviate the issue in the short term to save your client from becoming insolvent while you get more time to work on other buckets such as *Revenue* and *Cost*).

Principles to adhere to in every case interview framework

MECE-ness: Refers to a grouping principle for separating a set of ideas into subsets that are mutually exclusive, i.e., no overlaps between the different branches of the issue tree, and collectively exhaustive, i.e., covering all important aspects so there is no gap in your analysis. It is used to break down problems into logical and clean buckets of analysis. In our example, we look at a top-level bucket called *Transportation*, which must cover all parts of the transportation from suppliers to our client, from manufacturing to the distribution centers, from the distribution centers to the stores, etc. You should not have another top-level bucket called *Transportation*, nor can lower-level ideas related to transportation pop up somewhere else in your framework other than under the *Transportation* bucket.

Actionable: Your structure should consist of areas and ideas that you can exert influence on within the given time frame, focusing on the relevant levers only. For instance, if the case brief states that you need to come up with measures within one year, everything beyond that should not be part of your framework as it is outside of the solution space. If you are given six months to reduce CO_2 emissions, building a new, more sustainable production factory would not be an actionable area to investigate.

Granular: The ideas you come up with at the top level need to be supported by concrete and specific ideas at the lower levels. Granularity strongly correlates with the depth of your structure.

For instance, when looking at how to increase the revenue from a passenger on a flight, treating revenue as one big bucket is not enough. You would want to break down the revenue into its parts, e.g., the ticket price, booking fees, credit card fees, food and drink purchases on board, duty-free purchases on board, priority boarding fees, extra-leg room fees. You get the idea and can thank strategy consultants for your highly granular and annoying flight booking experience. In our example about CO_2 emission reduction, just looking at transportation is not enough. You need to break it down further, as discussed above.

A good test whether your answers are granular enough is what I call the *CEO recommendation check*. If your comment to the CEO who pays thousands of dollars per day for your advice is *"Have you considered looking into transportation?"* your team will be thrown out the door within minutes. On the other hand, if you say to the CEO, *"Here are five areas we should look into to reduce emissions related to the transportation of your company by 20%,"* they will be eager to hear your thoughts.

Logically coherent: Ideas should be logically coherent and consistent within their level and across levels of your issue tree. Ideas on the same level should stick to the same level of granularity or aggregation as well as importance and logic. For instance, if you are looking at *Revenue* and *Cost*, both items should be dealt with at the same level, and everything that influences the two should come below. General ideas at the top, concrete and specified ideas at the bottom.

If one of your top-level ideas is *Transportation*, another top level should not be *Change the machinery in our production process* as the latter is already a more concrete embodiment of another potential top-level area. Rather, the other top-level idea could be *Production*. At the same time, create frameworks with equally concrete ideas at the lowest level, otherwise you might miss out on investigating relevant areas. Frameworks should be balanced regarding the amount of content you come up with for each area.

Relevant: The content you discuss should be relevant for the case at hand, tailored to the client and their situation (as in driven by the objective of the client), and allow for a proper problem diagnostic. Avoid generic frameworks as they will not get you very far. Many of my clients in their first session try to force-fit frameworks they have memorized to a case that calls for a different and uniquely generated approach.

For instance, to reduce CO_2 for our client from above, some people would look at *Revenue* and *Cost* or *Customers*, *Competition*, and *Market*, which you could argue potentially cover part of the problem since the measures we discuss should not negatively impact profit of the company or some external observations could provide inspirations for ideas. However, these interviewees miss the core part of the problem, namely (quantitatively) identifying where the issues are coming from within the company (the what), then figuring out concretely how to reduce emissions based on further quantitative and qualitative analyses (the why and the how). Everything you say needs to be relevant and tailored to the question at hand.

Hypothesis-driven: While you should cover the problem exhaustively, you need to have a clear hypothesis of where the solution is buried or what lever is the most effective to pull right from the start. Always communicate what part of your structure you want to analyze, providing a reason and justification for your course of action and allowing the interviewer to understand your thinking. In that sense, the justification is at the intersection of your content and communication. While moving through the framework and gathering additional information, your hypotheses should be proven or rejected. More on how to move through the case with the use of hypotheses and syntheses in **Chapter 12**.

Below is an example of a typical short case prompt: *"What could be the reasons that our automated check-in machines break down at different rates in different locations?"*

■ Case interview framework example for machine rate breakdown

This example (which by no means is the only correct approach) adheres to the content criteria and principles. The ideas mentioned provide a roadmap for a more detailed investigation of relevant areas. Based on the investigation that follows, we would be able to understand what drives the issue (by how much) and suggest remedies.

Now that you know how proper frameworks should look, let's get one of the most common issues out of the way. This issue has such a huge impact on the performance of candidates that it greatly contributed to my desire to write a book about consulting case interviews.

Should you learn case interview frameworks by heart?

The short answer is *no*. Be aware that framework templates were applicable 10 to 20 years ago. Top-tier consulting firms have long caught up with this and the cases you get during the interviews are created to test your problem-solving skills, creativity, and ability to generate insights, not remember specific frameworks. In fact, it hurts your performance when you try to use a memorized framework in a case that calls for a completely different approach. Also, it gives you a false sense of security that translates into stress once you figure out that the cookie-cutter approach won't work during the live interview. I have seen this kill interviewees' performance and confidence many times. In fact, when you interview a new candidate, you are always eager to hear them perform well and listen to insightful answers. If they then start rehearsing some of the standard canned frameworks the energy level in the room drops and it is hard to turn it around from this point onward.

Your ambition should be to learn how to build custom frameworks, create tailored hypotheses, interpret charts, and perform math no matter the context, industry, or functional area of the case. It is one of the core pillars of my approach to train your thinking and ability to come up with deep, broad, and insightful issue trees for each case individually.

If you have a non-business background, it certainly doesn't hurt to glance over the classic business frameworks and concepts and pay attention to business terminology, which is different from case interview frameworks and cookie-cutter approaches. I cover all the relevant business concepts and terminology in **Chapter 20**. As mentioned earlier, it also doesn't hurt to regularly read business publications such as *The Economist*, *The Financial Times*, *Bloomberg Business News* and others as well as consulting firm research reports during your case interview preparation to get up to speed with business problems and concepts.

Lastly, be aware that there are no typical McKinsey or BCG frameworks or specific approaches for any other firm really. All firms use a diverse set of cases, which are usually developed by each interviewer individually based on a real consulting project they have worked on. If you are looking for real case examples, check out **Chapter 37**, where I link to free practice case resources covering all firms.

Now that pre-learned frameworks are out of the picture, let's have a look at effective ways to come up with creative frameworks on the spot.

How can a first principles approach help you create frameworks and not get stuck?

There are several ways to come up with and create meaningful, relevant, and targeted frameworks. Your approach usually depends on how familiar you are with the topic at hand. While you are never expected to have in-depth domain knowledge about an industry, function, or client, some high-level understanding helps with idea generation. I discuss in the preparation chapter how you can develop this understanding through:

- ☑ practicing a diverse set of cases
- ☑ regular reading of business publications and magazines
- ☑ becoming familiar with basic business concepts and terminology.

At the core of your idea generation should be first principles thinking, which refers to the process of systematically deconstructing a problem or situation into its constituent parts in a MECE way. Only by following this approach can you identify where the issue in a case comes from and how big it is (the what), then dive deeper to understand the reason (the why) to eventually work on a solution (the how). First principles allow you to break a situation down into its core pieces, then put it back together. For instance:

"What do we need to build an aircraft?"

- ☑ A factory (infrastructure)
- ☑ Tools and equipment

☑ Materials
☑ Staff
☑ Financial means
☑ Know-how

From there, you go into second and third order considerations; for instance, for staff:

☑ What qualifications are needed?
 ▸ Formal education and training
 ▸ Work experience
☑ How many people do we need?
 ▸ # of people in total
 ▸ # of people for different areas (e.g., engines vs. wings)
☑ How can we hire them?
 ▸ Supply of and demand for labor in the area
 ▸ Job advertisement
☑ How can we retain them?
 ▸ Working conditions
 ▸ Remuneration and benefits
 ▸ Training

There are several ways you can employ this type of thinking for creating case interview frameworks. First, we look at the top level of your issue tree, the foundation of your problem-solving, then explore in more depth the branches, all with a first principles perspective in mind.

Create a top level that covers the problem or situation exhaustively

Here I'll demonstrate eight different ways of coming up with a structured top level. Admittedly, not all of them work all the time, but at least one of the eight should work for any given case framework or brainstorming. Remember the following case brief, as it will guide your understanding of the first five top-level idea generation strategies:

"Our client, a sports goods manufacturer, offering shoes, apparel, and sports equipment, wants to come up with a new carbon reduction

strategy for the next five years without negatively impacting its profit. What areas would you look at to reduce emissions?"

1. Process steps or task perspective

If you are not familiar with an industry or functional area, it helps to depict the process of how a good is produced or a service is rendered. Think about the flow of goods as they are being produced and sold to the consumer as well as the overarching administrative functions. Alternatively, think about what tasks are needed to deliver a product or render a service from start to finish. For our case example, we could use the value chain to inspire our top-level buckets (in brackets are the associated tasks).

- ☑ Suppliers (sourcing raw materials and products) →
- ☑ Manufacturing (producing the final goods) →
- ☑ Transportation and Logistics (moving raw materials and finished goods) →
- ☑ Sale (selling products B2B or B2C) +
- ☑ Administration (organizing the whole process)

Now that you have the process in front of you, you can go further to identify sources of CO_2 and a potential impact on profit when evaluating measures.

Alternatively, you could come up with the following two top-level buckets:

- ☑ Value-adding activities (Suppliers, Manufacturing)
- ☑ Support activities (Transportation, Sales, Administration)

This would not be too different from the value chain, just more aggregated.

Depending on the case, you might want to dive even deeper into individual processes. For instance, if you are optimizing the customer experience in a store, think about the customer journey and the individual steps. If you want to decrease the boarding time of a flight, break down the boarding process into its elements. You get the idea. Looking at problems from a process perspective helps you create MECE top levels for many cases.

2. Components

Think about what components in the business are needed to deliver the finished product or service. For our CO_2 reduction problem, you could come up with these top-level buckets:

- ☑ Stationary infrastructure (e.g., factories, warehouses, stores, offices)
- ☑ Moving infrastructure (e.g., container ships, delivery trucks)
- ☑ Digital infrastructure (e.g., servers, data centers)
- ☑ Input factors (e.g., energy, fabrics, half-finished goods)
- ☑ Staff (e.g., travel)

Like the process perspective, these general top-level ideas cover most of the problem, just with a different lens.

3. Segmenting

You could also structure a case based on the different business or product segments. From the prompt we know that our client offers three different product categories:

- ☑ Shoes
- ☑ Apparel
- ☑ Sports equipment

You can use these three buckets as a starting point to delve further and identify which product has the highest emissions. The more you practice, the more you get a feeling about when to break down a problem by different business or product segments or by something else completely.

For this case, many parts of the analysis would potentially overlap. To remain MECE and structured, you could create a matrix framework by adding the process perspective.

4. The matrix approach

The result would look like this:

	a. Shoes	b. Apparel	c. Sports equipment
1. Suppliers			
2. Manufacturing			
3. Transportation and Logistics			
4. Sales			

With this matrix, you can pinpoint in a systematic manner which product/process cell is an outlier regarding emissions.

A matrix structure is also useful when comparing options across several aspects. For instance, you might work on a case where you have to think about different options related to the update of a current production facility. The columns could be three options, such as *Refurbish*, *Outsource*, and *Rebuild*. The rows could be *Investment Cost*, *Operating Cost*, *Product Quality*, *Implementation Timeline*, among other things relevant to the case. The resulting table enables you to evaluate and compare each option in a structured and systematic manner to reach a final recommendation.

5. Identifying problem or situational drivers

You can also identify the key direct drivers to influence. For our problem, there are six main drivers to consider:

- ☑ Energy consumed to produce and finish goods (e.g., own and outsourced production)
- ☑ Energy consumed to store goods (e.g., storage and logistics)
- ☑ Fuel used to transport and store goods (e.g., transportation)
- ☑ Energy consumed to manage the process (e.g., marketing, sales)
- ☑ Revenue generated by becoming more sustainable (e.g., price increase, quantity increase)
- ☑ Cost from making changes (e.g., investments, higher operating cost)

6. Mathematical representation of the goal

When dealing with a quantifiable problem and a clear target, you can always depict the initial structure mathematically. Since we do not have a clear reduction target in our prompt from above, let's use another example. For instance, if you are asked to improve the profit of your client by ten percent, your top level could be:

10% of current profit = Increase in revenue + Decrease in cost

You have two top-level buckets you can deconstruct to identify ways to increase revenue or decrease cost. The benefit of a fully quantified goal is that you can measure every proposed change against it to evaluate if the recommended action is worthwhile pursuing. For instance, by quantifying the impact of your ideas, you are able to tell if a specific measure (e.g., the introduction of a new product) is enough to reach the goal or if several smaller scale measures are needed (e.g., a combination of several cost and revenue initiatives) to achieve the desired increase in profit.

7. Using opposites as top-level ideas

A relatively simple trick to create a top level that covers a problem exhaustively is to work with opposites. For instance, if you are asked about incentivization mechanisms to drive customer purchases, your top level could be:

- ☑ Monetary incentives
- ☑ Non-monetary incentives

Alternatively, you could also come up with:

- ☑ Positive incentives (e.g., cash back)
- ☑ Negative incentives (e.g., loss of status)

By the very nature of their phrasing, both top-level ideas together cover the full solution space. This approach works best for brainstorming and idea-generation questions.

8. A stakeholder approach

Sometimes it might make sense to structure a problem from a stakeholder perspective. For instance, let's assume you are working on a case where you are asked to improve the patient satisfaction scores in a hospital. Your top-level buckets could be aligned with the relevant stakeholders:

- ☑ The patients themselves
- ☑ Nursing staff
- ☑ Administrative staff
- ☑ Doctors

To make this clearer, let's look more closely at one top-level bucket to identify more concrete drivers of patient satisfaction on the lower levels based on the touchpoints, e.g., for *Doctors*:

- ☑ Availability
  - ▶ Approachable during treatment
  - ▶ Responsiveness after and in-between treatments
- ☑ Expertise
  - ▶ Education and qualifications
  - ▶ Years of experience
- ☑ Treatment
  - ▶ Use of proper facilities/infrastructure
  - ▶ Use of proper instruments and medical devices
  - ▶ Use of modern, safe, effective interventions
- ☑ Patient interaction/communication
  - ▶ Friendliness
  - ▶ Openness/transparency

The stakeholder perspective is a creative approach that helps you consider a problem from a different angle, which would also resonate well with interviewers.

Avoid common errors in your top level

No matter what idea generation strategy you are using, you need to follow a MECE approach, capturing the issue in its entirety without overlaps. This is only possible if you have a certain level of aggregation for each top-level bucket. If your ideas are already too concrete at this stage, it is impossible to go deeper and develop them to create a meaningful issue tree, while at the same time you struggle to generate breadth and exhaustiveness at the top.

Don't forget about the purpose of the framework, which is to guide your analysis, and look for the relevant data to understand where the issue comes from and how big it is (the what), the reasons for it (the why), before working on solutions (the how). Do not make the mistake of thinking about solutions before understanding the problem, ideally both qualitatively and quantitatively. A common response I get for the top-level structure for our CO2 reduction problem focuses on items such as *Capabilities* or *Risks*. Apart from being generic, neither of these will help you understand our client's problem. Such top-level ideas skip the problem analysis and go straight to the implementation measures that potentially require certain capabilities and carry a certain risk.

Another issue I often encounter when I'm coaching is that my clients discuss items that are not relevant to the question. For instance, top-level buckets that might pop up for the same case are *Customers* or *Competitors*. Again, those buckets cannot help you understand where the emissions come from and how big they are to then devise strategies to reduce them. The ideas are not related to the question at all since they focus on external phenomena when that problem requires an internal analysis. What both examples have in common is that they are usually presented by candidates who have built their case preparation around memorizing frameworks instead of thinking for themselves.

Lastly, a reminder that your top level defines the solution space for your approach, which should correspond to the client request. For instance, when you are given a one-year implementation timeline for your measures, your top level for a brainstorming exercise should not contain ideas that take more than one year to implement. If you are asked to work on the satisfaction of B2B customers, your top level should not cover B2C customers, and the ideas that follow below should be tailored to the requested customer segment as well. When asked to improve the company profit through cost reductions, do not look at the revenue side. Yet, if you are asked to improve the profit of a company, your top level should not just look at one side but both revenue and cost.

Develop lower-level ideas to support your analysis

Once you have figured out the top level, you build on that to dig deeper. Here I highlight **three specific techniques to help you create meaningful and concrete issue trees**. All will make you think about where your ideas are "positioned in space".

For every idea you come up with, think about if you could make it into several more concrete ideas by expanding it, if you can aggregate it into a more general bucket above, or if it inspires another idea on the same level.

1. Expansion of ideas

Your top level needs to be supported by more concrete lower-level ideas. Let's use our process-based-view top level from before:

- ☑ Suppliers →
- ☑ Manufacturing →
- ☑ Transportation and Logistics →
- ☑ Sale +
- ☑ Administration

Now, let's go deeper by creating supporting areas you want to look at:

- ☑ **Suppliers:** 1. Standards 2. Materials 3. Processes
- ☑ **Manufacturing:** 1. Process 2. Machinery 3. Energy sources 4. Carbon offsetting programs 5. Products
- ☑ **Transportation and Logistics:** 1. Long-haul transportation 2. Short-haul transportation 3. Carbon trading schemes 4. Storage facilities
- ☑ **Sales:** 1. Stores 2. Packaging 3. Online
- ☑ **Administration:** 1. Offices 2. Corporate travel

From the newly generated sublevel, you can expand your ideas even further. For instance, for *Administration*, we could expand further to create a second sublevel with more concrete ideas:

Offices

- ☑ Investigate the change to renewable energy sources
- ☑ Look into installing passive cooling instead of air conditioning units
- ☑ Explore better building insulation

☑ Consider changing the light sources

Corporate travel

☑ Think about stopping travel completely and going fully virtual
☑ Look into reducing to only essential travel
☑ Investigate the potential to consolidate important meetings and travel
☑ Contemplate aligning travel schedules across the company

At the lowest level, you want to present as concrete ideas or areas to investigate as possible. Usually, this can be achieved by creating frameworks that consist of three levels that balance exhaustiveness at the top, with the required depth of analysis at the bottom.

Expansion works if you have a strong idea or concept and think about two or three related items to make it more concrete on a level below.

2. Think about extremes

Another trick to expand your ideas, which works especially well with (revenue) increase or (cost) reduction problems, is to think of extremes and lesser variations of those extremes. For instance, let's assume that we need to come up with ideas to raise our manufacturing client's cashflow in the short term to prevent them from going out of business. You might think about a top level such as:

☑ Increase operational cash inflows
☑ Decrease operational cash outflows
☑ Receive financing

Among the cash outflow levers you might identify *Production* as an interesting area to look at. Now, think about extremes and lesser extremes to generate depth and ideas:

☑ Stop production fully (extreme)
☑ Reduce production (less extreme)
☑ Shift production to areas where there is still demand (win-win idea)

Alternatively, you could look at another cash outflow bucket called *Staff.* For your second sublevel, you could create the following concrete ideas:

- ☑ Let everyone go (very extreme with many complications)
- ☑ Let part of the workforce go (less extreme)
- ☑ Put everyone on unpaid vacation (solves short-term cost issues, ensures long-term presence of workforce)
- ☑ Reduce everyone's salary for a while (less extreme)
- ☑ A combination of the measures above (a potentially worthwhile compromise for the short term)

Now let's consider a positive example for this approach. We are interested in increasing the short-term cash inflows. A sub-level bucket could be *Product related*. Based on that, you could generate a second sublevel with concrete ideas:

- ☑ Create a new product (extreme and probably not feasible in the short term)
- ☑ Create a new product variation (less extreme, still requires effort and a potential investment, which is a cash outflow and should be avoided in this situation)
- ☑ Improve existing product incrementally (even less extreme; the same applies as for the idea above)
- ☑ Rebrand an existing product (simple, potentially effective)
- ☑ Create product bundles (simple, potentially effective)

I added some talking points in the brackets for each idea to make it clearer and provide you with some things to say when justifying your ideas in front of the interviewer.

3. Linking of ideas and mind mapping

If you are stuck or not as familiar with an industry or topic, you could also work from the bottom up or backwards. Let's go back to the question about factors to look at to reduce CO_2 emissions. You might know that CO_2 emissions could potentially be related to the *Materials* used in the client's products. First, expand this concept by creating more concrete and insightful ideas one level below, just as I discuss above. For instance:

- ☑ Investigate the use and sourcing of new materials
- ☑ Look into sourcing existing materials from new suppliers

☑ Investigate the use of fewer materials either by making the products lighter or by producing less scrap

☑ Look into recycling either by recycling our own products or by recycling trash such as ocean plastics

Second, think about the other direction. What could be a potential top-level bucket that covers *Materials*? *Materials* are sourced from external parties known as suppliers, so you could create a new top-level bucket called *Suppliers*. Based on this aggregated new top-level bucket, you could think about where the materials go once they come from suppliers, which is our client's *Production*; potentially the next top-level bucket in your structure. Once the products are finished, they need to be delivered, which is your next top-level bucket, the *Transportation*, and, lastly, the products are sold, which is the *Sales* process – the fourth top-level bucket.

What I want to demonstrate with this example is that you don't always need to create your ideas in a top-down manner. You can come up with strong issue trees in all kinds of ways, going from general ideas down to more concrete ideas, going bottom-up, aggregating concrete ideas into a more general top-level bucket, or you could go sideways from one branch of your issue tree to the next. The trick is to learn and practice that one idea or concept can inspire you to create other ideas and concepts in a snowballing manner. If you combine any of the top-level idea generation techniques with idea expansion (top-down) and idea linking/mind mapping (bottom-up or sideways), you should be able to generate exhaustive and creative frameworks, even for industries, functional areas, or cases you are not particularly familiar with.

If you remember one thing from this section: **Whenever you create your issue tree, be mindful that you only need one idea/area to look at as a starting point.** Then, in your mind, go down, go up, or go sideways to create a full framework around it.

How to create a strong framework: example

Let's go back to the CO2 reduction example. Using the techniques described above we can devise an exhaustive framework as depicted below:

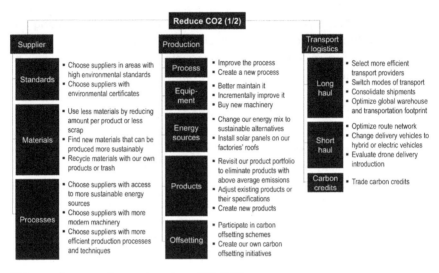

■ Structuring around areas to reduce CO2 (1/2)

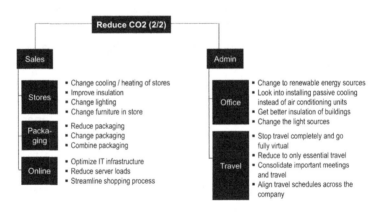

■ Structuring around areas to reduce CO2 (2/2)

How to create a strong brainstorming answer: example

Let's also look at a brainstorming question to apply some of the techniques described above. This time, we use a new question and look at it from scratch:

> *"Our client has decided to launch a new sustainable line of shoes. They want to become known as the most sustainable producer of this product. What concrete advertising channels can you come up with that would support their ambitions?"*

You might think something along the lines of *Social media*, a great idea. Now let's make more out of this. Think about where *Social media* is "in space." You could either expand into lower level more concrete ideas or aggregate it into a more general bucket one level above. First, expand the concept by listing the different types of social media or their audiences to create more concrete ideas:

- ☑ Target younger audiences via platforms such as Instagram, TikTok, and Snapchat
- ☑ Target more mature audiences via platforms such as Facebook, Pinterest, and LinkedIn

Moving up in the other direction, think about what aggregate idea could be above *Social media*? It could be *New media*, a new top-level bucket. With a new top-level bucket, consider expanding again to create more ideas one level below that relate to it, e.g.:

- ☑ Content creation
- ☑ Search engine placement

As well as up and down, you can also go sideways. If you have *New media*, create another top-level bucket called *Traditional media*. From this new bucket you can again generate more ideas by going down into several branches:

- ☑ TV
- ☑ Radio
- ☑ Newspapers and magazines
- ☑ Billboards

Now that you have two media-related channels, you might think about non-media related channels as well and come up with a top-level bucket called *Non-media*. From there, you can again create a couple of related sub-level ideas:

- ☑ Events
- ☑ Guerrilla

☑ Sponsorships

For each newly created sub-level idea across the three top-level buckets, think about a couple of concrete ideas to create the third level of your issue tree. You might end up with a brainstorming framework similar to the one below, all by starting with one idea right in the middle (*Social media*), then creating a whole issue tree around it.

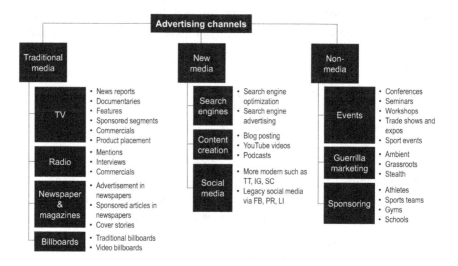

■ Brainstorming framework around advertising channels

Now that you know conceptually how to structure an issue tree, let's look at the approach that you should employ when setting up such a structure. It allows you to streamline the process and focus on the idea generation, not the logistics surrounding it.

What is the best step-by-step approach for structuring and brainstorming?

Follow these four steps for every structure and brainstorming question:

1. Understand the question you need to answer, play it back, and clarify with the interviewer if needed or if anything is unclear.

2. Ask the interviewer for one to two minutes to structure your thoughts. When preparing your answer create a top-down issue tree as displayed above.

   a. Let your thoughts be guided by one or more hypotheses, a preliminary answer to the case that you will test as you move through the framework
   b. List all areas and ideas that help you test those hypotheses
   c. Make sure that all ideas are MECE, tailored, concrete, relevant, and actionable.

3. Communicate your answer in a top-down manner by numbering and signposting your ideas, going from the top-level more general ideas down to the more specific and concrete lower-level ideas. While talking, make sure to qualify and justify every point you make. Interviewers not only care about your answer but also about your logic and thinking process, which you can demonstrate through hypotheses and proper communication. More on communication and hypotheses in **Chapters 12** and **13**.

4. Decide where you want to go next and ask the interviewer for specific data related to that branch of the tree, ordered by priority; start with the area where you see the biggest impact or potential.

When you think about your framework for one to two minutes, you will not create the perfect answer. In fact, you'll probably miss some details and more concrete ideas on the lower levels, potentially even an important top-level bucket. This is normal and expected. My experience shows that candidates usually create a structure that is 70% complete after they have thought about it. The remaining 30% of their answer is added once they lead the interviewer through their structure as they figure out new ideas on the spot. That is also why I advocate for practicing structuring drills, including the communication aspect. It not only develops your communication skills but also your ability to generate new ideas on the spot.

How can you train your structuring skills?

Structuring is the easiest part of the case to practice since you can work on it with plenty of examples in your daily life. For instance, when driving around your area, you might pass many different businesses. For each of those, come up with your own structuring or brainstorming questions. For example, you might drive past a retail outlet. What could be potential structuring questions related to that situation?

☑ *What factors would you look at when evaluating the brand positioning of this retail store compared to competitors in the area?*

☑ *How can you increase the profitability of the store?*

☑ *How can you increase the number of customers visiting the store?*

☑ *What factors would you look at when thinking about the ideal opening hours of the store?*

☑ *What ideas can you list that would drive up customer satisfaction?*

☑ *What ideas can you list that would drive up revenue per customer?*

☑ *What factors would you consider when evaluating the location for such a business?*

The list of potential business problems related to this one store is endless. I'm sure you get the idea. You don't need to open a casebook to practice this element of the interview. Work on structuring and brainstorming exercises in your daily life, even on the go. Deconstruct businesses and problems when you come across interesting situations. Of course, while you can practice structuring and brainstorming in your daily life, you can also make use of business publications, case libraries, casebooks, and consulting club case collections to work on real interview cases, either on your own or with peers. I cover detailed preparation strategies for the different parts and skills of the case in **Chapter 19**.

To become a master case solver, there are a couple more elements you need to learn about and internalize. Let's move on to the art of exhibit interpretation.

Interpret exhibits the right way

On your journey to solve the case, you must sort through and interpret data presented in the form of charts and data tables. The exhibit interpretation in a case is usually the most straightforward section since it is the only part of the case where you do not need to come up with new content, rather read and interpret what is already there.

What is the role of charts and data tables in consulting case interviews?

Exhibits usually come in two forms: 1. Charts that show data in the form of points, bubbles, lines, bars, and pieces of a pie amongst other means of visualization. 2. Tables that present data in an organized manner. Both are used to display values measured, for instance in a company (e.g., sales data), in a market (e.g., market growth), for a country (e.g., population data), for competitors (e.g., product data), among other areas. As a case interview candidate, you need to quickly skim through the data, elicit the key insights, and derive what it means for the situation at hand within the context of the case (the *so-what?*). Many candidates struggle with this part of the interview since they either do not have a clear approach or are unsure how to spot key insights.

In this chapter, I show you why exhibits are easy to decode and how it is done in the most impactful way. All you need is **a proper method to approach every exhibit, a trained eye to spot key insights, and a way to communicate and relate it back to the case**. You can train these three elements and improve your analytical approach to data tables and graphs and along the way improve your overall performance in the case. First, let's look at what types of charts you can expect.

What types of charts are common in case interviews?

The good news first: Consulting firms always use the same types of charts in their case interviews as well as on the job. I have compiled an overview of key charts and common variations below, covering ninety-five percent of what I have seen in interviews and on the job.

Side note one: You might be shown more than one chart and must interpret them by combining the information. Also, sometimes data that could be shown in multiple exhibits is combined so that, for instance, a bar chart, could also contain elements of a line chart. Lastly, charts might contain more data points than depicted in my illustrations.

Side note two: I have populated the charts with random data to make them appear as they would look in a case interview. In practice, each chart can display many elements. I have added a couple of takeaways on each chart, as would be done for a real client. Keep in mind that these observations or insights are meaningless without a case context as their purpose is to help you familiarize yourself with the different types of chart design. Due to the missing context, the charts do not show implications or recommendations either (the so-what?). We get to those later.

Bar charts

Bar charts are most commonly used when comparing values of several items at a specific point in time, or one to two items at several time intervals. Too many items or time intervals have a negative impact on the readability and clarity of such charts.

Bar charts can be presented in a column format (see below) or flipped by 90 degrees.

Revenue per year, in USD m

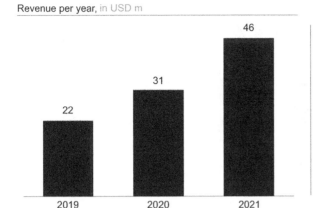

- Total revenue more than doubled over the last 3 years from USD 22m to USD 46m
- Growth has sped up between 2020 and 2021

■ Bar chart in a case interview

One variation you might come across in case interviews is the **stacked bar chart**. It extends the standard bar chart by one or more categorical variables. Each bar is divided into two or more sub-bars, each corresponding to a different categorical variable.

Revenue for three major geographies, in USD m

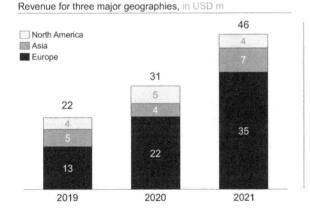

- Total revenue more than doubled over the last 3 years from USD 22m to USD 46m
- Growth is mainly driven by Europe with USD 22m revenue increase from 2019 to 2021
- North America's revenue has remained stable at USD 4m
- Asia's revenue grew by 40% yet overall only one fifth of European revenue with USD 7m in 2021

■ Stacked bar chart in a case interview

Another variation of the bar chart is the **100% bar chart**. It is a stacked bar chart that shows the relative percentage of multiple data series in stacked bars, with the total of each full bar equaling 100%. While all bars have the same height visually, they do not necessarily have the same total.

Revenue for three major geographies, in USD m

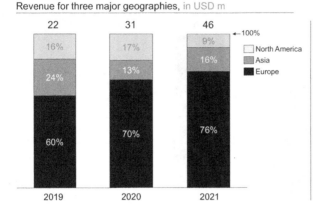

- Total revenue has more than doubled over the last 3 years from USD 22m to USD 46m
- Growth is mainly driven by Europe with a 16 percentage point increase in revenue share from 2019 to 2021
- North America's revenue share has almost halved and is now at 9%
- Asia's revenue share has decreased by 8 percentage points down to 16%

■ 100% bar chart in a case interview

The **clustered bar chart** visualizes multiple sets of data over the same categories (such as revenue of two products over three years).

Average number of support requests per product, in calls per hour

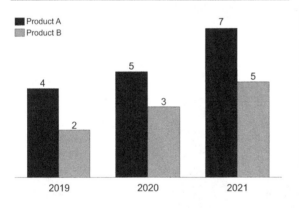

- Combined support requests for both products have doubled over the last 3 years
- Support requests for Product B have increased at a faster pace than support requests for Product A
- Last year, Product A had 40% more support requests than Product B

■ Clustered bar chart in a case interview

Bar charts are less suitable to illustrate parts of a whole unless they come as a **waterfall chart**. A waterfall chart can be either built up to a total or built down from a starting point to a new ending point. It can display all different kinds of data breakdowns.

Production time for sneaker model X, in average minutes

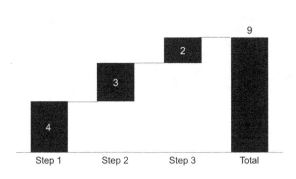

- The total production time for one shoe model X is 9 minutes
- The production consists of 3 steps with Step 1 lasting the longest with 4 minutes

■ Build-up waterfall chart in a case interview

Revenue & cost breakdown for sneaker X production, in USD m, 2021

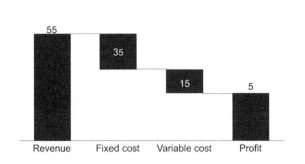

- The profit for model X sneakers was USD 5m in 2021, which represents a profit margin that is slightly less than 10%
- The revenue for the year was USD 55m with a production cost of USD 50m
- Fixed cost makes up 70% of the total cost

■ Build-down waterfall chart in a case interview

A specific form of the bar chart is the **histogram**, which displays an approximate representation of the distribution of numerical data. Histograms can be used to provide insights into mean and standard deviation.

Machine breakdowns, in # breakdowns reported per month, 2021

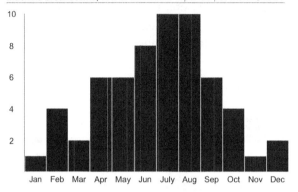

- Machine breakdowns increase over summer months with July and August showing peaks of 10 reported break-downs each
- Lowest machine breakdowns in winter months from November to March with 2 breakdowns on average each month
- Rapid increase in breakdowns from April and rapid decrease from September

■ Histogram chart in a case interview

Line charts

Line charts illustrate time-series data, i.e., development and trends in data over a specific time period. Contrary to bar charts, they consume almost no space since the points in time are connected by lines, which allows for the visualization of many time intervals.

Inflation rate, in %

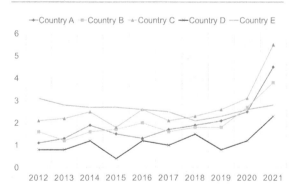

- Significant increase in inflation rates in 2021 across all countries
- Before, inflation rates in all countries moved in tandem in all years within a narrow band of around 2 percentage points
- Spread between lowest and highest inflation rate widens in 2021, with Country C at around 5.5% and Country D at around 2.3%

■ Line chart in a case interview

Line charts are not used to show data breakdowns and tend to become confusing with more than five simultaneous variables (lines).

Pie charts

The pie chart's core strength is to visualize proportions. They include all parts of a whole, without any overlap in their segmentation. Pie charts can also be displayed as donut charts. Time series cannot be displayed with pie charts.

Sales volume, in % of total number of sales for 2021

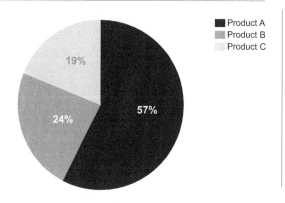

Product A
Product B
Product C

- Sales of Product A make up 57% of the total sales volume

- Products B and C with similar sales volumes make up 24% and 19% respectively

■ Pie chart in a case interview

Scatter plots

Scatter plots visualize how two variables relate to each other by plotting data points on a matrix. They are an extremely powerful tool to look at the correlation of variables by being able to display an infinite amount of data points, while keeping readability.

Scatter plots are limited by the number of axes (e.g., two axes can display two variables).

The **bubble chart** is a variation of the scatter plot that allows you to display the size of a certain data point, thereby introducing a third variable. The size of the bubble can visualize many things. It usually shows much fewer data points than a scatter plot.

Production cost vs. durability, in USD per toy and months until it breaks

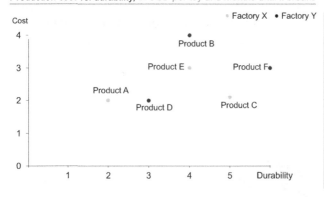

- There appears to be a positive correlation between production cost and durability
- The factory type does not seem to be related to durability

■ Scatter plot in a case interview

Universities vs. GDP, in # of universities per million & per capita GDP (USD), 2021

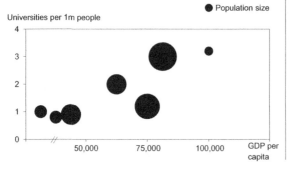

- There is a strong positive correlation between the number of universities per capita and the GDP per capita
- Countries in the data set with one or fewer universities per 1m people have an average GDP per capita of less than USD 50,000
- Countries with more than one university per 1m people have a GDP per capita of at least USD 62,500, above three universities it is at least USD 80,000
- The size of the country does not seem to be related to the per capita numbers of universities or GDP

■ Bubble chart in a case interview

Area charts

An area chart is a combination of a line and bar chart, visualizing how the values of one or more variables change over the progression of a second variable, usually time.

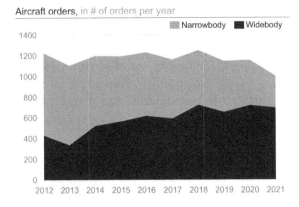

Aircraft orders, in # of orders per year

- The overall number of aircraft orders has remained relatively stable from 2012 to 2020, yet it has decreased from 2020 to 2021
- Over time, orders for widebody aircraft have increased from around 400 to around 700 per year
- Orders for narrowbody aircraft have decreased from around 800 to around 300 per year

■ Area chart in a case interview

Like a bar chart, there can be different variations such as stacked area charts or 100% area charts.

Spider charts

A spider chart, also called radar chart, can be used to display multivariate data in the form of a two-dimensional chart with three or more quantitative variables represented on axes starting from the same point. A line connects the data values for each spoke.

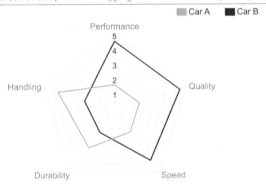

Comparison of cars, based on aggregated customer survey data (1-5)

- Customers rate Car A high for its handling characteristics and average for its durability
- They rate Car A poor for its performance, quality, and speed
- Customers rate Car B high for its performance, quality, and speed
- They rate Car B poor for its handling and durability

■ Spider chart in a case interview

Flow charts

Flow charts or process charts visualize a process or a system and its individual parts. They can be used to describe, improve, and communicate simple or complex processes in clear and easy-to-understand diagrams. Below, I have pasted your consulting interview journey again, which is well suited to demonstrate the merits of flow charts.

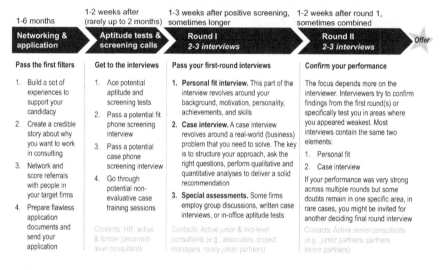

■ Flow chart in a case interview

Now that you know what types of charts can show up in a case interview, let's have a brief look at data tables.

What are data tables and how are they used in case interviews?

Data tables display information in tabular form with labeled rows and/or columns. They are commonly used to display client data (e.g., financial information), market data (e.g., sales information), economic data (e.g., GDP), and population data (e.g., demographics) amongst other things. Their format helps to organize disparate data and permits you to quickly digest it.

The way data is presented in tabular form can differ. For an example of the different stylistic elements a data table can contain, check out the table below.

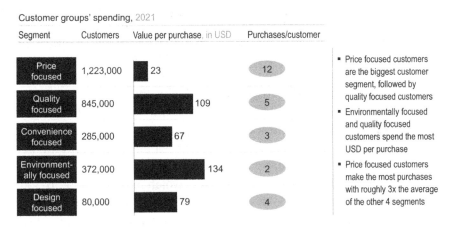

Customer groups' spending, 2021

Segment	Customers	Value per purchase, in USD	Purchases/customer
Price focused	1,223,000	23	12
Quality focused	845,000	109	5
Convenience focused	285,000	67	3
Environmentally focused	372,000	134	2
Design focused	80,000	79	4

- Price focused customers are the biggest customer segment, followed by quality focused customers
- Environmentally focused and quality focused customers spend the most USD per purchase
- Price focused customers make the most purchases with roughly 3x the average of the other 4 segments

■ Data table in a case interview

How do you interpret exhibits in case interviews with a step-by-step approach?

If you want to impress interviewers by interpreting exhibits in the most effective and time conserving manner, **follow these seven steps**:

1. **Restate and clarify the purpose of your exhibit analysis**, i.e., what you want to do with it (candidate-led format) or play back the question you are trying to answer (interviewer-led format). You must be clear about the purpose of the exhibit at the given stage of the case. The exhibit does not exist in a vacuum but is the result of your probing (candidate-led format) or the natural case sequence (interviewer-led format), and it should be looked at with a certain goal in mind, usually to verify a certain hypothesis of yours. An exhibit without context has no purpose. Only if you approach the exhibit interpretation with a clear objective in mind will you be able to spot and interpret the correct insights.

2. **Briefly describe what you see** on the exhibit by looking at the title, units, labels, legends, columns, rows, etc. You want to familiarize yourself with what you see and play it back to the interviewer in two to three sentences. Keep this part brief.

3. **Clarify whenever something is unclear.** Never interpret a chart before confirming your assumptions about what is displayed

with the interviewer. It could be that you are not familiar with a word, concept, label, or some explanations might be missing. Always be clear about what the chart is covering. For instance, is it our client's data, is it market data, or is it competitor data? Are you dealing with the general population or a subset of it? Is the chart backward looking or a forecast?

4. **Ask for time to structure your thoughts**, usually around 30 seconds to one minute. During that period, write down the key insights, the implications, and the next steps.

5. **Communicate your key insights**, which are the two to four most important data points on a chart, usually outliers or data points that surprise you. Communicate in a structured, top-down manner.

6. **Communicate the implications** (the *so-what?*) proactively, interpreting the data in the context of the case and highlighting what you would recommend based on the available data (what to do) or what the data tells you about the situation at hand (what it means).

7. **Communicate next steps**, discussing automatically how you would move forward in a structured manner, for instance, what additional analyses you want to conduct or what concrete implementation measures you would recommend.

This approach is highly effective in guiding your exhibit analysis and decision-making about what to do with the data. For now, remember the process; an example follows.

I want to stress **the importance of taking time to think about your analysis**, the fourth step of my approach. This habit is the biggest differentiator between successful and unsuccessful candidates, and I see its impact daily. Unsuccessful candidates try to rush through their analysis, reading and interpreting the chart on the go, all while talking to the interviewer. As a result, they miss key facts, fail to properly contextualize data for the case at hand, appear unstructured and chaotic, and overall take longer. I remember the disappointed faces of candidates that I challenged based on their rushed analysis and the aha moments that resulted. By thinking about these things beforehand, you can streamline your insight generation, contextualization, and communication. Taking time comes with two additional benefits:

1. You demonstrate to the interviewer that you can push back under pressure and are confident enough to take time to think (highly relevant when dealing with demanding senior clients).
2. You get additional time to identify what might be unclear related to the information from the interviewer or the exhibit itself. Exhibits might come with missing or unclear labels, units, or legends and you want to clarify what is displayed before discussing the correct insights and implications.

Avoid the two most common mistakes I see in almost every initial case with my clients:

1. **Do not read back every detail and data point from the chart.** A senior partner once told me in the early days of my career that he did not need *assisted reading* when I was guiding him through all data points on a chart instead of focusing on the relevant key insights only.
2. **Ensure you translate the data and insights into actual implications and recommendations.** Good candidates can elicit the key pieces of information from an exhibit. Excellent candidates interpret these findings in the context of the case and use them to sharpen their hypotheses, deduct implications, and plan a way forward.

What are the typical insights in an exhibit?

Usually you are confronted with many different data points and information on one or two exhibits. To figure out what the key insights are, group the data points on any given exhibit into three different categories:

1. **Data points that are relevant for you:** The key is to select the most important bits of information, usually outliers, unexpected data, or abnormalities that are relevant in the context of the case, and most striking when looking at the exhibit. Some of those insights might be generated by combining several data points.

2. **Data points that are not relevant:** There are always other things you could discuss, but in the interest of time, skip every data point that is not relevant for the case or your hypothesis or simply not interesting enough (e.g., a two percent drop in revenue for one particular product category is not that interesting if another product's revenue dropped by 23%). Think 80/20.

3. **Misleading data points:** Not all information shown to you is insightful or important, and some might even be misleading, just to create noise and distract you. Some exhibits might contain decoys that trick you into faulty conclusions. Hence, think before you speak and do not blurt out faulty statements that come to your mind quickly and might be based on wrong assumptions.

Let's have a look into the typical data points that are relevant for you – the first category from above.

Typical categories of insights

☑ **Comparison:** Compare different sets of data with each other, such as,

  ▶ internal vs. external (e.g., client vs. market)
  ▶ internal vs. internal (e.g., product A vs. product B)
  ▶ external vs. external (e.g., competitor A vs. competitor B)
  ▶ scenarios (e.g., supplier A vs. supplier B; option A vs. option B).

☑ **Segmenting:** Look for insights at a more granular level, do not look at averages and aggregates, for instance,

  ▶ breakdown of a process (e.g., customer journey)
  ▶ breakdown of financials (e.g., revenue)
  ▶ breakdown of business segments (e.g., sales)
  ▶ breakdown of geographic regions (e.g., growth).

☑ **Relationships:** Investigate a relationship or correlation between two or more variables:

  ▶ positive (e.g., cost and quality)
  ▶ negative (e.g., age and health).

☑ **Changes and trends:** Look for absolute or relative changes in one or several values over time to spot trends and trend reversals, such as,

  ▸ financials (e.g., revenue)
  ▸ customer data (e.g., purchasing behavior, satisfaction).

Types of insights, usually outliers

☑ A figure or group of figures is very small or very large compared to the others, often based on a comparison of patterns and correlations.

☑ A figure is very different from what you would have expected (rejects your hypothesis) or exactly what you would have expected (confirms your hypothesis).

☑ A figure or breakdown of figures is very different than others.

☑ A figure or group of figures shows high or low growth (decline) compared to the others.

☑ The data changes significantly at a certain point (e.g., spikes or bottoms, trend reversals).

☑ On average, the figures look good, however, when digging deeper into specific segments you see certain issues or deviations.

Learn how to spot those kinds of patterns quickly. When you are given two or more charts, the key insights often come from combining the data points of both. For instance, if you are comparing checkout speed across several stores the number of cashier desks alone is not enough. You might only get to an insight if you are able to relate the number of cashier desks to things such as the size of the store, the number of customers, the number of items purchased, etc.

How to solve a typical exhibit interpretation: example

The chart below is taken from the same case we have been working on from the start, the CO_2 reduction effort for our sporting goods client. The hypothetical practice situation is that you were keen to look into customer data since the interviewer nudged you in that direction. The interviewer has handed you a chart to investigate the customer purchasing behavior.

Customer data, 2020-2021

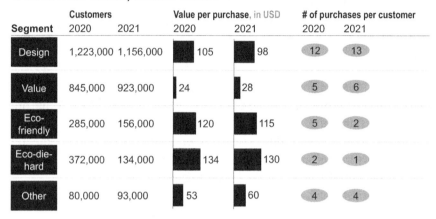

Segment	Customers		Value per purchase, in USD		# of purchases per customer	
	2020	2021	2020	2021	2020	2021
Design	1,223,000	1,156,000	105	98	12	13
Value	845,000	923,000	24	28	5	6
Eco-friendly	285,000	156,000	120	115	5	2
Eco-die-hard	372,000	134,000	134	130	2	1
Other	80,000	93,000	53	60	4	4

■ Customer segment and purchasing behavior chart

Let's follow the seven-step approach to interpret this exhibit effectively:

1. When you receive the exhibit, **restate the purpose of your analysis**: *"Using this data, I want to look at the different customer segments and their purchasing behavior to identify target segments for our effort."*

2. Now, **briefly describe what you see on the chart**: *"On the chart I see five customer segments compared across three metrics, the total number of customers, the number of purchases per customer, and the average value of each purchase. For each metric, we have data for Q1 2020 and Q1 2021, which allows me to look into changes."*

3. **Clarify** if something is unclear: *"I have two questions: First, what is the definition of eco-die-hard customers? Second, are these customer segments mutually exclusive?"* The interviewer tells you that eco-die-hard customers are making purchase decisions only based on environmental criteria (and are more extreme in that regard than eco-friendly customers) and confirms that the segments are mutually exclusive, even though it is client data, hence take it with a grain of salt.

4. **Ask for time** to structure your thoughts and write down your insights, implications, and next steps:

    a. Insights must be outliers that are relevant in the context of the case. The case is all about sustainability, so the eco-customers warrant a closer look. Indeed, the data for those customers are also outliers since we see the biggest changes here over the last year.

    b. Implications are the logical recommendation based on your insights. Now that you know that your client lost customers and their spend, it is time to interpret this information. Since in the past these customers were plenty, they had a high spend, and as we are currently working to make our client's products more sustainable, you should probably focus on getting those customers back.

    c. Next steps show how you are planning to put your recommendations into action. Think about what can be done to get the customers back in the context of the case.

5. Now it is time to **communicate what you have found:** *"I see four striking things that took place on this chart over the last year* (numbering and signposting). *First, we have lost almost 50% of our eco-friendly customers. Second, we have lost more than 50% of our eco-die-hard customers. Third, the number of purchases of eco-friendly customers has more than halved. Fourth, the number of purchases of eco-die-hards has decreased by more than 60%. Overall, we have lost significant revenue from those two customer segments."*

6. **Discuss the implication(s):** *"Based on this development, I would recommend prioritizing getting those customers back* (what you want to do) *for two reasons. First, they are very important customer segments, which made up large parts of our client's revenue in the past. Second, we are currently working on making our client's offering more attractive to such customers and could leverage our efforts in that regard* (why you think that's a good idea)."

7. **Put this implication into practice:** *"Going forward, I would like to examine two points next. First, I want to understand what product segment we could start with reducing CO2 emissions. I want to refer to my initial structure by getting an insight into the value chain and levers we have here to understand where the emissions come from, how big they are, how we can remove*

them, then understand how much that would cost us. Second, I want to identify potential marketing and advertising strategies that would help communicate our more sustainable message to said customer segments. For this I want to understand what our current marketing looks like (how you are going about it)."

As demonstrated, exhibit interpretation is a straightforward task. Still, it comes with ample opportunities to go wrong.

How can you avoid common pitfalls in exhibit interpretations?

Steer clear of these common pitfalls and you already fare better than 80% of the case interview candidates I've interviewed:

- ☑ Analyzing the chart without an objective in mind.
- ☑ Starting to talk about the data without thinking about it first, figuring out insights and interpreting them along the way without a proper structure or plan.
- ☑ Failing to clarify what the data covers and for what time period (market data vs. company data vs. competitor data, specific population data vs. general population data, historical vs. current vs. forecast, etc.), consequently drawing wrong conclusions that are based on faulty assumptions.
- ☑ Describing every data point on the chart without any direction or hypothesis.
- ☑ Discussing *non-insights* or *negative insights*. For instance, if asked, *"What data point on the chart could influence the customer waiting time?"* do not say, *"As we can see from the chart, data point A has no influence on waiting time."*
- ☑ Finding insights quickly, then rambling on about the same insights without adding anything to the discussion until the interviewer steps in to ask how to interpret them (*"What does it mean?"*) or how to proceed (*"What would you do about it?"*).
- ☑ Repeating the same points or using filler sentences or phrases without concluding or deriving a concrete plan of action.
- ☑ Taking too long to move through the exhibit. A proper exhibit analysis including interpretation and next steps can be

communicated exhaustively in less than two minutes (after thinking about it for one minute).

☑ Guiding the interviewer through the insights and the contextualization in a chaotic, non-structured manner (no numbering, no signposting).

☑ Failing to recognize or mixing up units and magnitudes, especially across charts and tables or failing to properly identify and read titles, units, labels, and different axes, basing the analysis on faulty assumptions.

☑ Failing to interpret the key insights in the context of the case or interpreting the data the wrong way, coming up with logically faulty implications for the case.

☑ Getting into lengthy calculations. Chart interpretations are usually only about what you can spot easily. Stay away from calculations if you are not being asked to calculate or if they are not needed to generate insights.

☑ Failing to recognize correlations and dependencies (e.g., on a graph with an x-axis and a y-axis).

☑ Failing to spot insights that can only be derived from the combination of two data points, so-called "hidden insights" (big-picture thinking).

☑ Failing to identify important information in the footnote or the source that might change the meaning or interpretation of the data (detail orientation).

Now that you know what to do and what not to do, let's work on building your skills.

How can you train exhibit interpretation?

You can quickly improve your exhibit interpretation skills by applying the approach, the right communication, and the tips above to practical examples. Prepare for case interviews by analyzing charts in magazines such as *The Economist* or *The Wall Street Journal*. A quick Google search for *"Chart of the day"* yields thousands of results that you can use to practice and hone your chart interpretation skills. To check your insights, compare them with the text of the articles accompanying these charts. Additionally, look for online case libraries and go through university consulting club casebooks that are linked in **Chapter 37**. When practicing, follow the steps I describe above.

- ☑ Internalize the seven steps.
- ☑ Time yourself to create realistic conditions and pressure (one minute to think, one to two minutes to communicate your analysis).
- ☑ Train your eyes to find insights quickly based on outliers and abnormalities.
- ☑ Train your mind to generate implications and next steps in the context of the case.
- ☑ Become comfortable with the top-down communication of your analysis by practicing out loud, including recording yourself and critically listening to your performance.

In addition, establish a case interview math practice routine since case math might be based – as a follow-up question – on the exhibits you receive during the interview. More on that next.

[10] Ace all case interview math problems

On your quest to solve a case, you need to work through quantitative problems. In this process, you first need to understand how such analysis would help you comprehend the problem, then get the right data, analyze it mathematically before qualitatively interpreting the result to provide implications and recommendations for the client. Most candidates fear this part of the interview and my experience shows that most errors and rejections do, in fact, occur in the quant section.

Why do candidates struggle with consulting math?

There is no need to fear quantitative problems in case interviews. The level of math required is not more complex than what you have already learned in high school and you do not need a specific degree to master case math. As with every other element of a case interview, there is a specific way of approaching it, which you might not be used to from your previous academic or professional experience. You cannot rely on assistive devices and tools such as calculators or Excel and must go back to mental math, which you probably last practiced five to 15 years ago.

Every consulting math problem consists of three parts: First, you need to plot a course of action, i.e., figure out what to calculate and how to set up your approach. Second, plug in the numbers and perform the calculations. Third, you need to interpret the results in the context of the case. Adding to that are the stressors from the time pressure and the interviewer observing you. In this section, I'll show you:

- ☑ **Logic, approach, formulas:** How to come up with the correct calculations
- ☑ **Basic arithmetic, tricks, and shortcuts**: How to perform swift and accurate calculations

☑ **Communication:** How to communicate your approach, results, and interpretation

☑ **The consultant's quant mindset**: How to stay cool under pressure.

What is the purpose of case interview math?

Fact-based decision-making and recommendations in case interviews are often based on quantitative insights and results. Formulating the correct logical approach to quantitative problems and following through with the correct calculations is one of the key skills needed for the case interview but also for every working consultant to support their daily decision-making. Hence, quantitative analyses are conducted for two reasons.

1. Finding the problem and quantifying its impact

Before solving a problem, consultants need to figure out *what is wrong* and *what is wrong by how much*. They run quantitative analyses to get to the root of the problem and understand its magnitude, a process that also gives them insights into potential solutions. During the case interview, you must do the same in a simplified task.

2. Supporting recommendations

Strong arguments are needed to support business decisions for the client, and every measure or recommendation that is proposed by consultants has a quantitative backing and rationale. The answers you get to by conducting quantitative analyses during the case interview are crucial for your recommendation(s) in the end.

Consulting firms check your quantitative skills. You are expected to perform well in such an environment. Consulting firms check whether you have what it takes for the daily quantitative consulting life before starting your fast-paced career. Hence, the math in case interviews is similar to the real-life math consultants deal with every day. Usually, the actual questions are built on sanitized and simplified client data sets that the interviewers worked with. Being able to set up equations and formulas, perform basic arithmetic (addition, subtraction, multiply, division, percentages, and fractions), and give reasonable estimates is usually enough to solve a typical interview problem. Some of the problems may include multiple steps and require a certain degree of logic, which should never be too difficult.

Advanced mathematical knowledge is not required, complex math or financial concepts are usually not part of a case interview unless you are interviewing for a specific position. For instance, corporate finance consultants and specialist hires are expected to be comfortable with the common corporate finance toolkit and concepts. I discuss the most common computations, formulas, and business math concepts in **Chapter 20** and later in this chapter. However, since for most roles you are not expected to have any domain knowledge, if you are not familiar with a concept, you can always ask for clarification.

Since the math is usually straightforward and simple, what else makes it so challenging? The fact that both planning your approach and then calculating happens in a stressful environment with the interviewer watching every step. Add to that the time pressure and the fact that calculators cannot be used. On top of that, you are expected to perform consistently well on quantitative problems within one case and across several cases in succession. To make this process easier, let's look at how to deal with the quantitative aspects of a case.

How should you approach case math questions with a tested step-by-step approach?

There are two types of candidates with different skill levels: those who need to (re)-acquire skills not used since high school, and others who need to simply dumb down their approach and become familiar with simple math questions again. The latter is especially true for engineers and other applicants with a quantitative background. Both types usually have to get used to mental math again since they have been relying on the comfort of calculators and spreadsheets. Additionally, both need to adapt to the specific case interview math principles and the process. Unlike math problems in school, the focus of case interview math is always on the context of the case. Getting to results is only the first step. You need to use your results to make sense of them in the overarching picture of the case. In turn, 100% accuracy is not needed most of the time, rather directionally correct results – think 80/20 – that are interpreted well. Approach case interview math with this mantra:

> *It's better to get directionally correct results swiftly and interpret them correctly in the context of the case than obtain 100% accurate results with 3x the time invested and not generating any insights for the client in the process.*

In the following section, I show you how to tackle case math, using my battle-tested approach.

A nine-step approach to every case math problem

To get rid of the stress and improve your quantitative analytics, you need to learn an approach that works for every type of case math question, regardless of the problem or context. **Use this nine-step approach** whenever you encounter a quantitative analysis:

1. **Figure out what you need to do.** Through probing and moving through your analytical framework, you might get to a stage that demands you to perform a quantitative analysis. First, you should understand what you need to calculate and why this is relevant in the context of the case.
2. **Listen and/or read.** Carefully and actively listen to what your interviewer tells you about the problem and the available data. Alternatively, once you have aligned what should be solved and what data is needed, interviewers might show you one or two exhibits.
3. **Clarify.** Before you dig into the problem, slow down: read back the numbers you heard from the interviewer or extracted from exhibits or discuss what additional information you would need to answer the question. Align with the interviewer on the desired objective and outcome of your analysis. You want to be clear what you are trying to solve.
4. **Draft your approach.** Set up your planned approach. For more difficult tasks, you could ask for a minute to get your head around the problem. Draft your logic on the piece of paper you have been handed by the interviewer. Most of the time, it is up to you how you want to approach the problem and there is not just a single correct way. The question could be asked in a way that makes it not entirely clear what you

need to do and there might be different potential approaches that could work. For instance, when investigating whether an investment is beneficial, you could decide what criterion you want to employ to judge that (e.g., positive ROI, breakeven point reached within a certain time period). In an interviewer-led case interviewers might not ask *"Can you calculate the breakeven of the investment here?"* but they would package it in a more obscure question such as *"Would you recommend that investment to the client?"*

In any case, break down your approach into individual steps and write it out on the piece of paper to cover your calculation plan from start to finish. When thinking about how to draft your approach, break the problem into small individual steps instead of creating one lengthy and complex formula. Focusing on what works quickly is better than trying to establish the most elegant solution.

5. **Communicate your approach.** Lead the interviewer through your approach and communicate in a structured step-by-step manner (*"I want to break this calculation down into three steps. First, I want to calculate X by multiplying Y with Z, second..."*). You appear structured and mistakes can be spotted early. Also, interviewers can provide targeted feedback about your plan. More on communication later in **Chapter 13**.

6. **Calculate.** When the interviewer agrees with your approach, follow through with the calculations. This can be either done alone and in silence or by guiding the interviewer while you calculate. I always recommend my clients do it alone so that they have the full focus on the numbers and their calculations. That way, they are quicker and make fewer mistakes. Do not feel pressured to talk while you calculate. You put yourself on the spot and mistakes are automatically picked up by the interviewer before you have a chance to correct them. If you prefer to conduct your calculations in silence, ask if the interviewer is okay with it. This is a hotly debated topic, but most interviewers are perfectly fine with this approach. If your calculations takes a bit longer, provide an update midway about which step you are currently at. This puts interviewers at ease as you are demonstrating progress and transparency. You

should usually finish the calculation part within a maximum of around three minutes.

7. **Sanity check your results.** Make sure that there are no mistakes in your calculations. Do the numbers make sense? Are they in the right ballpark? Do the magnitudes make sense? Did you plug in the right numbers to calculate? Can you spot any careless mistake or broader issue? Alternatively, you could already front-load your sanity check. For instance, if you calculate 780 million times 87, you know that the result will be somewhere around 70 billion (8 x 9 =72; 100 million x 10 = billion). Use the precise calculation to prove your point. If your result is completely off the mark, you have made a mistake with your precise calculation. You can state your intentions out loud before doing it: *"Just give me 30 seconds so I can run a quick sanity check on the numbers."* Keeping the interviewer in the loop about your thoughts and progress is key throughout.

8. **Simply answer the question.** Answer the question in a confident and assertive manner. Do not phrase the answer as a question and focus on the key results when communicating. For instance, if asked if an investment makes sense your answer should not be *"The investment breaks even after two years"* but rather, *"Yes, the investment makes sense since it will break even within two years"*. The final result of the calculation is usually just the supporting argument for your answer. If you follow the approach I discuss here, there is no need to communicate and go through each intermediate step of your calculation either. Focus on the outcome, not the process, in the same manner as you would do when presenting to a CEO.

9. **Relate it back to the case.** When answering the question, do not stop there. Automatically explain and interpret the numbers in the context of the case. Relate the outcome and the answer to the situation and problem as well as to your hypotheses. Remember why you set up the calculation in the first place. How does it tie into your planned analysis? How does it impact your hypotheses? Is it the result or just some intermediate outcome? Also discuss if the outcome is reasonable and makes sense or – in some cases – is achievable. At the end, plan ahead and discuss your next steps, either additional analyses if you have not fully grasped

the issue, or implementation measures, if you want to move toward a recommendation.

You want to focus on one thing at a time. When working on quantitative problems, always split communicating from thinking, thinking from calculating, and calculating from communicating. If you do two or three of those at the same time, for instance, thinking about the approach on the fly while talking to the interviewer about it and already performing initial calculations, chances are you'll get lost along the way, make mistakes, or – in the best case – just take longer and leave a less than perfect impression.

Dealing with data

The data you receive could be verbally communicated by the interviewer, presented via exhibits, or shared through a combination of both. There are three possibilities you need to think of:

1. **You have all the data to set up and perform the calculations.** Move on and think about how to manipulate the data to get to a desired outcome. This is the most likely scenario.
2. **You are missing some data.** Think about what data is needed to set up your approach, then ask the interviewer to provide you with the missing data. If they don't have it, make reasonable assumptions to get to plausible numbers to fill the gaps. This happens sometimes.
3. **You have too much data.** Not every data point that you see or that is communicated to you might be relevant for the calculation. Sometimes, data is just there to confuse you. Ignore. Focus on the signal, not the noise. This is a rare scenario.

Make sure that you consider all data that is available to you (sometimes not in the most obvious manner) before jumping to conclusions and asking for more data and new information.

Be cautious with mental math

A word of caution for all you mental mathematicians out there. Even if you are a math wizard, still take notes, also when you are performing calculations in your head. Every step, every intermediate result should be documented. Otherwise, you face a serious problem when you make a mistake. You have no track record of your process or documentation of your mistake and would have to start from scratch to think about your approach or re-do all calculations. With no paper trail, it is almost impossible to spot your own mistakes in time or perform a sanity check, which could save you from a rejection. Additionally, the interviewer is not able to help you effectively as they have no point of reference to hold on to.

At the very least, keep a record of your intermediate results for the interviewer to be able to follow and intervene and for you to be able to quickly go back to find and fix a mistake. At best, write down all your steps, calculations, and intermediate results.

What should you do when you get stuck on the approach?

Most candidates start to panic when they don't know how to structure a math problem. Not all is lost at this point if you stay calm and collected and have a plan to deal with the situation. So, what can you do when you get stuck and don't know how to proceed?

Before you ask for help, think through the following checklist:

- ☑ Do I know what the objective is? What do I need to solve? If you don't have an answer for that, clarify with the interviewer.
- ☑ Do I understand the problem and the details of the question? If you are missing some context, clarify with the interviewer.
- ☑ Do I have all the data that I need? Am I missing something, or am I confused due to a large amount of (irrelevant) data?
- ☑ What would be the simplest way to approach this? Am I approaching this from a too complex perspective? This is a big sticking point for most candidates.
- ☑ Is this similar to something I have worked on during practice?

If you are still not able to move forward, ask for help in a targeted way by offering the interviewer something in exchange. Do not say: *"I don't know what to do. Can you help me?"* Do not stay silent either. Rather explain your current understanding of the situation to the interviewer (e.g., *"I believe that in this case I would need to look at the net benefit of the decision."*). Discuss your thinking about how you would like to solve the problem on a higher level but are currently missing one or two steps to make it work; then ask for guidance (e.g., *"I need to compare the additional costs and revenues. It is clear for me how to get to the revenue numbers. For the additional costs I am not 100% certain that I am approaching this correctly, would you have any input on that"*). Interviewers want you to succeed and a little push on the math approach does not automatically lead to a rejection unless it happens more frequently in one case or across cases or you need support in more areas of the case.

I discuss more about what to do when you get stuck in a case in **Chapter 12**.

How to solve a typical case math problem: example

Let's go through an actual case math problem, based on the CO2 reduction case from earlier. Hypothetically, you have figured out that manufacturing seems to be one of your client's key issues and that an investment into new machinery would help alleviate it.

1. **Figure out what you need to do.** *"I know now that we should look into improving the sustainability of our client's manufacturing. In order to do that, I would like to look into the investment that is needed and the consequences and benefits for our client."*
2. **Listen to the interviewer's brief.** *"Our client would need to invest USD 500m to make their production more sustainable. As a result, the quantity of goods sold would increase by five percent and the average price for one item would increase by USD 5. The profit margin per item would remain at 20%. They want to know if the investment is worthwhile."*
3. **Play it back and clarify if needed.** *"So, I understand that an investment of USD 500m would achieve our sustainability targets. Customers would buy five percent more at USD 5 more per item. The future profit margin would still be 20%, and they want to know if the investment makes sense, with the decision criterion being to reach breakeven within five years since the initial brief told us that we have five years to implement all measures. Is my understanding correct?"* The interviewer agrees.
4. **Ask for time to think about your approach.** *"Can I take a minute to structure my approach?"* Write down a step-by-step

plan to solve the issue. You might have figured out that you would need additional data to solve the question, which is the current quantity sold and the current price of the product. You can ask the interviewer for those data points. As a reply, they tell you that the current quantity sold is 78 million items per year at an average price of USD 87 per item.

5. **Communicate your approach.** *"I want to approach this calculation in four steps: First, I want to calculate our current profit per year by multiplying the current quantity with the current profit per item. Second, I want to calculate the future profit per year by multiplying the future quantity with the future profit per item. Third, I want to deduct the current profit from the future profit. Fourth, I want to compare five times the delta of the future and the current profit to the USD 500m investment and see if we are able to break even within five years."* If the approach makes sense, the interviewer agrees (there are other ways to approach this, for instance, calculating the payback period which is the investment divided by the additional profit per year).

6. **Calculate.**

   a. Current profit p.a. = 78,000,000 x 87 x 0.2 = 1,357,200,000
   b. Future profit p.a. = 78,000,000 x 1.05 x (87 + 5) x 0.2 = 1,506,960,000
   c. Difference p.a. = 149,760,000 ≈ 150,000,000 (ask the interviewer if you can round this number up to make your life easier)
   d. Difference over five years = 750,000,000, which is bigger than 500,000,000.

7. **Perform a sanity check.** In this case you could think along the lines of:

   a. Check your intermediate steps, e.g., 78 x 87 x 0.2 ≈ 80 x 90 x 0.2 ≈ 70 x 0.2 = 1.4 → makes sense
   b. Check your zeros, e.g., 78 x 87 = 4 digits + 6 zeros from 78,000,000 (78×10^6) = 10 digits (6,786,000,000)
   c. Both current and future profit are in the same ballpark
   d. The difference is sensible
   e. The magnitudes seem reasonable and make sense.

8. **Communicate your answer.** *"The investment makes sense as we are breaking even in less than five years, hence I would recommend it."*

9. **Discuss and interpret it in the context of the case.** *"The investment achieves both goals of our client. First, the investment achieves our sustainability goal. Second, the investment would not only keep the profit stable but increase it over a five-year time period* (interpretation in the context of the case). *I would like to check the assumptions that we would really sell five percent more at a higher price point and that the investment will not exceed USD 500m as changes to these figures could quickly change my evaluation* (think about feasibility and reasonability). *Going forward, I would like to do two things. First, I want to think about how we can implement these measures and, second, we should start thinking about potential marketing and advertising strategies to promote these new sustainable products* (next steps and moving forward)."

Now that I have discussed the process and provided an example, let's look at the typical setup of math problems and key formulas you need to know.

What are typical math problems and key formulas?

Three types of case math problems

All case interview math problems fall into one of the following three categories with the objective to either figure out a problem or help you come up with a recommendation:

1. **Market or segment sizing**, e.g.,
    a. *"How many super sports cars can be sold in China in the next five years?"*
    b. *"If we expanded our offering to low-cost flights, how many additional passengers could we get every year?"*
    c. *"What is the size of the global market for tertiary education in 2025 in USD?"*

2. **Operational calculations and decisions**, e.g.,

    a. *"Let's compare the lead time for each production step across all five products. I want to see how much time we would save in total if we implemented the best practices from product A in the production of the four other products?"*

    b. *"If we added 25% more service space, how many additional customers would we be able to serve in three months?"*

    c. *"How many more units do we need to produce in factory A per year to increase the utilization rate by 12%?"*

3. **Investments and other financial and strategic decisions**, e.g.,

    a. *"Investment A would give us a 12% annual return and Investment B 5.5% every six months. What investment should the client go for?"*

    b. *"How much do we need to increase the price of product A to have a profit margin that is the same as the average of the profit margins for products B-D?"*

    c. *"On charts 1 and 2 you see different supplier contracts. Purely based on the cost, which supplier would you choose?"*

While case math problems can be categorized broadly into these three areas, within each area there is a wide variety of problems. Hence, the focus of your preparation should be on developing quantitative reasoning skills rather than memorizing approaches for a defined set of math problems. Still, there is a set of formulas, as well as approaches and memory items, you should be aware of.

Case math formulas and approaches for each type of problem

Market or segment sizing

There is no shame in asking the interviewer for certain numbers in a market sizing exercise (e.g., the population of a specific country), however, to make your life easier you could memorize some figures before you go into the interviews:

- ☑ World population
- ☑ Population of US, UK, Germany, China, India and other large countries
- ☑ Population of countries within your geographical region
- ☑ Average life expectancy

☑ Average household size
☑ Income levels

For market sizing, follow this simple approach based on a sample question, and do not overcomplicate it. *"How many new cars are sold in Germany every year?"*

1. **Define the outcome variable you are trying to solve for**: *Number of new cars sold in Germany per year.*
2. **Think of the three to four key variables that influence the outcome variable and their relationship to set up your approach:** *Number of households x cars per household / average age of a car.*
3. **Ask for data on the individual variables and, if not available, use assumptions for each.** Support your assumptions with actual data you might know, plausible arguments, or rational observations: *"There are roughly 80 million people in Germany, with an average household size of two, so we would have 40 million households. A household on average would have one car I would assume since many households, especially in urban regions do not have a car, while some households especially in the countryside might have two or even three cars. I would argue that a car is driven on average for eight years before it is replaced with a new one. This sounds like a long time but is in line with my observations of the cars on the street and of the cars of the people I know."*
4. **Plug in the numbers into your formula and calculate to get to your desired outcome variable**: *40m households x 1 car per household / 8 years average car age = 5 million new cars sold every year.*
5. **Refine your answer to showcase that you have the big picture in mind:** *"On top of private cars we should add cars sold for professional purposes such as taxis, so I would like to add 20% on top of that, which is 1m additional cars."*
6. **Answer the question and interpret the result**, providing some insight into how confident you are with your estimation and offering potential changes to refine the outcome: *"Six million new cars are sold in Germany every year; that is roughly eight percent of the total population. I believe that is reasonable given my assumptions. If I were to challenge this and reduce that*

number, we could reduce the cars per household since a greater part of the population lives in urban areas rather than on the countryside. We could also increase the average car age to 10 years."

Operational calculations

To solve operational problems, you would need to come up with formulas on the spot based on the situation and context of the case. The following formulas are a good starting point for your efforts.

- ☑ **Capacity** = Total capacity / Capacity needed per one unit (e.g., Total storage space in m^2 = 2,000, m^2 need per unit = 4; Capacity = 2,000 / 4 = 500 units can be stored)
- ☑ **Resources needed** = Demand / Supply (e.g., Employees needed per day = 80 hours of customer requests per day / 8 daily working hours per employee; 10 employees are needed per day)
- ☑ **Utilization rate** = Actual output / Maximum output (e.g., Actual output = 25 aircraft per month, Maximum output = 30 aircraft per month; Utilization rate of production = 25 / 30 = 83%)
- ☑ **Output** = Rate (per time) x Time (e.g., Rate = 5 pieces per hour, Time = 5 hours; Output for 5 hours = 25)

Investment, financial, and strategic decisions

To evaluate the financial impact of decisions, these few formulas are key:

- ☑ **Profit** = Revenue − Cost
- ☑ **Revenue** = Price x Quantity
- ☑ **Cost** = Fixed cost (the cost that cannot be changed in the short term, e.g., rent) + Variable cost (the cost that changes with the number of products produced or services rendered, e.g., material cost)
- ☑ **Contribution margin** = Price − Variable cost
- ☑ **Profitability (Profit margin)** = Profit / Revenue
- ☑ **Market share** = Revenue of one product / Revenue of all products (in one market)
- ☑ **Total market share** = Total company revenue in market / Total market revenue

- ☑ **Relative market share** = Company market share / (largest) Competitor market share
- ☑ **Growth rate** = (New number − Old number) / Old number
- ☑ **Payback period** = Investment / Profit per specific time frame (e.g., annual)
- ☑ **Breakeven number of sales** = Investment / Profit per product
- ☑ **Return on investment** = (Revenue − Cost of investment) / Cost of investment = Profit / Cost of investment
- ☑ **Depreciation (of an asset) per year** = Value at purchase / Years of useful life
  - ▶ Depreciation refers to the reduction in the value of an asset over time

There are also more advanced concepts, which are common for more specialized financial case interviews, not for generalist roles:

- ☑ **NPV (Net present value)** = Net cash flow of a period t / $(1 + \text{discount rate})^t$
  - ▶ The NPV is the present value of the sum of future cash in and outflows over a period (t = number of time periods, e.g., years) and used to analyze the profitability of an investment or project
- ☑ **Rule of 72**: To find out how long it takes for a market, company, or investment to double in size, simply divide 72 by the annual growth rate
- ☑ **CAGR (Compound annual growth rate)** = $(\text{Final value} / \text{Beginning value})^{1/t} - 1$
  - ▶ The CAGR shows the rate of return of an investment or a project over a certain period of years (t = the number of years), expressed as an annual percentage
- ☑ **Present value of a Perpetuity** = Cash flow / Discount rate
  - ▶ The perpetuity is an annuity that lasts forever
- ☑ **Return on equity (ROE)** = Profit / Shareholder equity
  - ▶ The ROE measures how effectively equity is used to generate profit
- ☑ **Return on assets (ROA)** = Profit / Total assets

▸ The ROA measures how effectively assets are used to generate profit

☑ **Price elasticity** = % Change in quantity / % Change in price

  ▸ It measures how a change in price affects the change in demand

☑ **Gross profit** = Revenue from sales − Cost of goods sold (COGS, e.g., materials)

☑ **Operating profit** = Gross profit − Operating expenses (e.g., rent) − Depreciation (the spread of an asset's cost over its useful lifetime, e.g., of a machine) − Amortization (the spread of an intangible asset's cost over its useful lifetime, e.g., of a patent)

☑ **Gross profit margin** = Gross profit / Revenue

☑ **Operating profit margin** = Operating profit / Revenue

☑ **EBITDA (Earnings before interest, taxes, depreciation, amortization)** = Operating profit + Depreciation + Amortization

  ▸ The EBITDA looks at the profitability of the core business

Regarding the latter formulas, have a look at a Profit and Loss statement, which I cover in **Chapter 20** (business concepts every case interviewee should know).

At the beginning of your preparation, you might still struggle with being too slow or making too many mistakes when performing your calculations. Let's work on that.

What are the important math concepts and the most common shortcuts?

Below are some tricks to become faster, more accurate, and more comfortable with case math as well as more advanced concepts that you might encounter during interviews. The more often you employ these tricks during practice and work with certain concepts, the more it becomes second nature to you. Sometimes you might be able to combine a couple of tricks to become even faster. While there are many specific calculation shortcuts (e.g., when multiplying a number by eleven), you should focus on a couple of shortcuts that are replicable and can be used for most situations. Don't try to memorize many different shortcuts that only have highly isolated use cases. Internalize and use a few shortcuts well. Like everything else in consulting interviews: *Do not boil the ocean.*

The basics: simple arithmetic calculations

Learn these simple shortcuts and use the examples below as pointers.

Additions

Build groups of 10

When adding up numbers, build groups of numbers that add up to 10 or multiples of 10.

$7 + 3 + 12 + 8 + 5 + 5 = 40$

$(10) + (20) + (10) = 40$

Go from left to right

$356 + 678 = (356 + 600) + 70 + 8 = (956 + 70) + 8 = 1026 + 8 = 1034$

This is a simple way to become faster and more accurate once you have internalized it.

Subtractions

Make it to 10

When performing quick subtraction, figure out what makes it to 10. For instance: $42 - 25$

1. Reverse the subtraction for the units digit $(5 - 2 = 3)$
2. Add the number that would make it to 10 $(3 + 7 = 10)$; this is the units digit of the result
3. Add 1 to the digit on the left of the number you are subtracting $(2 + 1 = 3)$
4. You end up with 7 on the units digit and $4 - 3 = 1$ on the 10s place, which is 17

Let's use another example: $3853 - 148$

1. Reverse the units digit $(8 - 3 = 5)$
2. Add the number that would make it to 10 $(5 + 5 = 10)$
3. Add 1 to the digit on the left of the number you are subtracting $(4 + 1 = 5)$

4. You end up with 5 on the units digit, 5 − 5 = 0 on the 10s place and 8 − 1 = 7 on the hundreds place, which gives you a result of 3705

With a bit of practice, the *what do you need to add to make it to 10* becomes an automated habit for your subtractions: 1 + 9, 2 + 8, 3 + 7, 4 + 6, 5 + 5, 6 + 4, 7+ 3, 8 + 2, 9 + 1

Go from left to right

You can use the same approach we've discussed for additions for subtractions as well:
42 − 25 = (42 − 20) − 5 = 22 − 5 = 17

Multiplications

Get rid of 0s

To make your calculations simpler, get rid of the zeros at first, adding them again at the end. For instance, if asked to calculate 34 x 36,000,000: convert it into 34 x 36m, which is 1,224, then add six zeros to that number which is 1,224,000,000

Use the label method ("*m*") or the scientific notation (x10^6). If you had to multiply 3,400 times 36,000,000: convert again to 3.4k x 36m, which is 122.4, then move the comma to the right side of the 4 and add eight zeros (the sum of the zeros you got rid of in the beginning: 3 + 6), which is 122,400,000,000. Using the scientific notation, we would end up with this: $(3.4 \times 10^3) \times (36 \times 10^6) = 122.4 \times 10^9 = 122,400,000,000$.

Expand

Break apart multiplications by expanding them and breaking one of the terms into simpler numbers. For instance: 18 x 5 = 10 x 5 + 8 x 5 OR (20 − 2) x 5 = 20 x 5 − 10 = 90

Factor with five

Factor common numbers to simplify your calculations when dealing with multiples of 5. For instance: 17 x 5 = 17 x 10 / 2 = 85.

Another example would be 20 x 15 = 20 x 10 x 3 / 2 = 300

The most common numbers to keep in mind are: 5 = 10 / 2; 7.5 = 10 x 3 / 4; 15 = 10 x 3 / 2; 25 = 100 / 4; 50 = 100 / 2; 75 = 100 x 3 / 4

Exchange percentages

Sometimes you can exchange percentages to simplify the calculation. For instance: 60 x 13% = 0.6 x 13 or 6 x 1.3 = 7.8

Convert to yearly data

If you want to convert daily to yearly data, instead of multiplying by 365, multiply by 30 and then by 12, which would add up to 360 days. For most cases, this is close enough and can be argued for well by using certain assumptions, e.g., bank holidays, downtimes. Always notify interviewers about your assumptions and simplifications.

Divisions

Convert percentages

Convert percentages into divisions. For instance: 20% of 500 = 500 x 1 / 5 = 500 / 5 = 100

Split into 10ths

Split numbers into 10ths. For instance: 60% of 200 = 10% of 200 x 6 = 120

Expand

Apply expansion in a similar manner as described already for multiplications:

- ☑ Simple example: 35 / 5 = 30 / 5 + 5 / 5 = 6 + 1 = 7
- ☑ More complex example: 265 / 5 = 200 / 5 + 60 / 5 + 5 / 5 = 40 + 12 + 1 = 53

This can be extremely useful when trying to estimate a number as you do not need to perform all calculations up to the last digit to get to a ballpark estimate, e.g., 200 / 5 + 60 / 5 = 52 ≈ 50

Learn divisions and fractions by heart

	1	2	3	4	5	6	7	8	9	10
/1	1.00	2.00	3.00	4.00	5.00	6.00	7.00	8.00	9.00	10.00
/2	0.50	1.00	1.50	2.00	2.50	3.00	3.50	4.00	4.50	5.00
/3	0.33	0.67	1.00	1.33	1.67	2.00	2.33	2.67	3.00	3.33
/4	0.25	0.50	0.75	1.00	1.25	1.50	1.75	2.00	2.25	2.50
/5	0.20	0.40	0.60	0.80	1.00	1.20	1.40	1.60	1.80	2.00
/6	0.17	0.33	0.50	0.67	0.83	1.00	1.17	1.33	1.50	1.67
/7	0.14	0.29	0.43	0.57	0.71	0.86	1.00	1.14	1.29	1.43
/8	0.13	0.25	0.38	0.50	0.63	0.75	0.88	1.00	1.13	1.25
/9	0.11	0.22	0.33	0.44	0.56	0.67	0.78	0.89	1.00	1.11
/10	0.10	0.20	0.30	0.40	0.50	0.60	0.70	0.80	0.90	1.00
/11	0.09	0.18	0.27	0.36	0.45	0.55	0.64	0.73	0.82	0.91
/12	0.08	0.17	0.25	0.33	0.42	0.50	0.58	0.67	0.75	0.83
/13	0.08	0.15	0.23	0.31	0.38	0.46	0.54	0.62	0.69	0.77
/14	0.07	0.14	0.21	0.29	0.36	0.43	0.50	0.57	0.64	0.71
/15	0.07	0.13	0.20	0.27	0.33	0.40	0.47	0.53	0.60	0.67
/16	0.06	0.13	0.19	0.25	0.31	0.38	0.44	0.50	0.56	0.63
/17	0.06	0.12	0.18	0.24	0.29	0.35	0.41	0.47	0.53	0.59
/18	0.06	0.11	0.17	0.22	0.28	0.33	0.39	0.44	0.50	0.56
/19	0.05	0.11	0.16	0.21	0.26	0.32	0.37	0.42	0.47	0.53
/20	0.05	0.10	0.15	0.20	0.25	0.30	0.35	0.40	0.45	0.50

■ Division table and fractions for consulting case math questions

Advanced concepts: other common mathematical operations

Averages

In case interviews, calculating the average is popular, since it is simple, yet demands several calculations to arrive at a result. It is a good pressure test for candidates. For example, you might be presented with a table containing data on three products, each with different production costs and the same production quantity. You might have to calculate the average production cost for one unit. The average is the sum of terms divided by the number of terms. For instance, the production cost of Product A is 5, of Product B, 10, and of Product C, 15. The average production cost is (5 + 10 + 15) / 3 = 30 / 3 = 10 for one unit.

A common variation is **weighted averages**. Instead of each of the data points contributing equally to the final average, some data points contribute more than others and therefore, need to be weighted differently in your calculations. If the weights add up to one, multiply each number by its weight and sum the results. If the weights do not add up to one, multiply each variable by their weight, sum the results, then divide by the sum of the weights.

To stick with the example above, Product A might be responsible for 20% of the sales, whereas Product B and C for 30% and 50% respectively. Alternatively, it could be written as the following: There are 40 units of Product A, 60 units of Product B, and 100 units of Product C. The weighted average is: 5 x 20% + 10 x 30% + 15 x 50% = 5 x 0.2 + 10 x 0.3 + 15 x 0.5 = 1 + 3 + 7.5 = 11.5. For the second set, you could calculate it as: (5 x 40 + 10 x 60 + 15 x 100) / 200 = 11.5. Other common contexts, where you are asked to calculate averages could be growth rates, demographics, economic data, geographies and countries, product categories, business segments and units, revenue streams, prices, cost data, etc.

Fractions, ratios, percentages, and rates

Fractions, ratios, percentages, and rates are all different sides of the same coin and can help expedite your calculations.

For instance, **fractions** can be used to represent a number between 0 and 1. Expressing numbers as fractions and using them for additions and subtractions as well as multiplication and divisions can help you solve problems faster and more conveniently through simplification. For example, you can write 0.167 as 1/6, or 0.5 as 1/2. You can also combine fractions with large number divisions. For instance, let's assume you want to see how much percent 400k is of 1.7m.

Write it as a fraction: 4/17 = 1/17 x 4

Now look at the division table for 1/17, which is 0.059, essentially 0.06.

1/17 x 4 = 0.06 x 4 = 0.24 or 24%

If you had calculated it more accurately by taking three times as long, you would get to 0.235 or 23.5%, rounding it up again to 24%.

As you can see, using fractions for larger number divisions can be a huge time saver. I would recommend you learn all fractions up to a divisor of 20 (e.g., 1/20) by heart, using the fraction table I shared earlier. It increases your speed and accuracy in interviews.

Ratios are comparisons of two quantities, telling you the amount of one thing in relation to another. If you have five apples and four oranges, the ratio is 5:4 and you have nine fruits in total. In case interviews, one tip is to write ratios as fractions of the total, e.g., apples are five out of a total of nine fruits, which is 5/9.

Percentages are a specific form of ratios, with the denominator always being fixed at 100. From experience, almost 80% of case interviews include some reference to or use of percentages, pun intended. Discussion points such as *"Revenue increased by 15%"* or *"Costs are down four percent over the last six months"* are common. Percentages are also useful when you want to put things into perspective, state your hypotheses, or guide your next steps. For instance, *"That would translate to a 15% increase compared to our current revenue. Now, is a 15% increase realistic? What would we need to do to achieve this?"*

Be careful not to mix **percentage points** with percentages. A percentage point or percent point is the unit for the arithmetic difference of two percentages. For example, moving up from 40% to 44% is a four-percentage point increase, but it is a 10% increase in what is being measured. Interviewers might ask for one or the other.

Rates are ratios between two related quantities in different units, where the denominator is fixed at one. If the denominator of the ratio is expressed as a single unit of one of these quantities, and if it is assumed that this quantity can be changed systematically (i.e., is an independent variable), then the numerator of the ratio expresses the corresponding rate of change in the other (dependent) variable. To make this more practical, let's look at common rates. One common type of rate is *per unit of time*, such as speed or heart rate. Ratios with a non-time denominator include exchange rates, literacy rates, and many others. Case interviews might include some of the following rates:

- ☑ **Growth rate:** the ratio of the change of one variable over a period versus the starting level
- ☑ **Exchange rate:** the worth of one currency in terms of another
- ☑ **Inflation rate:** the ratio of the change in the general price level in a period to the starting price level

- ☑ **Interest rate:** the price a borrower pays for the use of the money they do not own (ratio of payment to amount borrowed)
- ☑ **Price-earnings ratio:** the market price per share of stock divided by annual earnings per share
- ☑ **Rate of return:** the ratio of money gained or lost on an investment relative to the amount of money invested
- ☑ **Tax rate:** the tax amount divided by the taxable income
- ☑ **Unemployment rate:** the ratio of the number of people who are unemployed to the number of people in the labor force
- ☑ **Wage rate:** the amount paid for working a given amount of time, or doing a standard amount of accomplished work (ratio of payment to time)

If you are not familiar with these or others that might come up, it is always okay to ask the interviewer for a clarification of the definition. **Keep an eye on the time frames rates are expressed in.** This could be annually (per annum = p.a.), quarterly, per month, etc. Often, information is provided for different time frames, divisors, or units (e.g., *"the top speed of vehicle A is two miles per minute, the top speed of vehicle B is 150 miles per hour"*). Interviewers often use different units for different figures to trick you. For instance, when dealing with two different currencies, always convert all numbers to the same currency by using the exchange rate first. Otherwise, you are comparing apples and oranges. Convert to the same before conducting your analysis, calculations, or comparisons.

Growth rates

You should be able to work with growth rates, which is easy for one time period.

- ▶ (Increase of 30% in year 1): 100m x 1.3 = 130m

It gets trickier when you must calculate growth over multiple periods. You need to get the compound growth rate first.

- ▶ (Increase of 30% in year 1, 30% in year two): 100 x 1.3 x 1.3 = 100 x 1.69 = 169

The latter can be done quickly if you want to calculate growth over two to three time periods. Everything beyond that becomes tedious and lengthy. If you want to calculate growth for several periods, it is better to estimate the outcome. A shortcut is to use the growth rate and multiply it with the number of years.

▶ (Increase of 4% p.a. over 8 years): 4% x 8 years ≈ 32%; 100 x 1.32 = 132

If you use the exact compound annual growth rate (CAGR), you end up with roughly 137, more accurately $100 \times (1+0.04)^8 = 136.85$. The total deviation of five or roughly 3.5% (5 / 137) due to your simplified approach is close enough. However, be aware that the divergence (the underestimation) increases with larger numbers, higher annual growth rates, and the number of years. In a case interview, you can account for that by adding between 1% to 10% to your outcome value, depending on the numbers you are dealing with. Keep it simple. Adding 5% to the 132 brings us to 138.6, even closer to the exact number.

To use the same approach with varying growth rates, sum them up. For instance:

▶ (Increase of 4% in year 1, 10% in year 2, 5% in year 3, 7% in year 4): 4% + 10% + 5% + 7% = 26%; 100 x 1.26 = 126

If we calculate the exact number, it is 128.5; again, the shortcut is close enough and much faster. If you add 1% or 2% you are even closer.

You can apply the same tricks to negative growth rates, keeping in mind that you are overestimating the decrease. Lastly, you can use this trick for combinations of positive and negative growth rates as well.

Expected value and outcomes

You might have to compare the impact and success of different recommendations or the expected return on an investment. One way to do this is to work with probabilities and calculate the expected value (EV) for a course of action. The expected value for each recommendation is calculated by multiplying the possible outcome by the likelihood of the outcome. You can then compare the expected value of each option and make a decision that is most likely to achieve the desired outcome.

For example, if you have to decide between two projects and your analysis shows that Project A yields USD 50 million with a likelihood of 80% and Project B yields an outcome of USD 100 million with a likelihood of 30%, you will decide for Project A, with an expected value of USD 40 million (Project B: USD 30 million).

▶ EV(A) = 50m x 0.8 = 40m
▶ EV(B) = 100m x 0.3 = 30m

If you want to compare the outcome of bundles of recommendations, the expected value is calculated by multiplying each of the possible outcomes by the likelihood of each outcome and then summing all values for each bundle. Sometimes, interviewers keep it simple and set the expected outcome for each alternative to 100%. In such cases, just take the alternative with the better outcome, i.e., the one with lower cost or the one with a bigger (net) benefit, depending on the question or goal.

To work both on accuracy and speed *(in that order)*, let's look at how you can develop a winning case math mindset.

What comprises a winning case math mindset?

Keep the following 10 tips in mind to improve your case interview math performance and speed, while reducing the potential for errors and mistakes.

1. Tackle math aggressively

Consulting interviewers want to see highly driven candidates that show self-initiative and engagement. If you hesitate whenever a number pops up or make mistakes in the quantitative section of the case, interviewers will test if this was just an anomaly or happens repeatedly. Candidates that struggle with math get more quantitative challenges during the case, whereas candidates that proceed flawlessly through the initial math question(s) often get shortcuts for the remaining quantitative parts or even whole results readily delivered by the interviewer as they have collected enough positive data points about their candidate's performance in that area.

Hence, it is important to tackle math problems aggressively and with confidence. In most of my client interviews, I notice a hesitancy once the case moves into a more quantitative direction. Many are simply scared of digging into the numerical parts of a case or of discussing things in a quantitative context. Do not be that person!

If you mess up one calculation, you should not let this have a negative impact on the next one.

2. Re-learn and practice basic arithmetic

(Re-)learn simple arithmetic operations and practice until you can perform them in your sleep. While case math is never difficult, many candidates struggle with the concept of being watched while doing these basic operations. Therefore, the better your skill to compute quickly in a stressful environment, the bigger your quantitative muscle in the interview. Practice calculations both mentally and with pen and paper under time-pressure and the vigilant eyes of friends and peers. Go through number generators and math drill exercises to work on large number additions, subtractions, multiplications, and divisions. Work with averages, percentages, and fractions. This certainly helps to build resilience and stamina.

3. Consider the numerical impact in your analysis

Get a feeling for numbers, percentages, and magnitudes. You should be able to accurately and approximately estimate percentages, percentages of percentages, as well as magnitudes on the spot. This helps you to interpret results and put them into context as well as to spot more obvious mistakes.

You should always have a critical eye on quantitative aspects of a situation, even if the interviewer does not explicitly ask you about it. For example, relate numbers to each other (e.g., *"The total is x, which represents a y% increase"*) or automatically think about the potential financial impact of your recommendation (e.g., *"While these measures would definitely help improve our client's customer satisfaction, I would be curious to understand how much the implementation would actually cost."*). In addition, put numbers you hear into perspective (e.g., *"I heard you say a 12% decrease is needed to achieve our planned cost reduction. I believe that in the current market environment with increasing commodities prices, this could be a difficult undertaking."*). By interpreting numerical results in that way, you demonstrate strong business sense and judgment. You spot the implications of your outcomes and conclude correctly by discussing the *so-what?* of your analysis.

Putting numbers into perspective is also a valuable skill during a sanity check (e.g., *"Is it really possible that we could increase our revenue by 200 million if we currently only make 50 million? Let me check my calculations again because that doesn't seem right."*).

On the other hand, if you are basing your recommendation solely on the outcome of a calculation, it makes sense to also discuss qualitative arguments to demonstrate your holistic big-picture thinking. For instance, if you recommend choosing a supplier solely because it is cheaper than the others, you could discuss that you would also like to look at the quality of their products, the supply chain, the availability, etc. Supplement a quantitative result with qualitative factors and vice versa.

4. Express problems quantitatively

Instead of approaching problems purely from a qualitative side, make a habit out of using equations to describe relationships, ideas, and parts of the issue tree (if appropriate). It helps your thinking, shows that you are structured in your approach, and demonstrates that you are not afraid to get your quantitative hands dirty. A brief example: *"Our client's train tracks on Route A suffer from more than 100% utilization during the peak hours, leading to delays for many trains and passengers. What ways can you think of that could improve the capacity issue?"* To investigate and improve the over-utilization of the route, you could come up with the following equation: Utilization = demand / capacity. From this equation, you can instantly see that you need to either decrease demand or increase the capacity to improve the utilization situation. *Demand* and *Capacity* could be potential top-level buckets for your issue tree. You can now list investigative areas or ideas below each to structure your problem analysis. This approach would help you to quickly isolate quantitatively where the problem is coming from and how big it is, then quantify your remedies as you go along, indicating the best levers to pull and the best course of action.

5. Sanity check everything you do

Quantitative problems come with the most potential for errors and mistakes as they involve multiple challenging steps and actions you need to go through before reaching a sensible outcome. You want to avoid mistakes in the first place, but we all know that they do happen; even on the job later on. If you cannot avoid a mistake (which I discuss how to do in **Chapter 14**), at least try to catch your own mistakes before the interviewer does. How can you do that?

☑ Do not assume that the approach you came up with on the spot is correct without double checking or thinking it through properly *(the importance of taking time)*.

☑ Remain vigilant and aware that mistakes are common in the math section. Never communicate the outcome of a calculation before double checking that it is at least in the right ballpark and not the result of a careless mistake *(the importance of sanity checking)*.

This also applies (or even more so) when you think that the math seems to be relatively easy. I have seen many interviewees getting caught off guard with simple math problems since they pay less attention to them compared to more difficult examples, then falling into a trap or making avoidable mistakes.

In sum, sanity-check your approach to the problem and outcome of each (intermediate) calculation. Use your judgment to spot calculation and estimation results that seem out of line (e.g., 18.3% vs. 183%). There are eight typical error sources:

1. The logic is off or too complex.
2. Your calculation is wrong (e.g., forgetting to carry the one, magnitude errors).
3. You use the wrong numbers for the right approach. I see this often when candidates do not have organized notes and – in the heat of the moment – plug in the wrong numbers to calculate, even though their approach is correct.
4. Your assumptions are off.
5. You round numbers too generously or simplify the calculations too much (more on rounding later in this chapter).
6. You fail to keep track of units and compare apples and oranges (more on that next).
7. You forget one or several steps of your calculation. I see this often when candidates are glad to have made it through the math section yet forgot to work on the final step of their approach (e.g., adding up two numbers).
8. You interpret the results in the wrong way. I see this often when candidates are happy to have finished their calculation, then jump to a conclusion without thinking first. For instance, if we are comparing several scenarios and are interested in the alternative with the best net benefit, you would want to

recommend the alternative with the highest result (highest net benefit). Some candidates do not think and select the alternative with the lowest number (lowest net benefit) as they somehow confuse lower with being better in this situation, by mixing it up with costs in their mind. Always make sure to interpret your results correctly and define what your outcome should be when drafting and communicating your approach.

If you spot a mistake and have not yet communicated the faulty result, ask for more time to sanity check the calculation or the approach. If you have already blurted out a wrong number, state *"This cannot be right."* Then, go back to think about your approach or re-do the calculation. Provide reasons why your numbers might be off. Fix the problem quickly if the interviewer does not intervene. Most importantly, do not get thrown off by a mistake and keep your composure.

Do not go faster after a mistake. Often, follow-up mistakes occur due to your newfound sense of urgency and disappointment in your performance. From my experience, more than 50% of candidates that make a math mistake make another one in the next two minutes. Rather, slow down and take some extra time to pick yourself up! It is not necessarily over yet unless you let it impact your performance going forward.

6. Keep track of units

Do not lose track of your units. Is it kg or tons, is it USD or EUR, etc.?

- ☑ When receiving the brief for a math question, write down every number including its unit.
- ☑ While setting up the calculation already prepare (either mentally or preferably on paper) a space for the end result including the correct unit.
- ☑ Keep the units for your intermediate results organized and label every number.

Interviewers might use different units for different numbers to check if you are paying close attention or simply just to confuse you. Stay vigilant, play back the units to make sure you have noted them down correctly. You must track the units of the input variables, manipulate them correctly (i.e., convert all to the same unit), to then get to the right output. Do not compare apples and oranges. Sometimes interviewers also use multiple units for one variable. For instance, *"Our client would pay USD 500 per employee per year with option #1 and USD 1000 per three employees for 10 months with option #2."* Pay close attention in such cases and convert both options to the same units before comparing them, e.g., cost per employee per year.

7. Use shortcuts in your approach

Set up efficient and effective calculations. Most analyses in the business world rely on multiple assumptions and reasonable estimates, therefore not requiring a 100% level of precision. Hence, most of the time, close-to-correct answers are expected. Employ shortcuts in your approach to get to accurate and directionally correct answers. Less is often more. A couple of examples:

- ☑ When drafting formulas, always look for the simplest way to get to an accurate answer. For instance, if you are asked to decide between two potential suppliers by comparing the cost of both over a 40-week period, yet all information in the brief is on a weekly basis, for your decision it is enough to calculate and compare the weekly cost for each. If for some reason you want to calculate the difference over 40 weeks, first take the difference of the weekly cost, then multiply it by 40. Alternatively, you could calculate the cost for each supplier for 40 weeks, then calculate the difference, but you would end up with more calculation steps and more difficult calculations since larger numbers are involved.
- ☑ Think critically what outcome is needed to support your decision. For instance, if you must find out if the profit margin of a deal for 30 aircraft is more than 10% there is no need to calculate the profit margin for all 30 units but calculating the profit margin for one aircraft is sufficient to evaluate the deal. This leaves you with smaller numbers which are easier to handle and interpret.
- ☑ When evaluating which option out of several is the best, only look at metrics that differ for every option. For instance, if the fixed cost for every option is the same, yet the variable cost and revenue is different, you would only need to consider the latter two to provide a recommendation (given that you are

not asked to evaluate the total value of each option but just to pick the best).

Always explain your logic, shortcuts, and simplifications to the interviewer. They need to understand why your approach is enough to answer the question. Ninety-nine percent of the time, they will agree. Your final results won't be 100% accurate either way and are not expected to be for most cases. Use plausible shortcuts in your approach and calculation to reach plausible numbers. The same is true for rounding.

8. Round numbers

Like the point above, use rounding to make your calculations easier and minimize the risk of mistakes. Ask the interviewer if it is okay to round beforehand and explain exactly how you want to do it. For instance, if you come up with a revenue number of 82.5 million, ask to use 80 million instead. State beforehand that you will trim the fat a bit; if the interviewer agrees, proceed with your calculation. Similarly, if you get 42.65 as an intermediate result say that in the following calculations this will be rounded down to 40. Other examples include:

- ☑ 83 million Germans become 80 million
- ☑ 331 million Americans become 320 or even 300 million (by making some clever assumptions explaining why not everyone in the population should be included in your approach, e.g., by excluding certain demographic segments or areas)
- ☑ 365 days in a year become 350 or even 300 days (by making some clever assumptions about bank holidays, opening hours, weekends, etc.)
- ☑ USD 983 million in revenue becomes one billion.

The tricky part about rounding numbers is to know when it is a good time to do so. Some case math questions demand precise results. For example, if you are asked whether an investment has an ROI above 12% and you can already spot that the final result is close to that number, it would be wise to calculate with precision. Similarly, if you are comparing two alternatives or outcomes, be careful. Outcomes could be very close to each other so that extensive rounding might just flip their ranking and the direction of your answer. That is why you should always ask if you can round and provide details on how you would like to do it. That way, the interviewer could provide feedback on whether rounding is a good idea or not.

On the other hand, rounding is especially helpful when 100% precise answers are not needed. For instance, when you calculate a singular outcome, i.e., not comparing multiple numbers or outcomes. You might also round if your calculations yield only directionally correct results anyway, and precise answers are not expected, for instance, when you need to rely on (multiple) assumptions in your approach. Examples would be estimating the size of a market or the impact of a measure, which come with many assumptions and degrees of uncertainty.

What are best practices related to rounding? You should round only within a ten percent margin, ideally less and within five percent. Otherwise, you might skew the results, over or understate the outcome, and provide false recommendations. Think about the impact of rounding consecutive numbers. You can either get more precise results because the effects cancel each other out or magnify the blur of rounding.

For instance, if you want to calculate the revenue, which is quantity times price and the quantity is 9,500 units and the price is USD 35, you could calculate with a quantity of 10,000 and a price of USD 30. That roughly keeps you in a 10% margin of the precise result. If you round both numbers in the same direction, up or down, you would already be off by around 20% from the precise result.

To create a general rule: When you sum two numbers or multiply them, make sure to round one number up and the other one down, essentially rounding in the opposite direction. If you want to subtract or divide, make sure to round both numbers either up or down, rounding in the same direction. Lastly, whenever you deal with indivisible items, round them up to a whole. For instance, if you calculate that you would need to purchase 533.4 new cars for a taxi company to meet their demand, round it up to 534. There are no half cars.

9. Take your time

The single biggest lever to improve the outcome of your quantitative analysis is to take time and perform numerical tasks on your terms. What this means is that you should not get pressured to answer or calculate on the spot but rather ask the interviewer for some time to prepare your logic and then, again, to perform your calculations. One minute is usually fine for the logic and up to three minutes are okay for the actual calculations. Of course, faster is better but faster and wrong is worse than slow, steady, and accurate. Remember our initial discussion. You do not need to have a spike in every area of the case, yet you should avoid mistakes at all cost. A slow but accurate math answer helps you get the offer if you demonstrate spikes in other areas. A wrong but fast answer might lead to a rejection, even if you spike in other areas.

Do not feel pressured to talk to the interviewer while you are thinking or calculating. Focus on one thing at a time. Only communicate your logic, your results, or if you want, your intermediate outcomes once you are done with each step.

10. Watch the zeros and magnitudes

You would not believe how many candidates fall into this trap. Many people struggle with large numbers, simplify them by cutting zeros, then end up losing zeros along the way or even adding some to the result. Watch out for zeros that you have trimmed or left out to facilitate your calculations. There are two best practice solutions to deal with and keep track of zeros:

1. labelling
2. scientific notation.

For labels, add k for thousand (000), m for million (000,000) and b for billion (000,000,000) when manipulating larger numbers. That way you can simplify and keep track of your zeros.

Alternatively, by applying the scientific notation, you can trim the power of 10s and then perform simple calculations. Once you reach a conclusion you can add your zeros back. Let's look at one example: Calculate 96 x 1,300,000.

First, just calculate $96 \times 13 \times 10^5$, essentially getting rid of the five zeros of the second number. $96 \times 13 = 96 \times 10 + 96 \times 3 = 1,248$ Add the 5 zeros back, which makes it to 124,800,000.

Another example, a division: $1.4bn / 70mn = (1.4 \times 10^9) / (7 \times 10^7)$ $= 0.2 \times 10^2 = 20$

When adding the zeros back, for a multiplication you would add the superscripted numbers, for a division you would subtract one from the other.

Adopt one of the two options discussed above when practicing so it becomes second nature to you. You will never struggle with zeros again.

How can you train your case math skills?

Regardless of your current quantitative reasoning skills, devote time in your case interview preparation to brush up your mental and pen-and-paper math skills. If you are struggling with math or are dealing with a couple of insecurities in this area, there is no reason not to practice case math drills for at least two hours per day for a couple of weeks. At the end of your preparation, shortly before your interviews, you want to be in a state where you can tackle every problem you see flawlessly and swiftly with confidence and without anxiety. Your structuring, overall problem-solving, and chart interpretation can be in the highest percentile of all candidates, but if you do not fix your math issues and insecurities, you will still be rejected.

I want to stress this point because most candidates fail due to issues with their quantitative reasoning, something that is entirely preventable with effort and time. I would even go so far as to say that if you do not feel 100% ready to tackle any section of the case, postpone your interviews if you have the chance until you feel fully ready.

There are several things you could do to get up to speed with mental and pen-and-paper math. The trick is to be confident in your ability to efficiently work through simple math and resilient enough to face external pressures in the process. If you are starting out, (re)-learn and practice basic calculus such as additions and subtractions, multiplications and divisions, averages, percentages, and fractions. Get used to numerical reasoning by working with numbers you encounter in your daily life, be it the bar tab, the grocery store receipt, or figures and data you find in the news, especially business reporting. Perform simple arithmetic operations on the numbers you encounter in your head or with pen and paper. Do not use a calculator. Work on some simple business cases. For instance, while waiting at the doctor, calculate how much profit they make a month, a year, etc. The opportunities are endless. Practice with the following free iOS and Android apps.

iOS

- ☑ Magoosh Mental Math
- ☑ Mental Math Cards Challenge
- ☑ Coolmath Games: Fun Mini-Games

Android

- ☑ Magoosh Mental Math
- ☑ Matix Mental Math Games
- ☑ Math Games and Mental Arithmetic

Do all of this in a stressful environment. You want to build stamina and resilience to outside influences and stressors. Use the apps in the crowded and noisy subway, calculate during mock interviews with unpleasant interviewers who stress you out, in front of friends and family, or simply with time limits.

For more advanced case math exercises that also require you to think about the logic of the problem before calculating, take a look at the resources in **Chapter 37**. There you can find my own consulting case math video and practice course (25 videos and 2,000 practice examples), as well as freely available case math drills.

Now that we have the core sections of the case covered, there is one final component of every case interview that you need to deliver on strongly.

[11] Deliver the perfect recommendations

Why do you need to think about a recommendation?

The final section of the case revolves around your recommendation to the client. After you have collected and analyzed all relevant data, understood the problem and found a remedy, the best levers to pull or simply have an answer to the client's question, you conclude the case by providing your recommendation.

The recommendation is important since in a real consulting engagement it is usually the only thing the client sees that is built on the hundreds or thousands of hours the team has spent on the analyses and problem-solving. It is the business card of your team and your firm. Potentially one of the most difficult parts of the job, recommendations need to be delivered and sold in a way that convinces senior organizational leaders to take action, all while being built on imperfect information.

In a case interview it is – like every other component – an abbreviated task that you need to go through to demonstrate your ability to package actionable and effective advice in a top-down and concise manner to drive change for the fictitious client you are working for. Once you have solved the case, you are either asked directly by the interviewer to provide a recommendation or, if not, come up with it by yourself. For the former, the interviewer might introduce this final part by saying, *"The CEO is now in the team room and wants to know what you have found out."* Now is your time to shine!

How can you set up the perfect top-down recommendation?

To set up your recommendation, **follow this simple four-step approach**:

1. **Ask for 30 seconds to structure your thoughts.** Some interviewers want you to come up with the recommendation on the spot. This should not be an issue if you follow the proposed approach and remember the key points from the different parts of the case. You have spent the last 20 to 30 minutes working on it and everything is still fresh in your mind.
2. **State your recommendation** that you derive from your insights into the problem and the solutions you have worked on.
3. **Provide supporting arguments**, usually taken from the different analyses (e.g., exhibits, math) and the information you have received from the interviewer. Circle your supporting arguments while working on the case to be ready for the end.
4. **Discuss next steps** and (potentially) risks to showcase that you have the big picture in mind.

You can find examples of strong recommendations in **Chapter 13** on communication. Avoid the most common issues I've observed when candidates provide recommendations:

- ☑ **Do not repeat the objective and the work you have done.** The CEO is interested in what to do and not what you have done in the past to analyze the situation. In any case, both your interviewer and you are aware of the objective since you've been discussing it over the last 20 minutes; there is no value in repeating it.
- ☑ **Provide a clear recommendation.** Avoid vague and woolly answers. The CEO wants to hear a clear recommendation to know what to do. As a consultant, you need to derive actions from less-than-perfect information and the client is aware of that. You can hedge your recommendations when talking about the next steps and proposing new analyses.
- ☑ **Structure the recommendation.** Follow the clear line of reasoning I outline in the four-step approach above. Go from the top to the bottom, not from the bottom up (explaining your analyses and reasons before going into the recommendations). Do not ramble or go in circles. A strong recommendation can be delivered in less than one minute.
- ☑ **Do not bring in new content or new assumptions.** Everything you say should be based on topics you have come across and discussed during the case. Introducing new information

or assumptions would confuse the CEO and prompt further inquiry.

Each of the core components of a case presents a different challenge in itself. There is another crucial skill that defines case mastery, and that is the ability to move through the case effortlessly and connect the different components seamlessly.

You need to learn how to probe your way through the case, employing hypotheses and targeted questions, and connect the different components by sharing your insights, analyses, and outcomes through the right communication.

PART 5

Bringing It All Together: Become an Effective Problem Solver

Now that you know what the core elements are of each case, let's have a look at how they all tie together and how you can become an effective problem solver by moving through the case with a hypothesis-driven mindset and strong communication skills.

This part answers the following two questions:

- ☑ How can you move through the case with ease, letting hypotheses direct your investigation and course of action?
- ☑ How should you communicate with your interviewers and move through the interviews in a structured manner?

[12] Develop a hypothesis-driven mindset to move through the case

In a candidate-led case you need to drive the case, whereas in an interviewer-led case, you need to drive each question of the case while the interviewer moves the case forward. Hypotheses are important for both formats. For candidate-led cases, they are essential to help you move through the case with direction, intent, and focus while at the same time allowing you to justify and qualify your approach transparently in front of the interviewer. For interviewer-led cases, they help you deal effectively with each question.

How can hypotheses and synthesizing help you move through a case?

Let's look at a typical (candidate-led) case sequence:

1. The interviewer introduces the client, the context, and the problem or their request in a short brief.
2. You play back what you have understood, then ask clarification questions to understand the situation better as well as to operationalize the goal.
3. You take time to structure the problem and create an issue tree.
4. You present your issue tree to the interviewer and guide them through each branch, highlighting why certain areas are worth looking at.
5. You dive deeper into the issue tree to analyze the situation by asking targeted questions to elicit new information (through verbal input, exhibits, math problems).
6. You contextualize every new finding, synthesize what you already know and how it relates to the situation.

7. You drill until you understand the root causes of the issue or key priorities and levers to work on.
8. You can now devise a recommendation by synthesizing the findings and come up with a logical solution. Sometimes you will need to conduct additional analyses regarding the exact remedy or best course of action.
9. You provide your recommendation(s), supporting arguments, and next steps.

	Brief	Structure	Data/exhibit interpretation	Quantitative analyses	Recommendation
Interviewer	Introduces the case • Client and background • Question / problem / goal	• Listens to your framework • Provides hints if needed	• Listens to you and answers your questions • Provides new data verbally or in the form of exhibits • Provides hints if needed or if you get stuck		• Tells you that the CEO wants a brief update

You	• Play back the details of the case
	• Clarify
	  • Client and situation
	  • Operational goal
	  • Time
	  • Target
		• Draw your issue tree to analyze the situation and find a solution
		  • Exhaustive
		  • Insightful
		  • MECE
		• Communicate your framework
		• Discuss your starting point based on your hypothesis
		  • What?
		  • Why?
		  • How?
			• Interpret the information from exhibits (or verbally communicated data points)
			• Focus on
			  • Insights
			  • Implications
			  • Next steps
				• Perform quantitative analysis
				  • Set up your calculation approach
				  • Calculate
				  • Interpret the results
					• Create a top-down recommendation
					• 1-3 actions to answer the client's question
					• Supporting arguments for each
					• Next steps / risks

Iterative problem-solving process

Probing
• Dive into your issue tree to elicit qualitative and quantitative information to test your hypotheses
• Interpret verbal statements and exhibits
• Conduct quantitative analyses

Synthesis
• Interpret new data and findings in the context of the case and in relation to your initial hypotheses and issue tree
• Synthesize your findings as you move along
• Follow your issue tree or adjust your approach if needed until you are able to answer the client's question or achieve their goal

■ Overview of the case interview flow and process

The diagram above illustrates an overview of a typical (candidate-led) case sequence Let's look how hypotheses play a role in each step. **But first, what is a hypothesis?**

It is a statement that can be tested and verified through data. In simpler terms, it is an educated guess about the nature of things based on your understanding of the situation. It is relevant throughout the case, especially when thinking about the answer to your client's problem. As you move through the case (just as in your daily life), you are constantly using hypotheses, whether you are aware of it or not. Let's see how.

Playing back the brief

Before diving into problem-solving mode, you want to make sure that you have understood the situation and demands of the client. Therefore, play back the information you have received including all details. Even minor details might be relevant at a later stage; you never know.

Use of hypotheses at this stage: Hypotheses do not really play a role here.

Asking questions

Ask clarification questions. Generally, there are two types of clarification questions:

First, everything that helps you understand the client and the situation better (e.g., *"How do they operate? What does their value chain look like? What is their business model? What are their revenue streams? What are their key cost buckets? Are they like <well-known company in the same industry?>"*). Second, make sure to understand what the actual goal is. Ask if there is a specific success measure and how much time you have to implement this solution (e.g., *"You said the client wants to reduce emissions. Is there a specific measure, such as reducing it by 10%? What are we measuring CO2 in? In tons? Also, what is the time frame we have for implementing a new strategy here?"*).

Use of hypotheses at this stage: A hypothesis-driven approach helps you to define relevant questions for the situation at hand. You want to get value out of the interviewer's answers at this stage, i.e., information that is relevant for your understanding of the client, the situation, and the goal. If you are asking questions without a hypothesis in mind, they are likely useless for furthering your understanding.

- ☑ **Do:** Ask questions that are tailored to the client's situation and the question they are trying to have answered.
- ☑ **Do not:** Ask a generic set of questions that is the same for every case.

Creating your issue tree

Once you have understood the specifics of the case, start out with your initial framework to analyze the situation in the most effective manner. Later, you want to move through this framework to investigate the situation and answer your client's question.

Use of hypotheses at this stage: A hypothesis-driven approach helps you think of concepts, areas, and ideas as well as prioritize your time when dealing with a client's problem. When working on a case question, focus your analysis, problem deconstruction, and issue tree on the key items that can make the difference for your client and answer their question.

- ☑ **Do:** Cover the problem with a well-structured MECE framework, including concrete and tailored ideas, all supported with hypotheses about why they are relevant.
- ☑ **Do not:** Use generic frameworks and ideas, whose investigation would not yield any insights into your client's situation or problem, thereby *boiling the ocean*.

Probing for more data

The trick in candidate-led interviews is to move through the initial case framework, investigating each area by asking the interviewer targeted questions based on your hypotheses. You want to identify the root cause of the problem or understand the different aspects of the situation (the one component/area that influences the case the most) to answer your client's question in the most effective manner.

For instance, to stick with the case question about the carbon reduction strategy from an earlier part, let's assume that you suspect that the biggest impact lies in understanding the different products and making changes to their value chains. Naturally, you would start digging there. Once you've guided the interviewer through the ideas of your issue tree, you should now prioritize your analysis by answering three questions: First, what you want to look at first, second, why. And, third, how are you going about it? *"I first want to look at the different products our client offers and their value chain* (what?) *to understand what products they have and how many emissions they produce* (why?). *Hence, I want to know specifically two things: Do we have any data on a. the breakdown of products, and b. the emissions for each product along the value chain* (how?)?"

Use of hypotheses at this stage: A hypothesis-driven approach helps you steer your analysis, set the direction of the case, and prioritize areas of interest; hence it maximizes the value of your time and effort when working on a problem. It helps you tackle high-impact areas first, where you believe the solution of the case is buried. You want to identify and work on the 20% of the problem that generates 80% of the impact.

- ☑ **Do:** Ask about high-impact items first with clear logic and a goal in mind, looking for concrete information and data.
- ☑ **Do not:** Randomly propose areas to look at with badly defined data requests, i.e., fishing in the dark.

Analyzing data in the context of the case

By asking targeted questions, you receive additional information verbally or in the form of exhibits you need to interpret or math problems you need to solve. Analyze the data with a clear objective in mind. Think about what the data shows, why it can help you in this situation, and how insights generated from it can drive the outcome of the case. This way, it is easier to set up your focused analysis, make meaningful connections, spot relevant insights, and interpret information within the context of the problem you are trying to solve. At the same time, you are aware of the data's limitations and that you are generally dealing with imperfect information throughout the case.

Use of hypotheses at this stage: A hypothesis-driven approach helps you to effectively manipulate, understand, and use new information, as well as guides your interpretation of data and insights in the context of the case. The hypothesis tells you why you want to look at the data specifically and what the outcome of your analysis might mean for the answer to the client's question.

☑ **Do:** Focus on relevant data, analyze it, and interpret it in the context of the case.

☑ **Do not:** Collect and describe a wide variety of data, without interpreting or contextualizing it.

Bringing it all together through synthesizing and further probing

As the case progresses, with more buckets and ideas discussed, and with new data points collected, your hypotheses should become clearer, and each piece of additional information should add to a converging line of evidence. Some hypotheses might be rejected, others are confirmed, and new ones might emerge.

Throughout the process, keep your notes organized and constantly refer to your initial structure as this gives you security, direction, and control. Take stock of where you are currently in the case and keep the goal in mind. Constantly evaluate your position within the case in relation to the problem you are trying to solve or the question you are trying to answer. Additionally, think about interdependencies throughout the case. For instance, if you must make an investment to reduce emissions, consider how that would affect the profit, which is also part of the client's goals (based on our initial case brief to reduce emissions without impacting profit negatively).

If the interviewer offers additional information, move down that lane, drilling vertically into your framework. If they have no information or information that is irrelevant for the case, cross out those buckets and move to the next item in your issue tree based on the order of priority, moving horizontally within one branch of the tree, then again vertically. If you end up with no insights for a whole top-level bucket, cross it out, then go to the next top-level bucket and drill down into its branches again.

Using this approach, you might stumble across a new area that was not part of your initial structure. Acknowledge this, highlight why it is now relevant for the case, and dive deeper into the new area if needed. You could come across a new area if you are struggling and the interviewer proposes it to you, you just thought about it along the way, or new information you have received makes it a target of your investigation.

Use of hypotheses at this stage: A hypothesis-driven approach helps you bring all your insights together, combine and interpret them in the context of the case, keeps you focused and on track or might have you switch lanes if needed.

☑ **Do:** Recap how your insight generation and fact-finding impact your thinking and use it as a steppingstone to confirm ideas, formulate new ideas, or find a way forward.

☑ **Do not:** Fail to combine different data points and insights, forget to make inferences about their impact on the case, and lose track of what to do and where to go.

Recommending a way out through further analyses

Once you have gathered and analyzed enough relevant data, you should be able to understand the root cause of the problem or the different levers of the situation that you can pull, then provide one or more definite recommendations as well as next steps.

For instance, through digging you might receive a chart that shows that the client offers five product segments, yet one out of the five makes up 70% of their CO_2 emissions. Now that you have found the potential source of the issue, it is time to understand the root cause(s) and work on solutions.

Through further digging, you find out that the problem is due to an outdated production technique and could be fixed with an investment of USD 500 million. The 500 million would be balanced by new revenue generation due to increased customer demand. You ask for more data to evaluate whether this investment would make sense from a financial perspective and perform the calculation. You figure out that the investment would be paid off within three years. Based on the outcome, you conclude that the client should focus all efforts initially on this one category and recommend the specific investment to solve their issues.

Use of hypotheses at this stage: A hypothesis-driven approach helps you find the best course of action to answer your client's question.

☑ **Do:** Provide a relevant and targeted set of recommendations, which is based on facts and data and answers the client's question in the most effective way.

☑ **Do not:** Fail to provide a clear recommendation but have a long list of further analyses to conduct to understand and solve the situation.

Not so fast

While the case above sounds straightforward, in reality it might be much more iterative and tedious. Why?

☑ You might go down the wrong parts of the issue tree first, with your investigation yielding no results.

☑ Your initial issue tree does not cover the relevant parts of the case, i.e., the different product segments, their value chain, or the production.

☑ You probe for a few other things before receiving the right data and insights, i.e., the product breakdown chart.

☑ The data might be hard to interpret due to it being displayed across two pages, in different units, or just in a confusing format.

☑ You hypothesize different reasons for the anomalies in the data, i.e., the disparity in CO_2 emissions across products, hence not immediately figuring out that it is related to the production process.

☑ The math approach and/or the calculations are not as straightforward.

☑ A potential solution you discover might not work out, i.e., your proposed solution to reduce CO_2 emissions might not work out since it would reduce the client's profit, which is outside of the solution space the client has defined (*"Profits need to remain at least stable."*).

Setbacks are natural, and candidates rarely move through the case in the most linear manner. All these things are okay if you show that you are adaptable and capable of moving through the case with direction, logic, and in a structured manner, not giving up along the way.

One of the key reasons candidates fail is that they get stuck and do not know how to move forward. They might have exhausted all their ideas, or they do not see the link between the information they have received and the client's situation.

What should you do if you get stuck and don't know how to move forward?

Even if you are prepared and ready to ace the interviews, sometimes the actual case might not go as smoothly as you had hoped. Either you are not familiar with the industry, the functional niche of the case, the context, the specific question, or it might not be your day, the chemistry with the interviewer might be off, etc. In such situations, it can happen that you get stuck and don't know how to continue in a meaningful way. Whenever that happens, I recommend **a five-step approach to getting unstuck**:

1. Go back to the case brief and remind yourself of the client situation and the overarching objective of the case.
2. Go back to your initial structure, recap what you have already found out about the different branches of your issue tree, then synthesize those findings by relating them back to your hypotheses and the case brief (Do they confirm it? Do they reject it? Do you need a new hypothesis?). Often, candidates have the answer right in front of them and don't realize it.
3. If needed, ask the interviewer for 30 seconds to collect your thoughts about how to move forward.
4. If you have gathered all data to confirm your hypotheses, move forward by working on a solution. If you are still not sure what the issue is or have not fully understood the different aspects of the situation, delve deeper into branches of your issue tree you have not yet analyzed or think of new areas you have not yet considered. It might be that your initial issue tree did not cover the problem or situation fully at the top level, i.e., is not fully exhaustive or does not go deep enough with ideas to analyze the top level in a meaningful way, i.e., lacking depth and concreteness. Essentially, think about what parts of the situation you might have missed.
5. If you are truly lost and do not know how to continue, involve the interviewer, explain your current thinking and everything you know about the case. Highlight that this has not yet contributed fully to your understanding of the situation. This is the cue for them to jump in and give you pointers (*"Have you considered factors X or Y?"*). Alternatively, you could proactively ask when probing, *"Is there anything else I haven't*

looked at yet?" Do not blatantly admit that you are fully lost. Always offer some insights and a recap of the status quo before asking for guidance and help.

Getting stuck is not a big problem if...

...you do not admit that you are fully lost and do not know how to get out. Always provide some insights into your thinking and highlight the fact that there is a missing piece that you would need to move forward, implicitly prompting the interviewer to fill in the blanks for you.

For instance, if you get stuck with the framework right at the beginning of the case, think back to **Chapter 8** where I describe several tools and strategies that can help you create broad and deep issue trees. Focus on things such as the process-based view, segmentations, problem components, levers and drivers, quantitative frameworks or a stakeholder perspective. To generate more ideas, think about expanding current ideas or a bottom-up approach to idea generation and mind mapping.

If you are lost when receiving new data, try to put the data into perspective by comparing it to historical data, data from other segments of the client business, or data from competitors and the market. Sometimes you need comparison data or benchmarks to get meaningful insights. Sometimes you need to drill deeper into data segments as insights are rarely found when looking at averages or aggregate data.

If you get stuck during a math question, explain your current understanding of the situation as well as your thoughts about how you would like to solve it on a higher level but are currently missing one or two steps to make it work.

Also, be aware that you are not moving in a vacuum but are in constant communication with the interviewer, who might have a few pointers for you. Trained consulting interviewers notice quickly if you are stuck, spot your stalling behavior, and might offer to help you through the rough patch. For instance, at McKinsey, interviewers should not add to the tension of the interviewees but rather ease their stress. It is similar with most other consulting firms. Small hints, such as *"Have you considered X?"* or *"Why did you exclude Y in your consideration?"* go a long way. This by itself should cheer you up as you are working together with the interviewer on a solution to the case, not against them. Seeing it this way is a mindset switch. The only two things you should never do is to be openly defeated or be completely silent, not sharing your current thoughts and progress. Communication is key, even when admitting you are a bit lost.

Let's look further into the case communication to make this clearer. Now that you know about the different elements and parts of the case and how to move from one to the next by employing the correct thinking and problem-solving habits, you need to know how you can verbally guide the interviewer through your thinking and move with them through the case in the most effective manner.

[13] Communicate like a management consultant

Consultants follow a top-down communication approach to bring their CEO-level messages across most effectively and efficiently. You should follow the same style in case interviews. In this section, I show you battle-tested communication tools and communication principles. We go through the different parts of the case described above with examples of phrases you can learn, internalize, and use for every future case you go through.

What features characterize the perfect case communication?

The #1 consultants' communication tool: The Pyramid Principle

The Pyramid Principle was developed by the former McKinsey consultant Barbara Minto and enables impactful top-down communication. Its application is simple.

Start with the answer, then group and summarize your supporting arguments, ordering them based on a relevant logic. On top of this principle, I see four other principles that characterize strong consulting-style communication:

1. **Signpost:** Summarize what you are going to talk about before going deeper
2. **Number:** Give every idea or point a number to separate it properly from the rest
3. **Overcommunicate:** Always qualify, justify, and explain your thinking
4. **Energize:** Appear engaged and happy-to-be-here when speaking

Let's look at one best-practice example comprising all the principles mentioned above:

"I recommend that the clients focus their efforts on the APAC region for three reasons: first, growth; second, margins; and third, positioning (top-down answer, numbered, signposted). *First, we see the biggest growth in this region, which would further help us focus our efforts where they have the most impact. Second, profit margins are higher compared to other areas, which would help us optimize our global margins. Third, our client is uniquely positioned to target local demographics with their product offering, which gives us an advantage vis-a-vis potential competitors* (grouped supporting arguments, numbered, qualified)."

Adopting the Pyramid Principle and my four other principles for your communication transforms your answers into highly effective and structured messages. The energy aspect cannot be demonstrated in writing but should not be dismissed. Nothing is worse than interviewing someone who shows little engagement, presence, and energy, which often correlate with a lack of confidence.

Do not use empty phrases or sentences. Every sentence should add value and novelty to your spoken answers. This means you should stop talking once you have brought all your points across. I have noticed that when candidates are nervous or not confident in their abilities or answers that they start rambling. They either repeat points several times with different words until they are stopped by the interviewer or create endless sentences of different trains of thought, linking them with *"and"* or *"also."* Stick to the script!

Why and how should you overcommunicate?

I want to highlight the importance of full transparency and oversharing. You need to overcommunicate for two reasons. First, interviewers are not just interested in your ideas but also in your thinking and rationale. I discussed the importance of justifying and qualifying your ideas above. Second, interviewers do not know what you are up to, especially if the interviews are done in a virtual setup. For instance, when working on a math problem, instead of being quiet for three minutes, provide an update of what you are doing and why you are doing it along the way. You want to keep the interviewer in the loop about where you are in the process throughout the case.

What are the key communication phrases for each part of the case?

You can use the following phrases and communication strategies to effectively move through the case and share your insights in the most impactful way, while taking the interviewer along. We look at phrases for each relevant area of the case. All answers are related to our CO2 reduction case. For the sake of brevity, I focus on the phrases and the style (which are case-agnostic) and not the full context of the case. For full mock cases, check out **Chapters 17 and 18.**

Structure. When you present your issue tree, stick to a structured, numbered and signposted top-down approach, going from the top-level, more general ideas to the lower-level, more concrete and specific ideas. It is important to justify your approach implicitly or explicitly as well as highlight potential interdependencies. Here is the chart again to remind you of our issue tree from before:

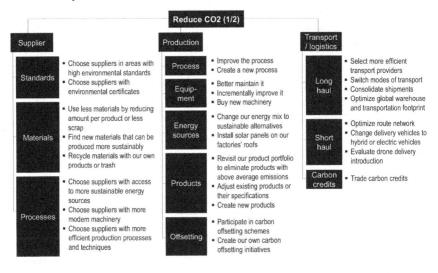

■ **Illustrative case interview framework (1/2)**

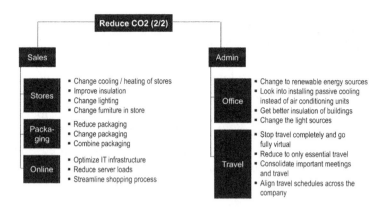

Illustrative case interview framework (2/2)

"Here, I want to look at five things, first the suppliers, second, our own manufacturing, third, transportation and logistics, fourth, the sales process, fifth, the administrative part of our client's business **(top-down, numbering, signposting)***.*

In my first bucket, I want to go through three ideas: First, I want to look at the standards that our suppliers have as they might drive their emissions **(example for justification)***. I want to look at if we a. could choose suppliers in areas with higher environmental standards or b. work with suppliers that have certain environmental certificates. Changing suppliers would have an impact on our transportation as well* **(example for interdependencies)***. Second, I'll look at the materials they are using as this has a significant impact on the CO_2 emissions. More concretely, I want to look at a. if we could use less materials by either making our products lighter or producing less scrap, b. if we should look at new materials that might be produced more sustainably, and c. if we could look at recycling, either our own products or trash such as ocean plastic. Third, I want to look at the processes of our suppliers. <Explain why and list more concrete things you want to look at in the same manner as above>.*

Now, I want to go back to my second top-level bucket, our own production. Here I'll look at five ideas. <repeat the process described above>..."

You might not have all your ideas on paper once you start talking, which is completely normal. If you do not know how many points you want to discuss, you can always say: *"Here, I have a few points"*. Then, number them as you go along. If you committed to a number, for instance, by saying, *"I want to discuss three things here"*, you can just add ideas by saying, *"Now that I think about it, there is a fourth point I want to discuss."* You can always add ideas on the fly as long as you make sure that you are communicating in a structured and clear manner. Do not jump around your framework.

Probing. Once you have guided the interviewer through your structure, you need to start probing for additional information in the areas in which you believe the case solution is buried based on your hypotheses. When probing, answer three distinct questions. Namely, **what** you want to do first, the area you want to investigate, **why**, the purpose of your investigation, and **how** you will go about it, plus the next steps detailing your data request or concrete analyses. If you want to look at multiple things, then again, number and signpost your ideas.

"Now having gone through all areas, I want to first look at our production bucket, and more concretely, the different products our client offers **(what?)** *to understand what products they have and how many emissions they produce* **(why?)**. *Hence, I want to know specifically two things: first, do we have any data on the breakdown of products, and second, the emissions for each* **(how?)**?"

Exhibits. When going over an exhibit, reading data and information back to the interviewer is not enough. You need to provide actual insights into the meaning of the data in the context of the case, the *so-what*? Focus your answer on the insights, the implications, and the next steps, considering potential interdependencies. Again, do this in a structured manner, employing numbering and signposting. Before you go into your analysis, briefly provide a high-level description of what the chart displays.

Shoe production data, 2021

Product	# produced, in k	Cost per item, in USD	Revenue per item, in USD	CO2 emissions, in tons
Sneaker X	120	13.4	79.9	879.6
Sneaker Y	154	13.6	84.9	1128.8
Runner Alpha	146	12.5	114.9	1053.3
Runner Beta	148	12.8	131.9	2134.2
Walker	113	12.1	59.9	820.7

■ Illustrative chart

Description: *"Looking at the chart, I see five different shoes that are produced by the client. For each, we have 2021 information on the production quantity, the cost of production, their sales price – both in US dollars – as well as the CO2 emissions in tons."*

Interpretation: *"I see three important things on this chart: First, Sneaker Y and both Runners Alpha and Beta are our client's top-sellers. Second, the profit margin of Runner Beta is by far the highest compared to the other four products, so combined with the high sales volume it seems to be most important product for our client. Third, Runner Beta seems to be responsible for a disproportionately high number of emissions. For instance, with almost the same quantity as Runner Alpha, the production is responsible for twice as many CO2 emissions, while all other products are relatively in line when looking at their production quantity and the associated emissions* **(the insights)**.

Based on that, I would recommend looking more into the production of Runner Beta shoes as I believe we should start decreasing emissions there as it is the most important product and the one where we could generate the biggest impact **(the recommendation/implication)**. *To do this, I would like to do three things next: First, do we have any data on the production process of this product that we can compare to our own production of other products? And, second, do we have any benchmark data that we can use to compare it to best practices on the market? Third, I want* *to understand how our costs would change if we implemented any measures here since we should keep the profit stable* (**the next steps/probing/interdependencies**).*"*

Synthesizing. Through extensive and focused probing, you collect several data points and new information. With every bit of new information received, synthesize your current findings and interpret them in the context of the case. Syntheses should lead to the confirmation of existing hypotheses or new hypotheses as well as converging lines of evidence that further your investigation into the root cause of the problem as well as the recommendation to satisfy your client's demands. At the end of your synthesis, move the case forward by recommending next steps such as probing for new data and information, going into new analyses, or discussing implementation measures.

"I know three things now regarding Runner Beta. First, it seems to have significantly higher CO2 emissions than any other product of our client. Second, its production process seems to be outdated and that is the reason for this emissions gap compared to other products. Third, I have gathered that the client would need to invest USD 500 million to remedy the issue (**recap of status quo**). *Based on this, I would like to investigate now if this investment would be smart, purely based on financial considerations* (**the implication**). *Hence, I want to look at the payback period to see the impact on our client's profit over five years. Do we know the impact on quantity sold and price due to the sustainability increase, as in, could we raise prices, and would people buy more sustainable goods? Will the production cost remain the same or is there any other cost we need to consider* (**the next steps/probing**)*?"*

Math. You should approach math problems in the most systematic way. This is also relevant for how you communicate your approach and results. For the approach, break it down into digestible steps, again numbering and signposting them. For the result, answer the question that was asked, interpret the result in the context of the case, and discuss how you want to move forward.

Approach: *"I want to approach this calculation in four steps: First, I want to calculate our current profit per year by multiplying the* *current quantity with the current profit per item. Second, I want to calculate the future profit per year by multiplying the future quantity with the future profit per item. Third, I want to deduct the current profit from the future profit. Fourth, I want to compare five times the delta of the future and the current profit to the USD 500m investment and see if we are able to break even within five years. If the answer is yes, then I would recommend this investment."*

Results and interpretation: *"I would recommend the investment as we are breaking even in less than five years* **(the answer)**. *The investment achieves both goals of our client. First, it achieves our sustainability goal by reducing emissions. Second, the investment would not only keep the profit stable but increase it over a five-year time period* **(the interpretation in the context of the case)**. *I would like to check the assumptions that we would really sell five percent more at a higher price point and that the investment will not exceed USD 500m, as changes to these assumptions could quickly change my evaluation* **(think about whether it's feasible and sensible)**. *Going forward, I would like to do two things next. First, I want to think about how we can implement these measures and, second, I think we should start thinking about potential marketing and advertising strategies to promote these new sustainable products* **(next steps and moving forward)."**

Recommendation. Once you have found a suitable answer, the interviewers might ask you for a brief recommendation to end the case. Communicate your recommendation in a top-down and structured way; no need to repeat the question. Back it up with supporting arguments, then discuss the outlook with risks or next steps.

"I would recommend the client make a USD 500-million investment into sustainable manufacturing of Runner Beta for two reasons **(top-down recommendation)**. *First, it would enable them to tackle their CO2 emissions most effectively since the product is by far the biggest contributor to the CO2 footprint due to outdated production equipment. Second, by making this investment, the client would not merely keep profits stable but increase them after 3.5 years due to higher demand and higher prices* **(supporting arguments)**. *Going forward, two main risks remain. First, we need to make sure*

> *the increases in sales and price will materialize, so we should also look into a marketing and advertising plan to support the measures. Second, we want to make sure the investment cost is capped at USD 500 million. Hence, we need to perform due diligence on potential machinery, the process, and the implementation efforts* **(next steps/ risks)**.*"*

Internalize this way of communicating so it becomes automatic as you move through the different elements of a case. This communication style can and should be used in every case, no matter the context, industry, function, or case question. Some phrases might repeat throughout the case (e.g., a synthesis or if you encounter multiple math problems). I used partially connected communication snippets of a case to bring my points across. To see how this would look like in a real case from start to finish, we go over a full candidate-led case and a full interviewer-led case in **Part 7**.

[14] Develop the right meta habits

I've noticed certain minor habits that correlate with successful outcomes of case interviews, which might not be super obvious when you start your preparation. I've highlighted my observations here, which to some extent go against common advice, by answering the following questions:

- ☑ How much time should you take to think about your answers and how long should you take to solve the case?
- ☑ How should you structure your notes?
- ☑ How can you avoid mistakes or recover from them?

How much time should you take to think and solve the case?

Time to think

Fifty percent of candidates are scared to ask for time to gather their thoughts. Thirty percent take time, yet not enough. Ten percent take too much time and about ten percent get it right. So why is asking for the appropriate amount of time to think about your answers important? There are two reasons.

First, your answers are more exhaustive, more coherent, better structured, and often also more concise the more you think about them. In short, never feel pressured to answer right away as this significantly decreases the quality of your answers. For a framework question, ask for time to draw your issue tree. When interpreting an exhibit, ask for time to think about the insights and implications. For a math question, ask for time to structure your approach, then again to perform the calculations.

By taking time to think about a proper approach, hypotheses, analyses, next steps, etc. your problem-solving is more effective, and you likely arrive at a conclusion quicker compared to when you do everything on the spot. I see this all the time. A candidate trying to analyze a chart on the fly will take twice as long compared to a candidate who takes 30 seconds to write down key observations and implications, then answers in the most top-down and concise way possible. Apart from the overall time needed to communicate insights and move through the analysis, the impression the interviewer has is also much better for the latter candidate.

Second, taking time is an essential skill when working with tough clients and senior leaders. A project manager's worst fear is a new hire consultant answering a senior client's question without thinking about it, just because they don't have the confidence to get back after some deliberation. You want to make sure that all your statements are well thought-out, coherent, and based on facts. Blurting out a quick but wrong answer could kill your client's trust in the whole effort of your team and in your firm. Case interviews evaluate your confidence and maturity to step back and take time in high-pressure situations. Consequently, demonstrate that you are confident enough to let your interviewer wait until you have formulated a strong answer or analysis.

How much time is too much time? What I wrote above is not carte blanche to take as much thinking time as possible. I recommend the following times both for thinking and answering/talking as an indication of upper boundaries for a standard case interview.

Element of the case	Candidate-led	McKinsey
Structure/Brainstorm	Think: 1.5 minutes Talk: 2-3 minutes (probing should follow)	Think: 2 minutes Talk: 6 minutes (prioritization included)
Exhibits	Think: 15-30 seconds Talk: 2 minutes	Think: 1 minute Talk: 2 minutes
Math	Approach: 1 minute Calculation: 3 minutes Talk: 2 minutes	Approach: 1.5 minutes Calculation: 3 minutes Talk: 2 minutes
Recommendation	Think: Up to 30 seconds Talk: 2 minutes	Recommendations are not common in McKinsey interviews (see the explanation below); if it comes up: 30 seconds thinking time and 2 minutes talking

■ Indication of time to take to think and talk about the elements of a case

Consider these times as a high-level guidance (more on the time to solve the case below). It goes without saying that the amount of time you take should be correlated with the quality and depth of your answer. If you take two minutes to think about an issue tree, then communicate two high-level ideas, it won't be received well. Similarly, if you talk for four minutes and just repeat the same talking points over and over again, your interviewer will interrupt.

Lastly, it always pays off to ask for time, however, be aware that some interviewers might not grant that request. Interpret this as yet another stress test and not as malicious interviewer behavior. If interviewers deny thinking time, their expectations about the structure, communication, and exhaustiveness of your answer are also lower.

Time to solve the case

A question I often get is: *"Will I score higher if I manage to solve the case in x minutes instead of y minutes?"*

For candidate-led cases, the time you take is an indirect indication of your case performance. Naturally, the faster you have arrived at understanding the root cause of the problem or the situation in general, then derived remedies or answers for the client, the more effective your skills related to problem-solving, analytics, creativity, chart interpretation, quantitative reasoning, and communication. While time alone is not that important, the other skills mentioned above are. Change your perspective. By mastering the right skills, the shorter time to solve a case comes naturally. And as I said, counterintuitively, taking time to think makes you faster at solving cases overall.

At top-tier firms, cases usually last between 20 and 30 minutes. In candidate-led cases, you are expected to identify the issue by going through the framework, hence your initial structure should focus on the most impactful items and quickly be followed by your probing efforts. Candidates often spend only two to three minutes on guiding the interviewer through the structure, briefly touching on the higher-level ideas, to have more time probing and investigating the lower-level more concrete ideas in a focused effort. For the latter, they are expanding the depth of their structure only for areas that have a high probability of helping them understand the problem and developing a recommendation.

For McKinsey cases, time plays more of an indirect role as it is the interviewers' responsibility to finish the case within a certain period, usually 25 to 30 minutes. Their goal is to get enough data points and observations on you in the different parts of the case, not to "finish the case." That is also why McKinsey cases often end abruptly without a recommendation. You should still manage to go through one question of each type, structuring/idea generation, exhibit, and math.

If your answers are insightful and well argued, you might take longer for each question. For instance, you could be talking about your initial structure for six minutes, covering the situation exhaustively at your top level, then going very deep with concrete ideas, guiding the interviewer through your thinking and problem-solving approach. If everything you are saying makes sense, is insightful, well structured, and does not overlap, you are free to continue. Interviewers recognize your spike in this area and might interrupt you at a certain point to make sure they can also gather data points on your exhibit interpretation and quantitative reasoning.

On the contrary, if you present your issue tree, yet your ideas are repetitive, not MECE, badly supported, etc. they might interrupt you much earlier and try to bring you back on track. Similarly, if you present your framework within one or two minutes, chances are that it is not very exhaustive in McKinsey-terms, prompting interviewers to intervene and ask for *"Anything else?"*

Exhibit interpretation and math problems usually take the same amount of time in candidate-led cases and interviewer-led McKinsey cases. For an exhibit, you discuss your goal or play back the question, clarify if needed, and take a minute to write down your thoughts, which you then communicate in one to two minutes. For a math problem, you play back the numbers, think for one minute about your approach, communicate it, then take two to three minutes to calculate and one to two minutes to answer and contextualize your results.

How should you write your case interview notes?

Note-taking is highly personal, as everyone processes data and information differently. Some people prefer not to take notes at all, potentially missing important bits of information, while others take notes in a chaotic and stressed manner, leading to confusion rather than order and control. On the other end of the spectrum are candidates who think visually and draft well-thought-out notes, which might take time away from actually thinking about the problem. You need to figure out what works best for you. However, there are a couple of principles you should stick to when taking notes, regardless of what type of note-taker you are.

Flip your pages by 90 degrees. Consultants think and work in the landscape format. To structure your inputs and outputs, flip your pages by 90 degrees. This format is more suitable for the creation of issue trees, chart interpretation notes, and calculations.

Keep your goal always visible. Write down the case goal(s) at the top of the sheet, underline or circle it to always remind yourself of what you're trying to achieve.

Keep your notes brief by using abbreviations and symbols. Focus on essential and relevant details and shorten what you write. Instead of writing: *"The client is wondering why their profits have decreased over the last five years"*, write: "5yr P ↓?" Find symbols that work for you during case practice and stick to those.

Make your notes visually appealing and keep them organized. For instance, use boxes, arrows, and lines to visualize the relationships between ideas. Show hierarchies and different levels of information by placing ideas at different levels of the sheet, for instance, when creating an issue tree. When highlighting certain aspects, circle them rather than writing them out again. Avoid repetitive or redundant notes.

Use a new sheet for every math question. Whenever you start working on a new math problem, start with a new sheet. You never know how long the equations and calculations are going to be and how much room you need. I have seen countless interviewees fumble as they reach the end of a full page, continue on a new paper, then miss important details from the previous page, leading to confusion and errors.

Do not forget information on other sheets. If you take a lot of notes, you might use two, three, or even four sheets of paper in one case. When starting on a fresh paper, number the new page and remind yourself of the important bits of information on the previous sheet(s).

Organize your sheets. You could separate the insights paper from the thinking paper(s). The insights sheet would only be used to write down the client name, case prompt, and the objective on the left side, and everything you learn throughout the case on the right side (e.g., all important findings and additional information that help you answer the case question). Thinking papers are used for your analyses, e.g., the initial structure or case math. Separating the two keeps your notes organized and clean.

You do not need to present your notes to the interviewer. While it adds a nice touch to the interview, you do not need to present your writing to the interviewer. Some candidates spend too much time creating a visually appealing notepad rather than coming up with exhaustive and meaningful ideas. That is a bad use of your time with a low return on investment. It is much more important to verbally guide the interviewer coherently through your ideas and thinking. At the end of the day, note-taking should not be an additional task that stresses you out. Find a process that works for you and stick to it.

How can you avoid and recover from mistakes?

No candidate is perfect. Consulting firms and interviewers know this. Hence, making a mistake during a case interview is not a definite deal-breaker for landing a top-tier consulting offer unless it happens more frequently within one case, you mess up throughout several cases, or one mistake triggers a chain-reaction of you losing your cool and falling apart in front of the interviewer. I've seen a range of negative emotions here, from people that almost started to cry or wanted to stop the interview to others that were so embarrassed that they could not recover from their mistake and made a follow-up mistake soon after.

Here are some key strategies to deal with and recover from your mistakes and errors.

Avoid mistakes in the first place. The most efficient strategy is to avoid making mistakes in the first place. Of course, this is obvious, but it is not a platitude. Eighty percent of the times I've seen candidates mess up, it is the result of them speaking before they think. Many candidates, at some point during the interview, have an epiphany and blurt out a random fact, a wrong conclusion, a statement not based on facts or based on untested assumptions, or wrong numerical results after having calculated hastily in their head. Develop a disciplined approach and be patient. Think before you speak, and you will already be better than the majority of candidates who make these simple mistakes.

Sanity check your results and outcomes. A general case interview habit you should adopt is to sanity check results and outcomes. Whenever you get a new insight, ask yourself: *"Does this make sense?"* *"Is it in the right ballpark or completely off?"* You can even do this out loud in front of the interviewer. Candidates that use this case habit generally perform better than others, both in the process (problem-solving, creativity, analytics, quantitative reasoning, business sense and intuition, communication) and the product (the recommendation) of their work. Also, sanity checking allows you to spot any mistake before the interviewer and correct it in a calm and natural way, leading the interviewer through the process (if they even noticed your mistake).

Keep your composure. If you make a mistake, keep calm, focused and carry on confidently. One thing I see often: Candidates let one mistake ruin their whole interview. Even if they perform well for 20 minutes and then make a mistake, they completely lose it and their performance for the rest of the case goes down the drain. Make sure that a mistake does not lead to a chain reaction of you breaking apart in front of the interviewer. Remind yourself that a one-off error is not a big deal for most cases. In fact, interviewers want to see how you deal with setbacks. Therefore, see it as an opportunity. If you don't make a big deal out of it, the interviewers normally won't either. Move on and focus all your mental resources on the next challenges. Thank the interviewer for helping out, then act as if nothing happened. Do not make the mistake of becoming faster but rather slow down after a lapse in judgment. Otherwise, chances are high that you will make a follow-up mistake.

Be coachable. Interviewers generally want you to succeed. So, if they point out your mistake or probe something you said, you should start going into problem-solving mode about what could be wrong right away. If they start to guide you, it is usually because they want you to get back on track. In that case, listen and demonstrate that you are coachable and able to receive feedback. Show that you are interested in what they have to say and take their feedback into account. The worst are candidates that are not willing to accept the help, become defensive about the intervention, and try to rationalize why they made a mistake or why they think they are still correct (even if they are not). This is one of the fastest ways to get a rejection. Additionally, avoid going back to the beginning of the problem or starting from scratch. If the interviewer intervenes, they want you to start from there and move on quickly due to the time limit of the interview.

Expect to be pressure-tested. Once you make a mistake in a specific area (e.g., problem structure, pen-and-paper math), interviewers might probe this area going forward to see if it was an exception or the rule. Hence, expect the area where you made a mistake to become the focus of more attention either in the same interview or in the next round after the interviewers have discussed your performance. The more confidence and strength you demonstrate going forward in these areas, the better you will fare in this pressure test.

PART 6

Unique Case Formats:
How to Ace
Interviewer-led and
Written Case Interviews

Let's take a look at two more case interview formats, the McKinsey case interview (officially, the Problem Solving Interview), which is interviewer-led, as well as the written case interview, which you must complete by yourself without any interaction. Most elements in each are the same as for a typical candidate-led interview. You still need to identify a goal, understand the situation, structure your approach, conduct analyses, interpret exhibits, and perform math, to come up with recommendations. The main difference for both is how you move through the case.

In this chapter, I focus solely on the differences between the respective interviews and the candidate-led interview to avoid redundant content and information. More specifically I answer the following two questions:

☑ What are written case interviews and how can you ace them?
☑ How does the McKinsey Problem Solving Interview differ from a typical case interview?

[15] Ace written case interviews

"The written case interview is a natural extension of the traditional case interview."

Bain & Company recruiting message

Some firms employ written case interviews, most notably BCG and Bain across several locations and offices, usually during the final round.

What is a written case interview?

A written case interview differs from a live case interview since you must work on the problem on your own, without interviewer guidance and discussion. Instead, you are handed a couple of pages with information about a client company and a problem it is facing or a goal it wants to achieve. You are asked to answer a set of questions and provide a recommendation. At the core, it most closely resembles an interviewer-led case interview, just in a written, non-interactive format.

To answer the questions and provide a recommendation, you need to perform several analyses within 30 minutes to one hour, as well as draft a couple of slides or flipchart pages to support your story. Once the preparation time is over, you must present your findings to one or several consultants and answer their challenges.

How do you approach a written case interview?

Follow this six-step approach to tackle this type of assessment effectively. It helps you to focus your efforts, swiftly analyze and synthesize relevant information, and provide a strong recommendation and presentation at the end.

1. Plan ahead: Be prepared when you start the written case

Since time is limited, you should know what to expect and plan how long you want to spend on each task of the assignment beforehand. For a typical 60-minute case take

- ☑ five minutes for a quick scan and to sort the documents
- ☑ five minutes to plan your approach (e.g., define the goal, what information you need, what analyses you can do, what output documents you need to draft)
- ☑ 10 minutes to draft your output slides as doing this early on helps you focus your analytical efforts
- ☑ 30 minutes for analyses, answering the questions, and working through the case
- ☑ 10 minutes to populate your slides with your findings and recommendations.

For 30-minute cases, cut every step down by roughly 50%. In total, you would need five minutes to scan the documents and draft a plan, spend five minutes to draft your desired output, then work 15 minutes on the material and use the last five minutes to populate your slides or flipchart.

2. Focus: Quickly separate the signal from the noise

Written cases come with an information overload that you need to sort through. First, figure out what you need to decide upon. Second, determine what analyses would help you make that decision. Third, think about what information you need to conduct the necessary analyses and see if it matches with your planned analyses. If you do not have the necessary data, adjust your analyses.

Write down the question you need to solve and constantly relate back to it when you work on the case. That way you can scan and read with an objective in mind and improve your comprehension speed. Dive into the relevant information, structure and conduct your analyses. Ignore every bit of information that is not relevant or insightful. Like in a live case interview, employ a hypothesis-driven approach to frame your structure and thoughts. Synthesize each bit of your analysis to draw proper conclusions. Always ask yourself whether what you are currently doing helps you with achieving your goal. You can practice your comprehension speed by looking at business school cases: HBS case studies, Ivey case studies, INSEAD case studies, MIT case studies (includes free materials).

Increase your reading speed with apps such as *Spreeder* or *Reedy*.

3. Spot insights: Interpret and distill key insights from exhibits

Written cases bombard you with charts, graphs, tables, and other visual depictions of data you need to interpret and distill insights from. Quickly read and interpret exhibits.

- ☑ What information is relevant for the case?
- ☑ What are the key messages and insights?
- ☑ How is the information of several charts and tables related?
- ☑ What are the implications of the data?

To work on those skills, go back to **Chapter 9** on exhibit interpretation. For written cases it also helps to go through *The Economist, The Wall Street Journal*, or similar publications and use their graphs or tables to train your interpretation skills. Alternatively, look at consulting club casebooks, online case libraries, older practice McKinsey Problem Solving Tests, and BCG Potential Tests. See the resources in **Chapter 37**. When practicing, time yourself, e.g., give yourself 30 seconds before communicating what an exhibit is about and what you would infer from it.

4. Perform quick math: Quickly draft equations and conduct pen-and-paper math

Get into the habit of quickly setting up and accurately performing calculations. Practice quick pen-and-paper math as well as estimations in a similar manner as you would do for a live case interview. To prepare and practice math for written cases, use the same resources I highlight throughout the book, specifically **Chapter 10** on case math. To get access to many (free) math practice resources, see **Chapter 37**.

5. Create a story: Draft a compelling storyline and support it with visually appealing outputs

When working on the output, create a top-down storyline with your recommendations first, then use supporting arguments to strengthen your position.

In practice, you create one key slide with your recommendation, i.e., what the client should do or what the best answer is for the client's question. Next, you have several supporting slides, discussing arguments for your solution, i.e., why your approach is the best based on the data you have seen and the analyses you have conducted. Lastly, place a slide about potential next steps to hedge your bets, i.e., what else you want to know to make your recommendation even stronger, what can be done to hedge risks, or what can be actions to implement your solution. You want to demonstrate that you think ahead and consider the bigger picture. For some written case interviews, you would only have one key slide or one flipchart page that combines your recommendation and supporting arguments.

As for the slide design, use an action title on each slide as well as visual aids such as a graph or table (with a title) and supporting bullet points, or if no graph is needed, just bullet points with your key supporting arguments. The action title should convey the *so-what?* of your analysis. You need to show the implication of what you present rather than a description of what you have found. The headings of each slide together should tell the full story. Everything below the action title are details of the story that should support the key message of that particular slide.

6. Present and defend: Communicate and defend your recommendation top-down

If you must present your findings at the end of the case to a consultant, follow the top-down approach of your slide deck. Be confident and engaging when going through your recommendation and supporting arguments.

First, present your headlines, e.g., *"The client needs to cut costs by x% to become profitable."* Then move on to the details of the slide such as *"There are three ways we can achieve this. First, we need to cut our manufacturing costs by y%, counteracting an increase of z% over the last three years..."*

Number and signpost your ideas. Approach this just like a recommendation you would give at the end of a live case interview. Go back to the sections on the Pyramid Principle and case interview communication in **Chapter 13** as well as **Chapter 11** on the final recommendation to read more about it. Discuss when you are using hypotheses and assumptions that you were not able to verify.

Lastly, be open and ready for debate. The interviewers might challenge your recommendation, no matter how strong and well thought out it is. It is important that you confidently stand your ground, coming up with arguments based on the data of the case as well as your interpretation of it and hypotheses about it. You should only yield to critique if the consultants make you aware of an obvious mistake. In this case, demonstrate that you are coachable and save the situation by providing a plan of action about how to change your analysis to cross-check or improve your results and recommendation(s). Do not appear overly defensive when being challenged.

[16] Ace the McKinsey Problem Solving Interview

The McKinsey case interview, also called the Problem Solving Interview by the firm, is arguably the hardest challenge for candidates on the journey to their offer. Forbes ranked McKinsey's interview process as the most difficult across all firms globally and the case plays a crucial role in that, besides the Personal Experience Interview.

I find that information available on the McKinsey application process and specifically the case interviews is often wrong, outdated, or assumed to be the same as for every other consulting firm. Consequently, the advice can be detrimental to your recruiting success with the firm. In this chapter, I'll shed some light on this elusive, often talked about and misunderstood interview by answering the following questions:

- ☑ What is the McKinsey Problem Solving Interview?
- ☑ What skills are assessed?
- ☑ What is the format of the McKinsey case?
- ☑ What are the questions in a McKinsey case interview?
- ☑ How is the McKinsey interview different from other case interviews?
- ☑ How should you prepare for a McKinsey case interview?

What is the McKinsey Problem Solving Interview?

The McKinsey Problem Solving Interview is, to some extent, a typical case interview like those employed by all top-tier consulting firms to test the problem-solving capabilities and communication skills of applicants. The interview simulates a client situation, where you are tasked to solve a specific problem that they are facing or achieve a certain goal based on their request. As in other firms, the interview is a dialogue between you and the interviewer, where you need to structure problems, propose ideas, gather information, spot insights in exhibits, solve quantitative problems, and communicate in a professional manner.

However, it comes with a twist. Instead of driving the case yourself and moving through the different layers of analysis autonomously as you would for other consulting interviews, you must answer a succession of questions from the interviewer. It involves several different skills that need to be demonstrated consistently across all questions and across multiple cases. Depending on the specific office and role, you need to go through four to six case interviews before receiving a full-time offer. In the process, you will have to convince all interviewers.

What skills are assessed by McKinsey?

There is essentially no difference in the skills assessed by McKinsey compared to other firms. What differs is how those skills are evaluated in a highly specific interviewing format. If you want to read up on the skills in more detail, go back to **Chapter 5**.

1. **Problem-solving:** Ability to deconstruct problems and situations into their constituent parts.
2. **Creativity:** Ability to come up with creative ideas and insights related to the situation at hand.
3. **Analytics:** Ability to quickly identify and prioritize key areas to look at, gravitate toward the right insights quickly, and to understand interdependencies with an inquisitive and hypothesis-driven mindset.
4. **Quantitative reasoning:** Ability to think through quantitative problems and perform calculations accurately and swiftly.
5. **Communication:** Ability to effectively and efficiently communicate your problem-solving strategy and insights.
6. **Maturity:** Demonstration of professional conduct, maturity, confidence, and genuine friendliness.
7. **Business sense and intuition:** Ability to quickly find your way in a new challenge and environment, ask pertinent questions, and provide the right recommendations that are relevant in the context of the problem.

What is the format of the McKinsey case?

A typical McKinsey case follows the Personal Experience Interview in a 50-minute to one-hour interview session. The case portion usually lasts between 20 and 30 minutes. The interviewer takes the lead and guides you through the case. Your role as the interviewee is to answer the questions asked by the interviewer exhaustively before they move on to the next question. While it is the interviewer's responsibility to provide hints and move you through the different questions, you should take the lead within each question. You take ownership of every question and should provide more exhaustive answers compared to a candidate-led case.

There is no requirement to go through a specific number of questions. Depending on your performance and speed, you might be asked between three to seven questions. Every interviewer has two questions per question type at their disposal to probe areas if needed. Receiving fewer questions can be a positive sign since the interviewer was happy with your exhaustive answers.

Going above three questions might happen if you are extremely fast, which is not necessarily a good thing and potentially means that you scratched the issues solely at the surface. For instance, if you communicate your initial issue tree in one or two minutes, it might be that you did not cover the problem or situation exhaustively or on a deep enough level. Alternatively, the interviewer might want to dig deeper into a specific question type to see if the (low) quality of a previous answer to a similar question was just an outlier or can be confirmed by another observation. For instance, you nailed the initial structuring and exhibit interpretation but took a little longer to come up with the right approach for the math question, then on top of that, you made a minor calculation error. Happy with your performance for structuring and exhibits, the interviewer likely uses the remaining interview time to ask you another math question. Most candidates need more than three questions to convince the interviewer. Do not be worried when your case goes above three questions.

Some McKinsey offices also offer a phone case interview as a first screening device. This follows the same structure as an in-person interview, except for the exhibit interpretation, which is missing. These phone cases are mostly conducted by former consultants of the firm.

What are the standardized McKinsey case interview questions?

In a McKinsey case, you must answer four different question types, which are the same as the core elements of a candidate-led case. The difference is that in the candidate-led interview you arrive at those questions yourself by probing and eliciting new information from the interviewer. In a McKinsey case, the interviewer asks you a question, listens to your answer, then moves to the next question. The questions fall into one of four categories: structuring/brainstorming, exhibit interpretation, math, recommendation (rarely). All you have learned about those four elements in the previous chapters is equally relevant for McKinsey as well. **The key differences are as follows.**

☑ McKinsey puts more emphasis on structuring and brainstorming, so you should take more time to think about those answers and take more time to guide the interviewers through broad and deep frameworks.

☑ For most questions, there is no real answer key or a single correct solution. The rating of your answer depends on the quality of your insights, your creativity, and the outcomes of your analyses as well as the interpretation of such.

☑ Instead of probing your way through the case, for every question you need to discuss the implications of your insights/ findings in the context of the case as well as potential next steps to indicate how you would move the case forward. This is almost like a mini recommendation at the end of each answer.

☑ The interviewer moves the case from question to question, regardless of your previous analyses and planned approach or direction. Do not be concerned if the case does not go in the direction you proposed. As long as what you said was sensible that is totally fine. The case has been prepared in a linear manner and you have no influence on the trajectory.

☑ There are sometimes multiple case goals which might be conflicting.

☑ Interviewers pay special attention to how you handle and consider interdependencies throughout the case.

☑ Self-standing recommendations at the end are usually not part of the case.

Let's quickly recap the different question types of a case and how they are important for McKinsey. In **Chapter 18**, we go through a live case to show you the similarities and differences to a candidate-led case with a practical example.

A **case interview structure** is used to break down the problem or situation you are trying to understand for the client into smaller problems or components. It is the roadmap you establish at the beginning of the interview that will guide your problem-solving throughout the case.

The difference at McKinsey: Since the McKinsey interview is interviewer-led, the firm's interviewers place extra emphasis on the structure. The way of structuring the case is also the biggest difference candidates encounter in McKinsey interviews compared to other firms' interviews. At the core, McKinsey wants to see creative ideas communicated in a structured manner, the more exhaustive, the better. Your goal should be to come up with a tailored and creative answer that fits the question. This means you can take up to two minutes to draft your structure. The structure you come up with needs to fully cover the problem at the top level, list key points related to each top-level bucket, which are specified further through a number of concrete ideas, recognize the interdependencies in your framework, be hypothesis-driven and make clear why your ideas matter. It should also highlight how and why you would move forward.

A big issue I see with my clients is that they take too little time to structure their thoughts because they feel pressured to be quick rather than exhaustive and creative. This is partially due to their experience with candidate-led interviews, as well as faulty information in online media and from non-McKinsey case coaches. Thirty more seconds often make the difference between a bad and a good framework or a good and a distinctive one. My battle-tested advice is to get rid of this time pressure mindset, *especially in a McKinsey interview*. McKinsey interviewers have the task of creating a comfortable environment where you can perform at your best.

Some structuring answers are better than others because they are broader, deeper, more insightful, fully MECE, considering interdependencies, are hypothesis-driven, and follow a strong communication approach, yet most of the time there is not one single correct solution. It is important that your answers display the characteristics specified above.

What also differs from other firms, where you might only have around two minutes to present your framework, is that you can take up to roughly six minutes to guide the interviewer through your structure, your explanations, and hypotheses. The firm wants to see exhaustive and creative approaches to specific problems.

Brainstorming/creativity questions are similar to structure questions. They can either be at the start of the case or come up at a later stage. Instead of focusing on your approach to a problem, brainstorming questions have you think about root causes, problems, solutions, or ideas more directly, usually in specific and narrow part of the case. For instance, instead of asking about the factors you want to consider when investigating an overarching problem, you might be asked questions such as:

- ☑ *"What reasons can you think of that led to an increase in conversion rates?"*
- ☑ *"What problems could drive this change in customer satisfaction?"*
- ☑ *"What ideas do you have to mitigate the delays in our rail network?"*
- ☑ *"What data would you need to analyze this?"*
- ☑ *"What analyses would you recommend for understanding the problem better?"*
- ☑ *"Who would you approach to get meaningful insights?"*

The difference at McKinsey: You should approach and answer brainstorming questions like normal structure questions since the same criteria are relevant for your evaluation. Pay attention to breadth, depth, and innovative ideas, all nicely structured in a logically coherent MECE framework. Also, think ahead about your priorities.

For **exhibit interpretation** questions, you are tasked to find the key insights of one or two PowerPoint slides and relate them back to the case question and the client situation at hand. In general, you approach those questions in the same manner as you would in a candidate-led interview. A chart's key insights are not negotiable, as there are specific data points or information you should mention and highlight, usually outliers.

The difference at McKinsey: The interpretation of those insights and the next steps are, again, up to your imagination and creativity; in many cases there is no specific answer that the interviewer is looking for. The evaluation depends on the quality of your arguments and the delivery of your points. You are free to say whatever you think makes sense as long as you support it with logical arguments and think about the bigger picture of the case and the goals.

Case math questions have you analyze a problem mathematically in three steps. First, you need to think about how to approach a quantitative problem by setting up your calculations. Second, you need to perform the calculations accurately and swiftly. Third, you need to answer the question, then interpret the data in the context of the case and provide next steps. There is an objective truth for every math question. Either answers are correct or wrong. If an answer is wrong it is due to a faulty calculation approach, the calculation itself, or a combination of both.

The difference at McKinsey: Your interpretation and next steps are again up to your imagination and creativity. For instance, you might want to qualitatively investigate the reasons for the numerical result or derive specific recommendations from the outcome before highlighting a couple of concrete next steps. You are free to say whatever you think makes sense as long as you support it well with logical arguments and think about the context of the case.

The **recommendation** is the conclusion of the case where you should provide clear recommendations based on insights from your analyses, which also act as supporting arguments. You then need to discuss a way forward.

The difference at McKinsey: In most McKinsey cases, there is no recommendation question. The case just ends after you have answered enough questions for the interviewer to collect their data or when the time has run out. This is something many candidates are surprised by when they get out of their McKinsey interviews, thinking they did not perform well. If you are asked to provide a recommendation, use the same approach as I discuss for a candidate-led interview in **Chapter 11**.

To sum it up, the interviewer guides you through a series of questions that you need to answer by coming up with structured ideas, providing insights into your thinking and reasoning, performing exhibit and quantitative analyses, synthesizing what you have learned along the way, and developing recommendations about what to do, the latter always within each question rather than at the end of the case.

The questions you receive are loosely connected and revolve around the overarching topic and context of the case. The interviewer provides clear directions and a flow of questions, which you need to answer with a hypothesis-driven mindset. However, do not be surprised if the case moves in a direction you did not anticipate, for instance, by focusing on a random area you have not prioritized or by jumping to different points in time. This is normal and does not affect your performance review as long as your analyses and arguments are sound. Interviewers have prepared the case logic, the exhibits, and the math way before you go through it. Hence, the case flow is based on their material, not your answers and hypotheses. That is also the reason why there is no single correct solution for your initial framework, your chart interpretation, and the interpretation of your quantitative outcome. On the flip side, you are constantly kept on your toes and need to pay attention to react to changes in the client situation that is presented to you.

McKinsey cases might be easier to prepare for and to go through if you understand their mechanics. The flow and types of questions are always the same (bar outliers), and you cannot get lost in the depths of your structure, walking down a wrong path of analysis, etc. One bad answer does not influence your chances with the next question and every new question represents a chance to gain back full control and confidence.

How should you prepare for a McKinsey case interview?

There are two things you need to remind yourself of when preparing for a McKinsey case interview. The format is highly standardized (in ninety-five percent of cases) and the content and client setting is usually very creative (in eighty percent of cases).

Use these two insights to guide your preparation. Do not learn frameworks by heart, expecting them to work for any McKinsey case you will encounter. Many of my clients ask if there is a specific interview for the different McKinsey practices such as implementation, operations, digital, etc., basically if there is a difference between interviews for generalist consultants and specialists. In fact, for both tracks, the case selection is a black box and randomized. You might encounter cases that cover domain-relevant problems as well as cases set in a completely different context. It is all about how you approach various problems and not about what you know about a certain area.

If you have not read it yet, I would like to point you to the section in **Chapter 8**, where I discuss the damage that memorized frameworks have done to candidates' performance over the last couple of years, especially at McKinsey. Even more so for McKinsey, it is important that you learn the right approach, habits, and conceptual strategies that help you tackle all types of cases. You need to study each individual question type and the associated skills and then learn how to approach them, regardless of the client situation, the context of the case, the industry, or function. You should learn how to build issue trees, interpret charts, and perform math no matter the case you are dealing with.

For McKinsey practice, splitting cases into their individual elements and working on them independently as drills is an even more fruitful endeavor since McKinsey cases are naturally divided into these question types anyway. When working with other candidates or coaches, specify that the case you go through and the feedback you are expecting should be based on McKinsey's format and standards.

PART 7

Real Case Examples: Work on Your First Full Cases

Let's integrate all that we have discussed so far by going through a real case interview together. For methodological details related to the different segments and elements of the case, please refer to the applicable chapters. To practice what you have learned, try working through every instruction yourself before looking at the example answer.

First, we work on a candidate-led case in **Chapter 17**, then we tackle a McKinsey interviewer-led case in **Chapter 18**. Pay attention to the differences and similarities.

Candidate-led case:
Public Sector Education

The brief

The interviewer introduces the case: *"Your client is the ministry of education of a relatively wealthy country with a population of 10 million people. It is the end of the year 2020, the first year of the COVID-19 pandemic. Due to lockdowns, schools in this country have been closed for a total of three months over the last year, which interrupted the education of students. On top of missing education, there are reports about the social and psychological issues related to the lockdowns for the student population. Also, we are expecting a negative impact on the lifetime earnings of those students. The ministry of education has now hired us to devise a plan that would enable students to receive their full education, without increasing infection rates in the country."*

Play back the brief and ask clarification questions

Play back everything in your own words and ask the correct clarification questions that are relevant in this context.

You say: *"I understand that we are working with the government of a small wealthy country with 10 million people. At the end of year 2020, students have missed three months of education due to lockdowns with significant negative effects on their education and future income. This also comes with social and psychological hardships. We are now asked to come up with a program that would allow students to receive their full education without driving up infection rates in the country. Is that correct* **(play back everything in your own words)***?"*

The interviewer confirms: *"Yes, you covered it well."*

You say: *"I would like to understand a couple of things before working on a solution. First, in the country we are looking at, can you describe the infrastructure, income levels, and the school system, plus how many* *students are we talking about? What is the COVID situation in the country? Second, what has been done so far* (**understand the situation better**)*? Third, when you say receive full education, what do you mean exactly? Do we have a specific target and a timeline to implement potential measures* (**operationalize the goal**)*?"*

The Interviewer answers: *"It is a high-income per capita country in Western Europe, infrastructure is great, everyone has access to the internet, the school system is public, meaning that more than 99% of students attend public schools. In total, there are 1.3 million students for which we are planning these measures. They are between the ages of 10 to 18. The COVID situation in the country is relatively stable.*

"Over the last year, what we have seen are a lot of individual solutions but no coherent framework or program that would yield strong results for all schools in the country. As regards the specific goal: What we want to achieve is that every student can receive the same content and information as if there were no pandemic and take the same tests and exams. For the latter, we expect the grades and performance not to negatively deviate from the results of the last couple of years. Since the school year is currently running, the sooner the measures are implemented, the better. Our client is looking at two months maximum."

Structure your approach

Now it is time to think about your structure by following the four-step approach discussed in **Chapter 8** (*What is the best step-by-step approach for structuring and brainstorming?*). Take two minutes to create your approach.

You say: *"Understood. I think I have everything I need. I would like to take some time, a minute or two, to think about my approach to this problem. We want to create a program and plan that allows students to get their education without increasing infection rates* (**clarify what you are going to do and ask for time**)*."*

The interviewer replies: *"Sure!"*

You create the following structure, adhering to the desired content creation qualities of being broad (exhaustive problem coverage), deep (three levels with concrete and granular areas to look at), and insightful, backed by hypothesis-driven thinking.

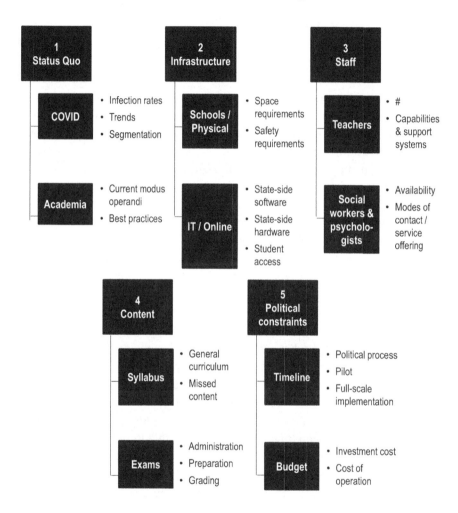

■ Example framework for the case

Next, you communicate your approach.

You say: *"In order to come up with a plan, I would like to look at five factors. First, the status quo, second, the infrastructure, third, the staff, fourth, the content, and fifth, potential political constraints* **(top-down, numbered, and signposted)**.

"Let's start with the first one, the status quo. I'd like to understand what is going on in the country to come up with sensible measures. Here, I want to look at two things. First, the COVID situation, focusing on infection rates and trends. Second, I want to understand the current academic status, figuring out potential best practices and how the content is taught **(deep dive into each branch with clear and concrete ideas and qualification/justification)**.

"Going to my second bucket, infrastructure. Here, I want to look at two things, the schools and the physical infrastructure as well as the IT/ online infrastructure to understand what we are able to offer to our 1.3 million students in terms of physical space and conduct of education as well as virtual learning opportunities.

"Third, I want to look at the staff in two categories, teachers and social workers/psychologists to understand their number, availability, and capabilities. They are the crucial liaison for the students.

"Fourth, I believe that we have to look at the lesson content in more detail. More concretely, two things: the content requirements and the exams to understand what we need to teach now and what has been missed so far, as well as figuring out effective ways to administer exams. We want to make sure that students can study and perform at their best and provide the necessary conditions for that.

"Lastly, I want to look into political constraints. Again, two things. First, the timeline to determine if we would be able to get our adjustments out within two months. Second, I want to look at budgetary constraints, more specifically the investment and the running cost **(presentation of your structure, interdependencies are implicitly clear throughout).**"

The interviewer replies: *"That sounds reasonable."*

Probe for more data

Now that you have presented your exhaustive approach, it is time to dive into your issue tree to work on a solution to answer the client's question.

You say: *"Based on my initial framework, I would actually like to look at the status quo first. More concretely, I was wondering if we have any data on the COVID situation in the country as this would influence my proposed approach whether we can keep schools open with safety measures, whether we have to close schools and come up with a distance learning plan, or if we have to go with a hybrid solution* **(the what and why of your prioritization)**. *Do you have any data on the infection rates in the country? Ideally segmented for students and other parts of the population or segmented based on any other metric* **(the how of your prioritization).**"

The interviewer replies: *"Yes, we have some data on the infection rates on these two charts."*

Interpret the exhibit

The interviewer provides you with two exhibits to look at. Interpret them in the context of the case. Follow the seven-step process as described in **Chapter 9** (*How do you interpret exhibits in case interviews with a step-by-step approach?*).

School size and infection rates

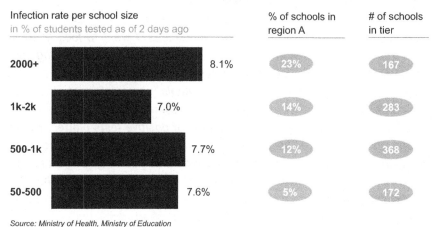

Infection rate per school size
in % of students tested as of 2 days ago

% of schools in region A

# of schools in tier

	Infection rate	% of schools in region A	# of schools in tier
2000+	8.1%	23%	167
1k-2k	7.0%	14%	283
500-1k	7.7%	12%	368
50-500	7.6%	5%	172

Source: Ministry of Health, Ministry of Education

■ Chart 1

Test positivity per region

Positive tests, in % of population tested as of 2 days ago

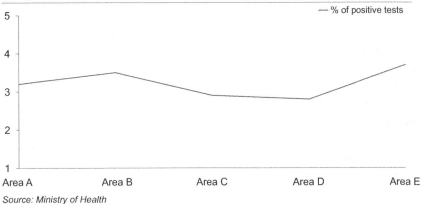

Source: Ministry of Health

■ Chart 2

You might have noticed that the exhibits are not in the best format/ shape possible and there might be some need for clarification. For instance, the way the data is visualized on the second chart is far from ideal, yet sometimes this is the type of presentation you must work with during a case interview.

You say: *"Thank you very much for the exhibits. I want to look at those with the goal of deriving implications for our proposed teaching plan* **(discuss the purpose of your analysis)**. *On the first chart, I see the infection rates for different sizes of schools, some information on the geographical distribution for region A, and some data on numbers in tier. On the second chart, I see the percentage of positive tests plotted against geographic regions of the country. The data for both charts is from two days ago, so a current snapshot* **(describe what you see)**. *Do you mind if I clarify something? On the first chart, am I correct in assuming that 23% of the schools with more than 2,000 students are in region A? Also, what is meant by schools in tier? On the second chart, does the chart cover just students or the general population* **(clarify)**?*"*

The interviewer answers: *"You are correct on the regions. Regarding the tiers, it shows you how many schools there are for a certain size category. For instance, for the first line, it shows you that there are 167* *schools with more than 2,000 students. As regards the second chart, it displays data for the general population."*

You say: *"All right, that's clear. I'd like to take a minute to write down some thoughts please (**ask for time to structure your thoughts**)."*

Take a minute to jot down your insights, implications, and next steps.

You say: *"I see two important things on these two charts: First, larger schools seem to have higher infection rates compared to smaller schools, yet the difference is minuscule. Second, and probably more important, infection rates in schools are significantly higher than in the general population (**discuss the insights**). Based on that, I'd actually argue for closing schools and creating a distance-learning program to achieve both goals of our client, providing students with access to their education without driving up infection rates (**talk about the implication**). Since my hunch is now to favor online learning, I would like to investigate a few things next to see if that would be feasible. Going back to my framework, if we want to create an online learning program, I think two elements are important to look into. The infrastructure and the teachers since they are needed and responsible for content delivery and exam administration (**discuss next steps**)."*

The interviewer replies: *"Okay, what do you need?"*

Since your analysis is going well and you are gravitating toward the answer to the client's question, the interviewer takes a backseat as they don't need to provide hints.

Probe further

Follow the areas of interest that you have identified when contextualizing the insights from the exhibit.

You say: *"Do we have any data on the infrastructure? (**what**). I want to understand if it would be possible to teach students at home via a distance-learning program (**why**). More specifically, I would like to know what infrastructure is in place from the school system's side and if all students in the country have access to digital media? (**how**)"*

The interviewer replies: *"Actually, the government has a framework in place that would need some development to be fully ready for 100% distance learning. However, it would be possible. A recent publication by the OECD shows that students should expect a three percent drop in their lifetime earnings due to lockdowns and missing their education. Our modelling now shows that by providing access to virtual lessons, students should only expect a one percent drop in their lifetime earnings since most of the lessons can be streamed and even missed content could potentially be made up for. The investment needed to make the platform workable would be around EUR 5,000 per student."*

You say: *"Interesting, it almost sounds like we have a solution at hand to reduce the impact on students. To evaluate the merit of this solution, I think we should investigate it further. I'd like to know a couple more things. Would this be for the 1.3 million students in the country? What were the expected lifetime earnings pre-pandemic? Am I correct in assuming that we are looking at the social benefit only, essentially, being in favor of this measure if the benefit for the students outweighs the investment cost for the state?"*

The interviewer replies: *"Yes, that would be for the 1.3 million students who each had average expected lifetime earnings of EUR 2.7 million before the pandemic started. You are correct, we care about the social benefit of these measures."*

Synthesize

Now it is time to synthesize what you have figured out so far.

You say: *"Okay, let me just quickly recap. We know three things now. First, it seems that schools are drivers of infections in this country, which points us to the fact that we need to work on a program that takes schools out of the equation, such as a virtual learning environment. Second, I understand that there is a framework for distance learning ready that would need some adaptation and investment to be fully rolled out. From a technical perspective, it seems feasible. Third, with this program, we would be able to teach all content and even make up for most of the missed classes in the past, which would also positively impact the income of students in the future. That sounds promising* **(recap of the status quo and implication)**. *Looking back at the case goal, I want to* *clarify if this could be implemented within two months and if teachers have the needed capabilities to work with such a system* **(the next steps/ probing)**.*"*

The interviewer replies: *"Yes, that's all correct. The investment I discussed would also include training for teachers to adjust and teach their content in a virtual setup."*

Now you need to move the case forward.

You say: *"Okay, I think I have a plan of action. I'd like to investigate the social impact of the virtual learning program. In short, I want to calculate the impact and the cost, then compare the two."*

Perform calculations

You want to support your plan with data that you can derive from a quantitative reasoning problem. Follow the steps I discuss in **Chapter 10** (*How should you approach case math questions with a tested step-by-step approach?*) on case math.

You say: *"I want to make clear what my plan is and play back some numbers to you. I'm going to evaluate the social benefit of the measures, and if the benefit is higher than the cost for the state, I would recommend the measures. To do that, you have already given me some data. We have 1.3 million students with an average pre-pandemic expected lifetime income of EUR 2.7 million each. Without any measures, there would be a three percent loss in lifetime earnings, with our virtual learning program, the loss would only be one percent. The investment would be EUR 5,000 per student. Let me just quickly think how I want to approach this. Please give me a minute, and I'll get back to you* **(clarify the objective and purpose, play back the numbers, ask for time)**.*"*

The interviewer replies: *"Sure."*

You say: *"All right, I think this is pretty straightforward. I want to approach this in three steps and calculate it on a per-student basis. At the end of the day, if the social benefit for one student outweighs the cost, it will do so for all, since the numbers scale linearly. So, to answer the question it is not necessary to calculate for all 1.3 million students. First, I want* *to look at the cost, which is EUR 5,000 per student. Second, I want to look at the benefit of the program, which is two percent of a student's lifetime earnings, essentially the proportion that they would not lose in a virtual setup. In absolute terms, I get the benefit by multiplying the EUR 2.7 million times two percent. Third, I want to compare the benefit with the cost and make my recommendation* **(introduce your approach)**.*"*

The interviewer replies: *"Sounds about right."*

You say: *"Perfect, please let me go ahead and perform those calculations then."*

There are two ways you can proceed now. Either you talk the interviewer through every step while you are doing it, or you perform the calculations on your own and provide a brief update along the way.

You say: *"Okay, for the first step, we know the cost is EUR 5,000. The second step is to calculate the benefit per student: one percent of 2.7 million is 27,000, so two percent is 54,000. Hence, every student would get back more than EUR 50,000 of their lifetime earnings. Third, if we compare the two, the benefit far outweighs the cost by more than a factor of 10. That sounds like a lot. Let me just quickly go over my approach and calculations to make sure I didn't miss anything...No, it's all correct* **(calculate and sanity check!)**"*

While this math seems easy, many candidates struggle with it. The most common issues I have seen in this case related to the math portion:

- ☑ Candidates do not know how to work with the cost and the benefit to define an outcome that would guide their decision.
- ☑ Candidates are not sure how to deal with the three percent and one percent. Most calculate the impact of three percent and the impact of one percent, then subtract one from the other, making the calculation unnecessarily longer.
- ☑ Some candidates even take 97% and 99% of the lifetime earnings, further complicating matters.
- ☑ More than 50% of candidates calculate the outcome for all 1.3 million students in the country. While technically not

wrong, the calculations become significantly longer and more complex, leading to more errors and issues along the way. What you need to find out is if the benefit is higher than the cost, not the total cost or benefit of the program. Pay attention to those details.

Finally, you must answer the question that you created for yourself, interpret it in the context of the case, and plan your next moves.

You say: *"Actually, I forgot one thing. What about the cost of running this virtual learning environment? We need to consider this as well."*

The interviewer replies: *"There's no additional cost to consider."*

You say: *"All right then. I'd definitely recommend the government implement this virtual learning solution since the benefit is more than 10x of the cost* **(answer the question)**. *Additionally, we would achieve what we set out to do. First, students would be able to receive their education. Second, with everyone studying from home, schools would no longer be drivers of infections in the country. The benefits are so high that even from a state perspective, due to increased tax income in the future, this investment appears to be sound* **(discuss and interpret the result/relate it back to the case)**.

"Now going forward, I would like to look at a couple more things: the exam administration, the availability of devices to access the classes from home for everyone, specifically for students in lower income households, and lastly the timeline, the political process, and the implementation **(provide next steps)**.*"*

The interview replies: *"The exams will also be administered through this new system and the investment cost we discussed also includes access and devices for every student in the country, if needed. As for the rest, I think you definitely identified a workable solution.*

We're having a quick chat with the minister of education. He wants to know what we've come up with so far. Would you mind giving him a brief update?"

Discuss your recommendation

Take 30 seconds to structure your answer.

You say: *"Sure! I recommend that we build a distance learning program for all students in the country for two reasons* **(provide a top-down recommendation)***. First, we have seen that schools are drivers of infections in the country. By going virtual, we eliminate this fact completely. Second, by offering a distance-learning program, we would also enable students to receive their full education, which in turn would yield significant benefits to their lifetime income that far outweigh the investment cost for the state* **(provide supporting arguments aligned with the client's goals)***.*

"Going forward, a few areas of investigation remain. First, we need to accompany the plan of action through the political process and decision-making to get the necessary approvals and budget. Second, we need to think about the implementation and timelines, as aiming to go live within two months from now could present a significant challenge. Third, one factor we have not looked at yet is the mental and social aspect of the situation. Going forward, we need to think about proper ways to address these issues as well **(discuss next steps, interdependencies are implicitly clear)***."*

The interviewer replies: *"Thank you very much!"*

The interview ends here on a strong note. A couple of thoughts:

- ☑ This is just one example out of thousands of potential cases you might face.
- ☑ Focus on the habits and the case flow, not the actual solutions and content ideas when you study the case.
- ☑ The initial framework is one of many equally powerful approaches to the question and is by no means fully exhaustive or perfect, yet more than enough for the purpose of a case interview and a distinctive evaluation by the interviewer. Keep in mind that you have only two minutes to think about it. The most important part of the framework revolves around understanding the situation. Many candidates make the mistake of thinking about solutions (the how) before understanding the situation (the what and why). You should only discuss in-person learning or virtual learning and what

it entails/what is needed once you understand the COVID situation in the country and the role that schools play.

☑ The framework is less exhaustively communicated compared to the interviewer-led McKinsey case (follows next) where you have more time to discuss your lower-level ideas.

☑ The case flows very smoothly. In reality, not every case you go through might go as smoothly or flawlessly. That is okay too, as long as you stick to the habits I describe in the earlier chapters. You can still get a distinctive evaluation if you need to probe and drill a bit more until you get on the right track. However, focusing your investigative mind on what drives a situation usually will lead you down the right path of analysis quickly.

☑ As you can see, not every idea from your initial framework might be relevant. At the end of the day, you do not have time to go through each in detail. Interviewers usually answer questions to unrelated/unimportant items swiftly (e.g., *"We don't have any data on that." "That's not relevant for now." "This has already been considered and would work."*).

☑ Make sure to consider interdependencies throughout implicitly or explicitly (e.g., two conflicting goals of the client, factors in your structure, implementation measures).

[18] Interviewer-led (McKinsey) case: Public Sector Education

Now let's integrate all that we have discussed so far in the context of a McKinsey-like case. For methodological details related to the different segments and elements of the case, please refer to the applicable chapters.

The brief

The interviewer kicks off the case interview.

The interviewer introduces the case: *"Your client is the ministry of education of a relatively wealthy country with a population of 10 million people. It's the end of the year 2020, the first year of the COVID-19 pandemic. Due to lockdowns, schools in this country have been closed for a total of three months over the last year, which interrupted the education of students. As well as missing education, there are reports about the social and psychological issues related to the lockdowns for the student population. Also, we are expecting a negative impact on the lifetime earnings of those students. The ministry of education has now hired us to devise a plan that would enable students to receive their full education, without increasing infection rates in the country."*

Play back the brief and ask clarification questions

Play back everything in your own words and ask the correct clarification questions that are relevant in this context.

You say: *"I understand that we are working with the government of a small wealthy country with 10 million people. At the end of year 2020, students have missed three months of education due to lockdowns with significant negative effects on their education and future income. In addition, this comes with social and psychological hardships. We are now asked to come up with a program that would allow students to receive"* *their full education without driving up infection rates in the country. Is that correct* **(play back everything in your own words)***?"*

The interviewer confirms: *"Yes, you covered it well."*

You say: *"I'd like to understand a couple of things before working on a solution. First, in the country we are looking at, can you describe the infrastructure, income levels, and the school system? Plus, how many students are we talking about? What is the COVID situation in the country? Second, what has been done so far* **(understand the situation better)***? Third, when you say receive full education, what do you mean exactly? Do we have a specific target and a timeline to implement potential measures* **(operationalize the goal)***?"*

The Interviewer answers: *"It is a high-income per capita country in Western Europe. Infrastructure is great, everyone has access to the internet, the school system is public, meaning that more than 99% of students attend public schools. In total, there are 1.3 million students for which we are planning these measures. They are between the ages of 10 to 18. The COVID situation in the country is relatively stable.*

"Over the last year, what we have seen are a lot of individual solutions but no coherent framework or program that would yield strong results for all schools in the country. As regards the specific goal: What we want to achieve is that every student can receive the same content and information as if there were no pandemic and take the same tests and exams. For the latter, we expect the grades and performance not to negatively deviate from the results of the last couple of years. Since the school year is currently running, the sooner the measures are implemented, the better. Our client is looking at two months maximum."

Structure your approach

The interviewer takes over and asks you the first question: *"Now that all questions are out of the way, I'd like to ask you what factors you would like to look at when designing a program that enables students to receive their education while at the same time not driving up infection rates?"*

Now it is time to think about your structure by following the four-step approach discussed in **Chapter 8** (*What is the best step-by-step approach for structuring and brainstorming?*). Take two minutes to create your approach.

You say: *"Just to make sure: You want me to come up with factors that I'd look at to create an education program while also considering infection rates? I'd like to take some time, a minute or two, to think about my approach to this problem* **(clarify what you are going to do and ask for time)***."*

Interviewer replies: "Sure!"

You create the following structure, adhering to the desired content creation qualities of being broad (exhaustive problem coverage), deep (three levels with concrete and granular areas to look at), and insightful, backed by hypothesis-driven thinking.

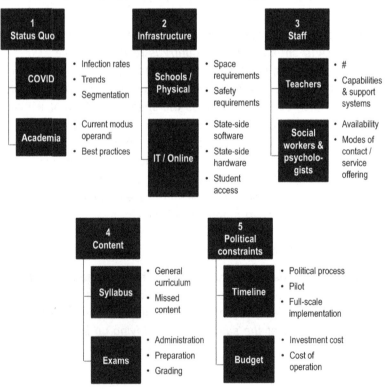

■ Example framework for the case

Now communicate your structure.

You say: *"In order to come up with a plan, I'd like to look at five factors. First, the status quo, second, the infrastructure, third, the staff, fourth, the content, and fifth, potential political constraints* **(top-down, numbered, and signposted)**.

"Let's start with the first one, the status quo. I want to understand what is going on in the country to come up with sensible measures. Here, I want to look at two things. First, the COVID situation in the country. I want to know a. what the infection rates are, b. if there are any positive or negative trends, and c. how the infection rates compare across the general population and the student body. Second, I want to understand the current academic status. I want to a. learn how schools are operating today, and b. identify potential best practices among schools and teachers. You said there were a lot of individual solutions, maybe there are some gems that we can use as inspiration **(deep dive into each branch with clear and concrete ideas and qualification/justification)**.

"Going to my second bucket, infrastructure. Here, I want to look at two things, the schools and IT/online infrastructure. First, with the schools we have to look at: a. the required space for our 1.3 million students; do we have enough schools, classrooms, etc. to safely teach? b. the potential safety requirements within that space. Do we have enough room dividers, air conditioning units, masks, hand sanitizers? How much would we need, etc.? Second, if we were to decide to close schools, we would need to look at alternative teaching methods, for instance, distance learning. To see if we would be able to do this, I'd be interested in the online infrastructure of the country, more concretely, two things: a. What does the infrastructure look like from the state side, e.g., does the ministry of education have access to online learning programs and modules (the required software); and do they have the required hardware infrastructure (the servers) to run an online learning program for that many students? and b. What does the infrastructure access look like for the student body? Does everyone have access to the internet and does everyone have the necessary IT access points at home such as computers and laptops?

"Third, I want to look at the staff in two categories, teachers and social workers/psychologists. First, the main stakeholders in the process are teachers. I want to understand if we: a. have enough teachers, and if b. the teachers have the needed capabilities and knowledge to teach content offline and online under the required circumstances or if we

potentially need specific training and support systems here as well. Second, since you mentioned there are also rising cases of social and psychological issues, I want to look at social workers and psychologists and how we can best utilize them to help students. Here, I want to look at: a. the availability of such staff, and b. the potential modes of contact/ service offering for affected students.

"Fourth, I believe that we have to look at the lesson content in more detail. More concretely, two things: the content requirements as well as the exams. First, regarding the content I am interested in a. what needs to be taught going forward, and b. what has been missed over the three months already, so we can make sure to adjust the content through whatever means of teaching we are going to use on top of making up for what has been missed. Second, I am interested in exams that students need to take, more specifically: a. how they can be administered, b. how students can best be prepared under these conditions, and c. the grading aspect. We want to make sure that students can study and perform at their best and provide the necessary conditions for that.

"Lastly, I want to look into political constraints. First, at the timeline. I know we need to have the measures implemented within two months ideally. I want to look at: a. the political process, b. a potential smaller scale pilot, then c. a full-scale implementation. Second, I want to look at budgetary constraints, more specifically: a. how much investment is needed, and b. how high the running cost would be **(presentation of your structure, interdependencies are implicitly clear throughout)**.

"Based on my initial framework, I would actually like to look at the status quo first, more concretely, I was wondering if we have any data on the COVID situation in the country as this would influence my proposed approach whether we can keep schools open with safety measures, whether we have to close schools and come up with a distance-learning plan, or if we have to go with a hybrid solution **(the what and why of your prioritization)**. *I would propose two next steps. First, I want to look at the infection rates in the country and in schools to understand the magnitude of the problem we are dealing with here. Second, I think we should also look at the current school situations to understand what is currently being done and potentially identify some next steps* **(the how of your prioritization)**. *"*

The interviewer replies: *"Sounds great."*

Interpret the exhibit

The interviewer provides you with two exhibits to look at. Interpret them in the context of the case. Follow the seven-step process described in **Chapter 9** (*How do you interpret exhibits in case interviews with a step-by-step approach?*).

The interviewer says: *"Now, we actually have some data I want you to look at. Based on the data provided, what would be potential implications for the minister of education?"*

School size and infection rates

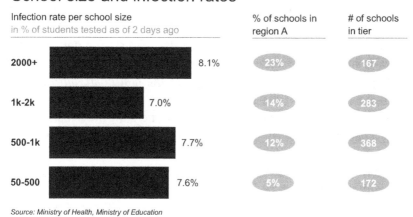

Source: Ministry of Health, Ministry of Education

■ Chart 1

Test positivity per region

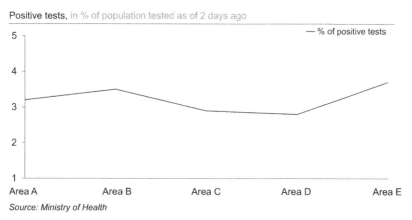

Source: Ministry of Health

■ Chart 2

You might have noticed that the exhibits are not in the best format/ shape possible and there might be some need for clarification. For instance, the way the data is visualized on the second chart is far from ideal, yet sometimes this is the type of presentation you must work with during a case interview.

You say: *"Thank you very much for the exhibits. I want to look at those with the goal of deriving implications for the minister of education* **(play back the question)**. *Let me just quickly recap what I see here. On the first chart, I see the infection rates for different sizes of schools, some information on the geographical distribution for region A, and some data on numbers in tier. On the second chart, I see the percentage of positive tests plotted against geographic regions of the country. The data for both charts is from two days ago, so a current snapshot* **(describe what you see)**. *Do you mind if I clarify something? On the first chart, am I correct in assuming that 23% of the schools with more than 2,000 students are in region A? Also, what is meant by schools in tier? On the second chart, does the chart cover just students or the general population* **(clarify)**?*"

The interviewer answers: *"You are correct on the regions. Regarding the tiers, it shows you how many schools there are for a certain size category. For instance, for the first line, it shows you that there are 167 schools with more than 2,000 students. As regards the second chart, it displays data for the general population."*

You say: *"All right, that's clear. I'd like to take a minute to draw up some thoughts please* **(ask for time to structure your thoughts)**.*"*

Take a minute to write down your insights, implications, and next steps.

You say: *"I see two important things on these two charts: First, larger schools seem to have higher infection rates compared to smaller schools, yet the difference is minuscule. Second, and probably more important, infection rates in schools are significantly higher than in the general population* **(discuss the insights)**. *Based on that I would actually argue for closing schools and creating a distance-learning program to achieve both goals of our client, provide students with access to their education without driving up infection rates* **(talk about the implication)**. *Since my hunch is now to favor online learning, I'd like to investigate a few things* *next, going back to my initial framework. If we want to create an online learning program, I think two things are important to look into. First, I want to look at the IT infrastructure in place to see how the content could be delivered, what we would need to build and what is already there. Second, I want to look at the teachers as they are responsible for the content delivery, more accurately, I want to look into the demand and supply of teachers as well as their capabilities* **(next steps).**"

The interviewer replies: *"Sounds reasonable."*

Perform calculations

Follow the steps I discuss in **Chapter 10** (*How should you approach case math questions with a tested step-by-step approach?*) on case math.

The interviewer says: *"We have some additional data I want to share with you on that. The government has a virtual learning framework in place that would need some development to be fully ready for 100% distance learning. However, it would be possible. A recent publication by the OECD shows that students should expect a three percent drop in their lifetime earnings due to lockdowns and missing their education. Our modelling now shows that by providing access to virtual lessons, students should only expect a one percent drop in their lifetime earnings since most of the lessons can be streamed and even missed content could potentially be made up for. The investment needed to make the platform workable would be around EUR 5,000 per student. Would you recommend this investment and solution?"*

You say: *"Interesting, it almost sounds like we have a solution at hand. Let me play that back quickly: We would be able to develop and roll out a distance learning program within two months. The cost would be EUR 5,000 per student. The benefit would be that instead of losing three percent of their lifetime earnings, students would only lose one percent. Is that correct? I'd recommend that investment if the social benefit is bigger than the cost for the state or the taxpayer in that case* **(play back the numbers and clarify the objective).**

The interviewer replies: *"Yes, that's correct!"*

You say: *"I'd like to take a minute to think about it, is that okay* (**ask for time**)*?"*

The interviewer replies: *"Sure!"*

You say: *"I think I have an approach, but before I share it, I'd like to know a couple more things. Are we still talking about the 1.3 million students? What were the expected lifetime earnings pre-pandemic per student* (**ask for more data if needed**)*?"*

The interviewer replies: *"Yes, 1.3 million students, who each had average expected lifetime earnings of EUR 2.7 million before the pandemic started."*

You say: *"All right, I think this is pretty straightforward. I want to approach this in three steps and also just calculate it on a per-student basis. At the end of the day, if the social benefit for one student outweighs the cost, it will do so for all, since the numbers scale linearly. So, to answer the question it's not necessary to calculate for all 1.3 million students. First, I want to look at the cost, which is EUR 5,000 per student. Second, I want to look at the benefit of the program, which is two percent of a student's lifetime earnings, essentially the proportion that they would not lose in a virtual setup. In absolute terms, I get the benefit by multiplying EUR 2.7 million times two percent. Third, I want to compare the benefit with the cost and make my recommendation* (**introduce your approach**)*."*

The interviewer replies: *"Sounds about right."*

You say: *"Perfect, please let me go ahead and perform those calculations then."*

There are two ways you can proceed now. Either you talk the interviewer through every step while you are doing it, or you perform the calculations on your own and provide a brief update along the way.

You say: *"Okay, for the first step, we know the cost is EUR 5,000. The second step is to calculate the benefit per student: one percent of 2.7 million is 27,000, so two percent is 54,000. Hence, every student would get back more than EUR 50,000 of their lifetime earnings. Third, if we* *compare the two, the benefit far outweighs the cost by more than a factor of 10. That sounds like a lot. Let me just quickly go over my approach and calculations to make sure I didn't miss anything...No, it's all correct* **(calculate and sanity check!).**"

While this math seems easy, many candidates struggle with it. For the most common issues I have seen in this case related to the math portion see **Chapter 17** (in the *Perform Calculations* part of the Candidate-led case example, as the same issues apply here).

Finally, you must answer the question of the interview, interpret the result in the context of the case, and plan your next moves.

You say: *"Actually, I forgot one thing. What about the cost of running this virtual learning environment? We need to consider this as well."*

The interviewer replies: *"There is no additional cost to consider."*

You say: *"All right then. I'd definitely recommend the government implement this virtual learning solution since the benefit is more than 10x the cost* **(answer the question)**. *Additionally, we would achieve what we set out to achieve. First, students would be able to receive their education. Second, with everyone studying from home, schools will no longer be drivers of infections in the country. The benefits are so high that even from a benefit perspective for the state, due to increased tax income in the future, this investment appears to be very sound* **(discuss and interpret the result/relate it back to the case)**. *Now going forward, I'd like to look at a few more things: the exam administration, potential running cost, the availability of devices to access the classes from home for everyone, specifically for students in lower income households, and lastly the timeline, the political process, and the implementation* **(provide next steps)**."

The interview replies: *"Thank you very much!"*

OPTIONAL: Discuss your recommendation

Ninety-nine percent of the time, McKinsey case interviews do not come with a recommendation section. They just end midway, sometimes even randomly once the interviewer has collected enough data points about your performance or if the time runs out. For the one percent chance, see *Discuss your recommendation* in **Chapter 17,** which applies here as well.

The interview ends on a strong note. A couple of thoughts:

- ☑ This is just one example out of thousands of potential cases you might face.
- ☑ Focus on the habits and the case flow, not the actual solutions and content ideas when you study the case.
- ☑ The initial framework is one of many equally powerful approaches to the question and is by no means fully exhaustive or perfect, yet more than enough for the purpose of a case interview and a distinctive evaluation by the interviewer. Keep in mind that you have only two minutes to think about it.
- ☑ The framework is more exhaustively communicated compared to the candidate-led case where you do not have much time to discuss your lower-level ideas but rather focus on the top level, then only dive deeper into areas you want to prioritize.
- ☑ Your answers, especially the next steps, match the interviewer's direction and the direction of the case. But in a McKinsey interview, this does not necessarily have to be the case. In fact, you could come up with completely different answers, implications, and next steps. As long as what you are saying is thoughtful, covers the issues well, is hypothesis-driven, and well-communicated, you are fine. In reality, the interviewer might want to prioritize a different area. Sometimes, there might even be time leaps incorporated into a McKinsey case, where you are still working in the same context, yet the next question takes place three months into the future of the previous question. For McKinsey interviewers, it is mostly about the quality of your answer and arguments, not if you are wrong or right or discuss a singular solution to a case.
- ☑ Instead of recapping and synthesizing in between elements of the case, every answer contains mini-syntheses and contextualization.
- ☑ Make sure to consider interdependencies throughout implicitly or explicitly (e.g., two conflicting goals of the client, factors in your structure, implementation).

PART 8

Killer Preparation Strategies: Maximize the Impact of Your Efforts

[19] Employ the most effective preparation strategies

It's time for you to put what you have learned to the test, internalize and master it. I have already laid out a plan in **Chapter 4** about how to split your preparation time. In this part, I want to take a few of the concepts and explore them in more depth. I answer the following questions:

- ☑ Should you learn case interview frameworks by heart?
- ☑ How should you prepare for case interviews alone?
- ☑ How should you prepare with peers?
- ☑ Should you work with a coach and, if yes, how can you get the best out of your coaching relationship?
- ☑ What business concepts and lingo do you need to know?

Why should you stay away from memorizing case interview frameworks?

Most candidates prepare for consulting cases by focusing on memorizing generic frameworks. Alternatively, they are looking for common case interview questions and answers with the hope that the cases are the same within and across firms, interviewers, and interviews. I want to highlight this one last time: There is no such thing as a shortcut or a consulting case interview cheat sheet and everyone who wants to sell you one is a scammer. It is all about the process of problem-solving, which should be the focus of your preparation. **Do not learn case-specific interview frameworks by heart**, expecting them to work for every case you might encounter.

There is no specific McKinsey, Bain, and BCG or other firm case study framework or framework book. It is much more important to learn the right approach and methodology that help you tackle all different types of cases. This is even more relevant for MBB interviews compared to tier-2 consultancies and boutique firms.

How can you practice alone?

Peer practice and mock interviews can be inefficient and ineffective for two reasons. It is difficult to find enough strong interview partners to practice. Also, a full case interview mock session takes 90 to 120 minutes, including a feedback discussion, which has you work only on one case and a couple of issues within the case. There are shortcuts and more effective ways to prepare. In other words, how can you get more exposure to cases and case questions in less time?

Work through cases and drills on your own. It complements your interactive case practice with others while saving time and improving your effectiveness in solving problems. When practicing alone, employ the same habits and communication as you would in a live session as the communication is as important as the content itself.

In general, I recommend my clients invest 80 to 90% of their time in honing their skills on their own, only using the remainder to practice with high-quality case partners. Let's look at one example to illustrate why that makes sense: If you practice with someone else, you might manage to work through two structure/idea generation problems within two hours because you go through a case including the feedback, then act as an interviewer for the other person. If you practice on your own, you can easily go through 15 structure/idea generation problems within the same time frame. Candidates who make individual preparation the focus of their training solve significantly more problems than candidates who solely go through peer case practice. Since mastery of every element of a case interview depends on internalization, practice, repetition, and exposure to new situations, the more problems you solve, the better you become (providing you are working on high-quality problems). Keep that in mind when dividing your time between working on your own and practicing with others. There are several ways you can practice for case interviews on your own.

Learn everything about case interviews

At this point in the book, you have already familiarized yourself with how case interviews work, what skills are needed, and how to score high on the interviewers' scorecards. You have made the first step toward case mastery. This is important before diving into the actual practice.

Read through cases

Get a hold of some case interview collections from your university's consulting club or online case libraries. For free resources, have a look at **Chapter 37**. Then, read through the cases presented to get an initial perspective on the mechanics of different example cases. Look at the natural case flow, the similarities and differences across cases, and how the habits I discuss can help you crack them. Additionally, as you go through cases you learn more about different industries and solutions to common case prompts. The more cases you read, the more you build your repertoire of ideas, approaches, insights, hypotheses, etc., and the easier it will be for you to recall some of it during a live case interview in the future. I recommend reading through cases every now and then during your preparation to get exposure to a variety of cases as well as to effectively use times when you don't have the energy or focus to actively work through cases. The process of reading through cases is a good complement to your problem-solving skill development.

Turn cases into drills

Do not always go through full cases on your own. It is much more effective to focus on building the right skills for each element of the case first, before bringing it all together. Focus on developing your individual skills for structuring, charts, and math as this quickly improves three things:

1. You internalize the steps to approach each element of the case, creating a series of automated habits, allowing your mind to solely focus on content creation and problem-solving.
2. You train your mental muscles and your resourcefulness to come up with insightful content and answers for different issues. For instance, the more cases you structure, the faster you become and the broader and deeper your structures will be. The more quantitative problems you work on, the easier it will be for you to structure such questions and perform calculations in the future, etc.
3. You become an effective consulting communicator by internalizing the right phrases for each part of the case, making you appear more in control and lifting the mental burden of thinking how to communicate.

For instance, if you have two hours to practice and want to use this time to work on your issue trees: Sit down, open a book or a compendium of sample cases, and only focus on the structuring question of each case. Read the first question of a case out loud, ask for two minutes to think about an answer, write down your structure, then communicate, also discussing where you would like to go next or what you would like to analyze at the end of your answer (in the same way as you would do in a live interview).

Whenever you work alone, do it out loud to practice not only the thinking aspect but also the full flow through the different case elements and the communication of your insights. If you are struggling with communication, now is a good time to record yourself and then listen to those recordings, spotting issues related to top-down communication, clarity of thought, repetitive points, rambling, filler words, filler phrases, as well as the speed of your presentation.

For structuring parts of the case, practicing the communication even on your own is especially relevant since large chunks of your answer might only come together when you lead the interviewer through it. I have noticed from my clients that around 70% of the structure is on the paper once they start guiding me through it. They make up the remaining 30% on the go as they continue to think about their answer while they speak. This makes sense since one to two minutes is not a lot of time to deconstruct a problem and talking about something automatically yields new ideas. Hence, when working on structuring drills, include the communication aspect since it also covers part of your content creation.

Once done, move to the next case and create your next framework. Within two hours, you can go through 10 to 20 structure drills. Repeat the same process for the other two main case elements, exhibits and math, and you will quickly improve in all crucial areas. Spend more time on case elements you are struggling with. Along with sample cases – see the relevant resources in **Chapter 37** that cover structuring, chart, and math drills. Below are three other sources you can leverage to work on different case elements:

Convert articles into case prompts

Open a magazine or newspaper, find a headline and turn it into a case prompt. For instance, at the time of writing there is an article in *The Economist* with the headline *"Britain's energy strategy is both timid and unrealistic."* Turn this into a case brief: *"What factors would you look at when defining a new energy strategy for Britain?"* This allows you to practice crucial skills such as problem structuring, creative thinking, and communication. Using the headline as a case prompt, think about clarification questions, then draft your initial structure on how you would approach the analysis, going broad and deep, displaying maximum creativity and hypothesis-driven thinking, then communicate out loud in the same way as you would do with an interviewer.

Practice reading and presenting exhibits

Similar to the above suggestion, use *The Economist, The Wall Street Journal*, or any other suitable medium to scout for exhibits. Analyze them and present your findings top-down, including the implications for the context at hand. What have you learned from the chart, and what does it mean in the context of the article? Google *"Chart of the day"* for an unlimited amount of practice exhibits on top of working through the exhibits you find in university casebooks or on other online resources.

Practice simple math

In articles, look for numbers and create your own math problems. For instance, if the article above states that it will cost GBP 40 billion over the next five years to build new power plants in the UK (hypothetical), think about how much each taxpayer would have to contribute per year to finance this. The opportunities to come up with math problems on your own are endless. Lead the imaginary interviewer through the calculations as you would do in a real interview. Work on such calculations on top of using casebooks, apps, consulting math practice courses, and other resources to develop your abilities to come up with equations as well as to perform pen-and-paper calculations.

Go through full cases

Once you have internalized how to ace the individual case elements, it is time to bring it all together and go through full cases on your own, leveraging several resources.

Use case libraries and case books

Go through cases in an interactive manner, including probing out loud, then reading the sample answer for comparison. With new information, continue to move through the case, step-by-step. It is a bit of a tedious process since you will rarely get it right the first time. Every case is different, and the sample solution could be buried in all different kinds of branches of the issue tree.

Prioritizing a *wrong* (as in *different than the proposed case solution*) branch for your analysis does not automatically mean that your problem-solving was bad if you had the right arguments for it. It merely means that the authors of the case placed the solution in a different part of the issue tree. You can evaluate your problem-solving by looking if you have covered the situation exhaustively, including the area the case authors placed the issue in. Exhibit interpretation and math are more straightforward. Move through the case by combining your analysis, probing, and reading the sample answers for each step until you arrive at a recommendation.

Leverage interactive cases from firm websites

Consulting firms such as McKinsey, BCG, Oliver Wyman, and others offer interactive cases on their career websites that mirror all elements of a real case interview. Go through them, practice every step like you would in a real interview, for instance, communicating your structured thoughts. Most of these virtual cases provide you with a multiple-choice answer format to test your skills and lead you through the process in a more linear manner.

Whenever you practice on your own, talk out loud and record yourself. Listen to it to spot minor (e.g., filler words) and major issues (e.g., lack of top-down communication, missing insights) in your presentation.

Take an interviewer's hat

A worthwhile exercise to improve your skills is to change gears and put yourself in the role of an interviewer. When reading through business newspapers and magazines, think about the article headlines from an interviewer's perspective. Think about what questions the case interviewer could ask and draft a list related to that topic, focusing on structuring, brainstorming, chart interpretation, and math problems. This helps you develop an intuition about what directions case interviews can go and what typical case problems could be.

How can you practice with peers?

While practicing alone can help you become much better quickly, your preparation schedule should incorporate regular mock interview sessions with other candidates as this is the best way to simulate live interview conditions. Live practice is an important aspect of your preparation if used wisely, taking a couple of things into account. When working with other candidates, there are three principles you should adhere to:

Work with high-quality case partners only. Not everyone might take consulting applications and interviews as seriously as you do. In fact, one of the most common complaints I get from my clients before I introduce them to my coaching network is the lack of quality case partners. If you randomly find and meet with people on platforms such as PrepLounge, chances are high that the people you practice with

- ☑ are not very skilled in solving cases themselves
- ☑ have little knowledge about how to conduct an interview from the interviewer's perspective
- ☑ cannot provide proper feedback about your performance, including insightful observations and actionable improvement advice
- ☑ are not reliable and do not show up for meetings.

Your aim should be to get a network of five to 10 strong case solvers and interviewers. That is the sweet spot. Practicing with the same one or two people all the time bears the risks that you become too comfortable, do not get different perspectives on your casing skills, or might internalize the wrong habits that are not corrected. On the other hand, practicing with too many people makes it harder to track your progress and increases the chance of receiving lower quality interviews and feedback. Within your network, find new case partners via referrals. If you are practicing with a strong case partner and they recommend someone, connect with them as well. I would advise against practicing too often with close friends as the familiarity and friendship impacts your experience.

Do not waste your time with bad case partners. If a case partner does not show up, is always late, or you can see that they do not know how to conduct an interview, do yourself a favor and politely cancel the session. At best, there is no value in bad case partners and only a loss of time, at worst, the session negatively impacts your performance and skills due to badly conducted interviews and wrong feedback.

Work with high-quality cases. If you work with bad quality cases, chances are that you are more confused at the end of a session rather than getting the feeling of making progress and having learned something. Here are a couple of pointers to identify good cases:

- ☑ contains all elements of a case interview (brief, structure, exhibits, math, recommendation)
- ☑ contains enough information about the issue and the goal in the brief
- ☑ provides the interviewer with additional information to be prepared for questions of the interviewee
- ☑ contains explanations on the different elements of the case (e.g., a sample structure, a clear math approach)
- ☑ follows a logical sequence to get from the initial issue tree to an answer
- ☑ challenging but can be solved with some effort and problem-solving prowess within 20 to 30 minutes
- ☑ does not follow cookie-cutter frameworks
- ☑ displays exhibits that are up-to-par with top-tier consulting firm standards (compare charts from consulting firm websites with charts practice cases and stay away from 1990s-style PowerPoint design cases)
- ☑ covers relevant topics for our times
- ☑ states if it is interviewer-led or candidate-led (which is going to be most cases).

These are just a couple of ideas that help you spot good case material. Refer to **Chapter 37** to find free and paid case resources and drills.

Learn how to conduct interviews yourself. If your aim is to practice with high-quality case partners, you need to make sure that you become a high-quality case interviewer to assure mutual benefits for both parties. Becoming a good case interviewer also helps you understand your own case interview performance better and, in turn, makes you a better case interviewee.

Before going into a mock case interview as an interviewer, set aside 20 to 40 minutes and read through the case properly. Ideally, you fully work through the case yourself before you employ it as an interviewer. Take notes about the initial structure, the logical follow-up probing questions and make sure you understand all exhibits and math problems. Think about different approaches to the math as well as potential calculation shortcuts. Reflect on the logical flow through the different elements and the recommendations at the end. Familiarize yourself with the additional information that can be provided to the candidate should they ask for it.

Before the case starts, clarify the learning goals with the interviewee. During the interview, take proper notes about the candidate's performance, using the case evaluation sheet from **Chapter 5** of this book. You can download and print the sheet from a link in the resource section in **Chapter 37**. Answer all questions of the interviewee. If you do not have additional information or a data point that they are asking for, simply say that the data is not available. If they get stuck, try to nudge them in the right direction, at first in a subtle manner and if they still do not know how to move forward, help them in a more direct way. Provide hints or shortcuts if needed. Monitor the time and make sure they finish the interview within 25 to 30 minutes.

After the interview, discuss the performance of the candidate in detail, again referring to the feedback sheet and the associated performance levels from 1 (insufficient) to 5 (distinctive) detailed in **Chapter 5**. Go through each section of the case and highlight your impression of the interviewee. Talk about strengths and weaknesses related to the different skills assessed and propose exercises and practice for them to improve based on what you have learned in this book and are employing yourself.

Learn from their performance and compare it with your own approach in the same context. They might have devised a smart or creative way to deconstruct the case, or they might have used an elegant and quick approach to a quantitative problem. Be opportunistic. Getting exposure to someone else's thinking and communication can boost your own case interviewing skills tremendously. Take note of everything that is relevant and meaningful for your own learning and development journey. Write it down in your case notebook that I'm going to talk about shortly.

Should you hire a case coach and how can you work with a coach?

Hiring a case coach

The case interview coaching topic is very dear to my heart as I have done more than 1,000 coaching sessions over the last two years alone and helped hundreds of clients get their desired offer.

Coaching is not for everyone. It might be too expensive for you, or you want to make it on your own, which is perfectly fine. Many years ago, when I was preparing for case interviews, I would never have thought about getting professional help. However, if you decide to go down the coaching route, you should consider two things:

1. How can you select the best coach to support your ambitions?
2. How can you best utilize a coach to improve your performance?

To answer the first question, many factors might play a role in your decision, but I see the following three as essential:

1. actual experience with recruiting and/or interviewing candidates
2. worked multiple years in top-tier firms or the firm of your choice
3. consistent proven-track record of success over time (third-party verified).

By looking out for the first two factors, you make sure that you are not working with a scam artist who has never even worked for a consulting firm. There are highly paid interview coaches out there who fake their resumes, claiming to have worked at McKinsey or any other top-tier firm, while they did not even manage to get an internship there. They work with candidates and teach them dangerous superficial knowledge that they have read about on the internet. They barely scratch the surface in the best case and set you up for failure in the worst case by teaching you the wrong habits.

I have seen this firsthand with a couple of my clients who previously booked sessions with such coaches and had less-than-ideal experiences and outcomes. These scams are hard to spot since they prey on the information asymmetry that exists in the field of case coaching. Case interview candidates usually know little about the industry and the process when they start preparing and can easily fall for bad actors in the space.

You should ensure that coaches have a fair number of third-party verified reviews to their name, which state that their coachees received offers with their respective target firms due to the impact of the coaching. You can find such third-party reviews on coaching platforms such as PrepLounge. (Interviewing) experience plays a role, however, it is only one of many factors. In the end, no metric is better than the success rate of their candidates in relation to the time the coach was active. If after five years, a coach can only show a handful of client successes, look the other way. You want someone who consistently achieves offers every month. There are a few additional factors that I would consider:

- ☑ Number of meetings vs. time registered on a specific platform, which shows undistorted demand within a given time frame. For instance, coach who has 300 meetings over seven years is less in demand than someone who did 300 meetings over the last year.
- ☑ Recommendation rankings if the platform is offering such features (only if there is a clear logic behind them).
- ☑ See who the reviewers are. If 20% to 50% of the reviews come from the same person, avoid the scam artist.
- ☑ The personal comments in the reviews. Read what people write about the person, their approach, their mentorship, availability outside of sessions, the time they take to make sure you succeed, etc.
- ☑ Normalized success rate (get a feel how it is defined, e.g., offer in Big Four vs. MBB offer rate). Many coaches claim they have a 100% success rate. If you read that, look the other way. No one has a 100% success rate. In a similar fashion, if someone has a 90% success rate of getting people into consulting, you could not compare this to someone who has a 90% success rate of getting people into MBB since you are comparing apples and oranges.

☑ Identify the copycats. It is no surprise that successful coaches are often copied. This can range from adopting the same marketing text and elements to stealing and re-publishing case preparation products or adopting a similar case coaching approach. If you read carefully between the lines when comparing coaches, you get a feel for it. I know all the players in the space and would be happy to point you in the right direction if you are looking for a strong coach for your ambitions. In fact, I do this regularly as demand for my sessions exceeds the hours that I can offer.

To filter out the bad actors and work with top-tier experts, perform proper due diligence on the coaches you consider working with. Find their LinkedIn, write to people who have left reviews for them and ask about their experience, or ask friends in your target firms if the person shows up in the alumni database. Just from my personal experience and access, a surprising number of McKinsey coaches on the internet do not show up there.

Also, prepare some questions and request a free introduction call to get more information about their experience, coaching approach, consistent success rate (across different firms and geographies), preparation plans, and usage of their own proprietary cases developed based on the firm-specific guidelines. Ask them about their insights into the interviewing and application process, mentorship, and availability between and after sessions, on top of everything else that is important for you. Personal liking also plays an important role.

If you select a coach based on your target firms, plus follow the checklist of criteria from above and have an introductory call, you should be able to screen and select the best coach for your needs and goals.

Working with a case coach

Once selected, how can you best work with a coach? If you decide to work with a coach, I recommend you start as early as possible in your preparation for two reasons. First, the sooner you have your first session, the sooner you learn the right approach, the right content creation strategies, and the right communication habits. A strong coach teaches you everything they know in the first session and from then on it should be a fine-tuning process, guiding you along the way as you practice on your own and with other candidates. Early sessions are a productivity multiplier. The longer you wait, the higher the chance that you learn bad habits and focus your efforts on the wrong things. Working on unlearning the wrong habits and re-learning new ones is a time and performance killer, which is especially critical for candidates on a short timeline or professional hires with limited preparation time during the week.

Second, you want to get meaningful feedback early on. A strong coach can tailor a focused preparation plan that should help you work on your skills in the most effective manner from day one, again saving you tons of time and making sure that you are improving. Within one session, a strong trainer can identify your strengths and weaknesses, then link those to targeted exercises and your timeline to have you improve quickly. Additionally, good coaches usually offer further preparation materials tailored to your preparation plan as well as access to their client network. The sooner you get access to such resources, the faster you progress and the higher the chance that you get to the desired skill level. You want to get the highest quality advice, then practice with the highest quality resources available, as well as with the best performing peers. As for the personal fit interview, an early session helps you tailor your stories ahead of the interview so you don't need to worry about their content and presentation and can focus your preparation fully on the case.

In short, if you are willing and able to pay for preparation, the sooner the better as the return on the investment is highest in the very beginning of your journey. Do not be afraid to bomb your first case with a coach. This is completely normal, and this is where the biggest and fastest gains are made. However, by reading this book you have a condensed version of what I've been teaching over the last 1,000 sessions with my clients and, based on that, already have a significant head start.

If you decide to work with a coach, do not go for the cheapest options available. Quality over quantity. There is no benefit in booking five sessions with a poor or average coach, who focuses on the wrong skills or doesn't know what they are talking about. One session with an experienced and successful coach can make all the difference in your preparation and interview performance.

All benefits of coaching aside, it is not a guarantee that you will get an offer. You still need to put in considerable effort on your own between each session to internalize the habits and to practice and hone your skills.

I'm still offering several case coaching sessions per week, and you can find more information on that in **Chapter 37** if you are interested.

How should you measure your progress with case preparation notes?

When practicing you want to continuously improve and spend your limited time in the most efficient and effective manner. One important tool that I use with my clients is what I call case preparation notes.

Think of it as a preparation diary you use every day after practice to write down your observations of the day. I cannot tell you how to write it since this is a personal process that should support your development; however, I can provide you with a couple of pointers about what the daily notes should contain in combination with your preparation plan that you have created earlier.

- ☑ Types of problems and questions you have worked on today.
- ☑ Feeling of improvement across different elements of the case.
- ☑ Feedback you might have received in a peer or coaching session.
- ☑ Evaluation if your preparation timeline remains realistic.
- ☑ Adjustments needed to your preparation plan.
- ☑ An error log (If you approach every setback with an error log you will a. quickly spot what areas you are struggling with most and b. not repeat the same mistakes).
    - a. Write down the types of problems you have struggled with today (e.g., a specific math problem)
    - b. Write down a sample answer for that problem (e.g., the approach and calculation)
    - c. Think it through until you understand the solution and your mistake fully.
- ☑ New ideas and concepts or different approaches and habits you came across or have learned about today.
- ☑ General thoughts about your preparation and progress.
- ☑ Potential (business) problems you have encountered in your daily life that you want to deconstruct later.

- ☑ New resources (e.g., websites) you have found today.
- ☑ New case partners you have found and/or reached out to.
- ☑ Flashcards of certain concepts, math formulas, communication phrases, etc.
- ☑ Answers for personal fit questions (which I cover later in **Part 10**).

These are just a few ideas. Use them to guide your own preparation notes. Journaling about your preparation process and keeping track of your errors are two powerful tools to reflect about your experience, monitor your progress, and improve your performance in a short amount of time, all in a targeted manner.

[20] Learn these business and problem-solving concepts

In this chapter, I provide an overview of the most important business concepts (not frameworks!) and problem-solving considerations that are relevant for case interviews. Study them, understand them, but do not learn them by heart to implement them with every case you are going through. The goal is to provide you with an overview of concepts that allow strategic thinking to blossom rather than frameworks (e.g., buckets for market entry cases) to be memorized and replicated during case interviews.

Business majors do have an advantage since they are more familiar with certain business concepts, terminology, and have gone through business school case studies. They simply have more experience in dealing with problems in a business context. Nonetheless, I believe that everyone can benefit from going through this, regardless of their background. On top of the collection below, go back to **Chapter 6** to dive into the potential functional areas and industries that are covered in case interviews and **Chapter 10** to look at common math formulas.

What are simple business definitions that you need to know?

Analytical tools

Benchmarking

Benchmarking relies on the comparison of two or multiple things, either internally within your own business or externally with the competition or the market. For instance, if your client is an airline, you could benchmark the speed of the boarding process both within the client's own aircraft fleet or across multiple locations as well as with competitors' metrics. Alternatively, benchmarking also works on a historical basis. For instance, you might want to compare specific client metrics to historical data to see how it has changed or to spot specific trends. Benchmarking allows you to understand weaknesses and issues and define improvement potentials.

Best practice

Consultants often refer to best practices, i.e., the best possible way of doing something. For instance, if you are working on improving the production process of your client's shoe manufacturing business, you should look into how it is done by industry leaders or your client's more advanced factories to learn and adopt their processes.

Cost-benefit analysis

Whenever comparing alternatives or the impact of a specific measure, consultants conduct a cost-benefit analysis. For individual measures, it would help to gauge the (incremental) impact and whether the measure's benefits outweigh its cost within the period under investigation. When comparing alternatives, the cost-benefit analysis shows which alternative comes with the higher net benefit (benefit − cost).

Functions in a business

A business consists of several functions, each with different responsibilities. Some functions are present in all companies (e.g., commercial), others are present only in specific companies (e.g., research and development), whereas some are more important in certain companies than in others (e.g., IT in a tech company). Several functions might be bundled together (e.g., operations and production).

- ☑ Commercial: strategic planning and steering of the company
- ☑ Business Development: growing business through interactions with customers, markets, and relationships
- ☑ Marketing & Sales: advertising, selling, and distribution of goods/services
- ☑ Finance: managing of a company's finances
- ☑ Operations: managing of a company's operations
- ☑ Production: managing of a company's production
- ☑ Legal: managing a company's legal affairs
- ☑ IT: provision and maintenance of IT backend and frontend

- ☑ Human Resources: hiring and retaining employees
- ☑ Research and Development: researching and developing new or improved products and services
- ☑ Sourcing: purchasing of input factors (e.g., raw materials)

Levers

Consultants deconstruct businesses into a collection of levers they can pull to reach their goal. If they want to raise the revenue of an airline, they could pull several levers. See the example about granularity of airline revenue in **Chapter 8** (in the section *Principles to adhere to in every case interview framework*), where I break down revenue per airline passenger into things such as ticket price, booking fee, baggage fee, seat reservation fee, etc. Whenever you look at a business problem, think of it as a series of levers you can manipulate *short-term and long-term.*

Opportunity cost

Opportunity cost is the benefit from an option that is not realized since another option is chosen. You look at the cost and benefit of every option to determine the opportunity cost. Just because an option has a positive net benefit does not mean it is the best course of action if another option has a higher net benefit. By choosing the lesser option, you incur an opportunity cost of not choosing the other option.

Short-term and long-term

Whenever you discuss your ideas, think about their position in time as well as the requirements stated in the case brief. If your interviewer asks you to solve the client's problem or answer the question within six months, solutions that would solve the situation in three years are not relevant as they are outside of the solution space. Alternatively, when you have more time to implement your ideas, you could divide them into short-term quick wins that would immediately generate results and long-term sustainable changes that would take some time to move the needle. By adding the time dimension to your considerations within your problem-solving, you demonstrate that you have the big picture in mind.

Trends

Consultants often look for trends in data to see if there is a general direction of development or movement reversals in certain metrics. When analyzing high production costs, they would look at their development over the last years to see if it has been steadily increasing, is just a recent phenomenon, or has always been this high.

Value chain

A value chain is a distinct set of activities or process steps in product creation and sale or service delivery to the end customer. The value chain is useful when you want to understand how a business operates. For your shoe manufacturer above, you could use a simplified five-step value chain:

Sourcing of materials > Production >
Logistics and transportation > Sales > Aftersales

The value chain is usually accompanied by support functions such as infrastructure, human resources, development, etc., which are not directly related to the flow of goods or delivery of services.

Financial concepts

Breakeven

The breakeven point is the point at which the costs of a business are equal to its revenues. If you want to calculate how many units need to be sold to break even, the breakeven point is equal to the fixed costs divided by the contribution margin per unit sold. The **contribution margin** is the amount of revenue available to cover fixed costs after variable costs are deducted. For instance, let's assume that you own a tire manufacturing company. You know that you have USD five million in fixed costs per year. The production of one tire costs USD 50 and you can sell it for USD 100. Hence, the contribution per tire is USD 50, or 50%. The breakeven quantity is now 5,000,000 divided by 50, which is 100,000. You would need to sell 100,000 tires per year to break even. The breakeven analysis also helps to evaluate the merits of an investment. For **payback period**, see below.

Cash flow

The cashflow of a company is similar to the profit (revenue − cost), yet it is not synonymous. It depicts the net flow of cash that flows in and out of the company in a period. It is not the same as profit since not every revenue generated or cost incurred, which are accounting terms, goes together with a flow of cash. A company might make a large sale in year 1, hence generating revenue. Yet payment will not happen until year 2, which means that in year 1 no cash inflow is occurring. A positive cash flow is crucial for a firm's survival.

Cost = Fixed cost + Variable cost

A firm's costs can be divided into fixed costs that cannot be changed in the short term (e.g., rent), and variable costs that can be changed in the short-term and are related to the quantity of products produced or services rendered (e.g., material cost).

Depreciation

It refers to an accounting method that allocates the cost of a physical asset over its useful life. For instance, if you purchase a machine and depreciate it over eight years in a straight line, one-eighth of the machine's value is accounted for as a cost every year.

Payback period

The payback period is the time it takes to recover the cost of an investment, the time until reaching the breakeven point. Let's assume you own a boutique shoe manufacturing business. To make this business more sustainable, you would need to invest USD 500,000. The contribution of a new pair of sustainable shoes sold is USD 50 and you are able to produce 5,000 pairs of shoes a year. To calculate the payback period of this investment you would need to divide the 500,000 by the contribution per year. 50 times 5,000 is 250,000. Dividing 500,000 by 250,000 yields two, which means that the payback period of this investment is two years or in other words, it would take two years to break even (not considering any other costs of the business).

Profit = Revenue − Cost

At the end of the day, every problem consultants solve should lead to an increase in their client's profit. Hence, profit considerations often accompany you during case interviews. Profit refers to the money the company makes (the revenue) minus the money the company spends (the cost) in a period.

Profit and loss statement (Income statement)

The P&L indicates − for a specific period − how the revenues of a firm (called the top line) are converted into the net profit (called the bottom line) after all revenue and cost items have been considered. In its simplest form it looks like this:

Revenue
− Cost of goods sold (COGS)
Gross profit
− Operating expenses (e.g., selling, general, and administrative)
EBITDA (Earnings before interest, tax, depreciation, amortization)
− Depreciation and amortization
Operating profit
+ Financial income − Financial expenses
Profit before tax
− Tax
Net profit

Formulas that are relevant and related to the P&L:

- ☑ (Net) Profit = Revenue − Cost
- ☑ Revenue = Price x Quantity
- ☑ Profitability (Net profit margin) = (Net) Profit / Revenue
- ☑ Gross profit = Revenue from sales − Cost of goods sold (COGS, e.g., materials)
- ☑ Operating profit = Gross profit − Operating expenses (e.g., rent) − Depreciation (the spread of an asset's cost over its useful lifetime, e.g., a machine) − Amortization (the spread of an intangible asset's cost over its useful lifetime, e.g., a patent)
- ☑ Gross profit margin = Gross profit / Revenue
- ☑ Operating profit margin = Operating profit / Revenue

☑ EBITDA (Earnings before interest, taxes, depreciation, amortization) = Operating profit + Depreciation + Amortization

Profit margin = (Revenue-Cost) / Revenue = Profit / Revenue

The health of a business is often displayed with the profit margin, which shows profit as a percentage of the revenue, highlighting how much of the revenue generated is converted into profit or how many cents of profit the business has generated for each dollar of sale. It is calculated by dividing the profit of the business by the revenue for a period. You should be able to calculate any one of the three given two of the others. For instance, if you know the revenue and the profit margin, you can also calculate the cost.

Revenue = Price x Quantity

The revenue of a company is the number of distinct products or services it sells times the price for each in a period.

Sunk costs

Sunk costs are costs that have already been incurred in the past. They cannot be recovered and have no impact on the future evaluation of a project. For instance, just because you spent USD 10 million in the past on an investment does not mean that you should pursue it further if the return is lower than something else or even negative. *Do not throw good money after bad.*

What are more advanced business concepts and analytical tools?

Analytical tools

3 Cs

The three C's model looks at every business problem from three angles, the company, the competition, and the customers. It can be used to analyze and improve a business or a specific strategic effort, considering what competitors do at the same time.

4 Ps of marketing

The four Ps of marketing help consultants to improve a client's marketing mix, the way the client approaches the market with the goal to meet a profitable customer need:

- ☑ Product: What product or service to sell?
- ☑ Place: Where to sell it?
- ☑ Price: How much to charge for it?
- ☑ Promotion: How to advertise it?

The four Ps might be helpful when thinking about the overall direction of the company, its product portfolio, as well as marketing and advertising strategies.

Ansoff Matrix for business growth

The Ansoff Matrix is a simple two-by-two matrix that can help you decide on how to grow your client's business by looking at the market and the product:

- ☑ New market + existing product: Market development → enter a new market with an existing product (e.g., a car manufacturer entering a new country with their existing product portfolio of small cars)
- ☑ New market + new product: Diversification → enter a new market with a new product (e.g., a car manufacturer creating a new product line of SUVs and entering a new country which is characterized by high demand for larger cars)
- ☑ Existing market + existing product: Market penetration → dominate an existing market with an existing product (e.g., a car manufacturer increasing marketing and sales efforts for their product portfolio of small cars within their existing geographic presence)
- ☑ Existing market + new product: Product development → develop a new product for an existing market (e.g., a car manufacturer creating a new line of high-performance sports cars for their existing country presence)

B2B (business-to-business) and B2C (business-to-consumer)

B2B and B2C refers to the customers of your client. B2B means that the client is selling its products or services directly to other businesses and companies, e.g., wholesalers, retailers. B2C means that it sells directly to the final consumers. Think about the target customer when investigating your client's go-to-market strategy as B2B and B2C customers have very different characteristics. The **go-to-market strategy** refers to a firm's plan of bringing a product to the market by identifying the right customers, creating the right marketing and sales approach, and finding ways to deliver its products and services.

BCG Matrix

The BCG Matrix is a two-by-two matrix that classifies products or services based on their market share and overall market growth. Products with high market share in high growth markets are star products, products with high market share in low growth markets are cash cows. Products with low market share in a high growth market are question marks that need to be investigated. Products with low market share in a low growth market are poor dogs and no resources should be invested. The BCG matrix helps consultants to decide where to allocate resources. Talk about these considerations explicitly only in BCG interviews as an interviewer from another firm might not like to hear about a competitor's model or framework.

Business model

A business model is the way a company translates its strategy into action. In its most commonly agreed upon definition it consists of (based on Osterwalder's and Pigneur's, and influential book *Business Model Generation: A Handbook for Visionaries, Game Changers, and Challengers*):

- ☑ Finances
    - ▸ Revenue streams
    - ▸ Cost structure
- ☑ Infrastructure
    - ▸ Key activities
    - ▸ Key partners

- ▶ Key resources
- ☑ Offering
  - ▶ Value proposition
- ☑ Customers
  - ▶ Customer segments
  - ▶ Customer relationships
  - ▶ Channels

The business model can help you understand the different components of a business and define levers you would like to investigate and focus areas you can prioritize.

First-mover advantage

The first-mover advantage explains the benefits a business can reap when being the first on the market with a new product, or when entering a new country, or just by doing something differently than competitors for the first time.

Implementation

Implementation refers to the execution of a decision, usually in the form of a process. In case interviews, you sometimes must think about implementation measures for your proposed solutions. Companies often run a pilot program before making significant changes (see below).

Incremental changes

Incremental change refers to the change in the value of a specific target variable, e.g., the revenue of a company. In case interviews, you might need to consider the incremental change from proposed measures. For instance, when thinking about an investment, establish the incremental change in cost and revenue to evaluate it.

Industry and product life cycle

Industries on the macro level and products on the firm level go through typical sales cycles. A life cycle consideration helps understand the environment of your client, which usually has four steps:

1. Introduction: New industry takes off or product is launched
2. Growth: Industry grows with existing players and new players entering or product sales are growing due to increased adoption
3. Maturity: Industry size and product sales reach a peak
4. Decline: Industry shrinks, and product sales decrease as new technologies, industries, and products appear

Market share

The market share is the portion of a market that is made up of a product or company, often accounted for in terms of revenue or number of units sold. For revenue, it is calculated by dividing the company or product revenue by the revenue of the total market for a period. The market share helps you understand the competitive control and market power of one company or product, as well as its size compared to the industry.

PESTEL

The PESTEL analysis is a corporate tool to evaluate opportunities and threats related to political, economic, social, technological, environmental and legal factors. You might use some of those considerations when evaluating a situation or potential strategies.

Pilot

A pilot program is a smaller-scale, short-term trial to evaluate and test the implementation of certain measures or ideas. For instance, instead of launching a new feature or product globally, it is only made available in a certain country or for a certain user group initially. In case interviews, you might recommend a pilot before going for a full-scale implementation.

Porter's Five Forces

With one of the oldest business frameworks in existence, Porter looks at the strength of companies based on a powerplay of five angles, the customers' bargaining power, the suppliers' bargaining power, the competitors' strength, the threat of new entrants, and the threat of substitute products. Consultants can use these areas to balance the power in their client's favor by improving the competitive position across the five areas.

Porter's Generic Strategies

According to Porter, firms can position themselves on a two-by-two matrix based on the scope of their business and their competitive advantage.

- ☑ Total market scope + high competitive advantage: Differentiation → create products that clearly separate you from the others, covering the whole market
- ☑ Total market scope + low competitive advantage: Cost leadership → create products that are cheaper than competitors' products, covering the whole market
- ☑ Niche market scope + high competitive advantage: Differentiation focused → create products that clearly separate you from the others within a niche
- ☑ Niche market scope + low competitive advantage: Cost focused → create products that are cheaper than competitors' products within a niche

If a company tries to cover all or several of the four, they are stuck in the middle and not effective at what they are trying to achieve. These considerations can help you when thinking about strategic decisions and the positioning of your client and its products.

Price sensitivity

Price sensitivity shows the percentage change in a product's demand resulting from a one percent change in its price. It is a measure of how sensitive customers react to price changes. Certain goods, such as luxury products, attract fewer price-sensitive customers compared to high price-sensitive goods such as commodities. Price sensitivity considerations are relevant when thinking about changing prices of a client's product offering. In general, higher prices would lead to lower quantities sold, except for a few notable exceptions such as luxury products.

Product adoption

Buyers can be classified into five categories once a new product is launched. Innovators, who buy early and are real fans of the product, early adopters, who are important to drive adoption of the product, the early majority, who help the product reach the mass market, the late majority, and laggards, who buy at the very end.

Supply and Demand

Every market consists of two sides, demand and supply. Demand refers to buyers, who are willing to pay a certain price for a product or service and supply refers to sellers, who are willing to sell a product or service for a given price. Generally, the more desirable the product and the lower the price, the higher demand and vice versa. Generally, the higher the price, the higher the incentive to supply and vice versa. The **price** of a product or service is usually influenced by its quality and desirability as well as the availability of substitutes or alternatives on the market.

SWOT-analysis

The SWOT Analysis helps evaluate a business or project based on four key factors:

- ☑ Company internal
    - ▸ Strengths (e.g., low-cost production)
    - ▸ Weaknesses (e.g., limited product offering)
- ☑ Company external
    - ▸ Opportunities (e.g., low-income segment is growing)
    - ▸ Threats (e.g., substitute product will soon be available)

In a case interview, it could be used to evaluate a company or a project to devise strategic actions and ideas or compare it to another company or project.

Synergies

Synergies refer to the interaction of two or more components (e.g., strategic initiatives, collaboration of departments or organizations) that produce a combined effect greater than the sum of their separate effects. Synergies are an important concept in the business world and drive many initiatives. In a case interview, you might have to evaluate ideas based on their synergistic effects. For instance, when merging two businesses, there are certain synergies related to costs and revenues.

Triple bottom line

The triple bottom line approach is gaining more traction. Historically, a business was only concerned with its bottom line, which refers to its profits. A triple bottom line approach also considers the social and environmental impact of the business. Do not ignore the latter two aspects since many case interviews today touch upon them.

Financial concepts

Balance sheet

A balance sheet is a financial statement that summarizes a firm's assets (what it owns), equity (the amount invested by shareholders) and liabilities (what it owes) at a given moment. It can be used for financial analyses, for instance, to analyze a firm's health. A balance sheet would usually not be part of a generalist case interview, but it is something you might encounter if you apply for more specialized financial consultant roles. The balance sheet contains two sides, with the sum of each side needing to be balanced. On the left side are assets, on the right side are liabilities and equity:

> *Assets (current, such as cash and fixed, such as machinery) =*
> *Equity (capital stock, retained earnings) +*
> *Liabilities (e.g., loans, outstanding taxes, rent, wages, utilities).*

A word of caution: Use these concepts only to sharpen your strategic thinking and to familiarize yourself with the logical constructs that support certain business decisions. Do not overly rely on them and do not assume that this is all there is to know. The business world is complex and if you work through cases or read business publications, you might encounter further business concepts or ideas. If you are not familiar with them, learn about them in the context of the case or the article, write them down in your preparation notes, then move on to the next case or article. That way, you organically build your business knowledge, sense, and intuition. Stay curious and keep an open mind throughout your journey.

PART 9

Introduction to Fit
Interviews: Become
a Well-rounded Candidate

[21] Understand the importance of the personal fit

Apart from case interviews, consulting firms want to get to know you on a more personal level. While the case interview focuses on your problem-solving skills, the aim of the personal fit interview is to understand more about you, your skills (both soft and hard), your personality, background, and motivation. This type of consulting interview has many names, such as personal fit interview, behavioral interview, resume interview, personal experience interview, and can consist of different questions and components depending on the firm, the interview round, and the role you are applying for.

Interviewers want to understand who you are, what you are passionate about, and what you have done in the past to see if you have the potential, traits, and skills to develop into a world-class consultant. That is why they spend a considerable amount of time during the interviews focusing on questions relating to your personal fit. This is usually done during the same interview slot as the case (with the same consultant interviewers) and lasts between five to 30 minutes. The importance of this interview varies across firms and interview stages, however, for most, it is as important as the case interview. If you fail to impress your interviewers here in one way or another, your application might very well be rejected.

Yet many candidates neglect this part of the interview and focus their preparation solely or almost exclusively on the case, later receiving feedback that they are *"strong problem-solvers but they do not seem to fit the company culture and the consulting lifestyle, or their story does not make sense and they might lack the right motivation."* Unfortunately, that's why they do not receive an offer. To avoid this type of feedback and the rejection that comes with it, I cover everything you need to know about fit interviews in the following parts.

[22] Understand what you need to demonstrate in a personal fit interview

Your fit will be evaluated throughout the whole process, starting with the resume screening, personality tests (in some firms), as well as several dedicated interviews with junior and senior stakeholders of the firm. There are three important reasons why consulting firms spend so much time evaluating the personal fit, each tested on its own:

What is the airport test?

Top-tier consulting firms hire people that are likable and pleasant to be around. Your team spends 12-to-16-hour days with you in the same room under difficult circumstances, travels with you, and spends their breakfasts, lunches, and dinners with you for weeks on end. The people you work with spend more time with you than with their families, spouses, and friends combined. Hence, interviewers constantly have the *airport test* on their mind – consciously and unconsciously – while they evaluate you. They think about whether they would enjoy being stuck with you in an airport. If the answer is yes, you have passed this important step.

What is the skills and development potential test?

Interviewers evaluate whether you are a good fit with the firm, looking for the right skills right from the start, the potential to develop into a world-class consultant, the right mindset to fit into the distinct company culture, and the right fit with the tough working environment that is consulting.

Once you start at a top-tier consulting firm, you are thrown into your first engagement within a week or two. You need to bring a certain level of skills and traits to the table to add value to your team from day one. What is even more important is that you can quickly develop your skills as you are constantly stretched to meet personal and professional development goals. As soon as you have barely mastered one thing, you are asked to take on new responsibilities. Further, consulting firms have distinct cultures and operate in a stressful, long-hours work environment where you need to hold your ground. If relevant traits and skills are visible from your resume and confirmed by the stories you tell during the fit interview, you have passed this test as well.

What is the client-readiness check?

Top-tier consulting firms are prestigious organizations with decades of experience in advising the most important corporations and public institutions on impactful matters. When you – as a newly minted consultant – are sent to the client for the first time, you are expected to represent that legacy and uphold the reputation of your employer. Unexpected behaviors, strange remarks, or a quirky demeanor might quickly erode your client's trust in you, your team, and your whole firm.

Consequently, consulting interviewers also evaluate whether they would feel comfortable putting you in front of their clients in often challenging interpersonal situations, representing your team and your firm's legacy beyond the purely analytical problem-solving aspects of an engagement. Consulting is very much an interaction-focused and people-driven business, where people and social skills matter. Apart from looking at your behavior during the interviews, your interviewers look for stories about how you handled difficult interpersonal situations in the past. If you can talk about strong stories that cover these areas and have a professional, friendly, and mature appearance during the interview, you should pass this test as well.

Key takeaway: Do not neglect the fit part of the interview. I often see candidates investing ninety-five percent of their time in case interview preparation, neglecting to prepare proper answers to fit, behavioral, and skills questions.

Work on answers and stories to common personal fit questions before the interview and practice them. This is the part of the interview where you don't want to think and make up stories on the spot, but merely remind yourself of your prepared answers. This way you make sure that your answers are structured, communicated effectively to the point, and hit the right characteristics that the questions try to assess. Like during the case interview, your answers should be built on an easy-to-follow top-down structure with a concise story arc that conveys your key messages effectively. Do not memorize and recite answers by heart. Your replies should still feel natural. Often, I see candidates trying too hard to impress interviewers in this regard.

In the next part, I show you the most common consulting fit interview questions with potential answers as well as my SCORE framework to answer such questions in the most systematic and impressive manner. I cover probably north of ninety-five percent of personal fit questions you can expect, however, it is impossible to cover every question that interviewers might pull out of their hat. Most consulting firms give their interviewers a lot of leeway in how they conduct the interviews, what questions they ask, and how they score the answers. For McKinsey with their highly standardized fit interview format, I cover all the questions you are asked.

PART 10

Types of Fit Interview
Questions: Prepare the
Most Impactful Answers

In this part, I answer the following questions, with a focus on making yourself stand out:

- ☑ How can you best introduce yourself, and what answers should you prepare about your resume?
- ☑ What answers should you prepare about your fit?
- ☑ What answers should you prepare that cover your skills and expertise?
- ☑ What is the McKinsey Technical Experience Interview?
- ☑ How can you best prepare for story questions?
- ☑ What questions should you ask the interviewer at the end?

As a consulting interview candidate, expect and prepare for five types of questions:

1. Introduction questions, which are commonly employed as icebreakers and have no impact on your evaluation, yet it is still important to manage the impression you give.
2. Questions about your resume and your educational, professional, and extracurricular experiences.
3. Simple fit questions, which cover your motivation, personality, and certain skills on a higher level.
4. Skills questions that ask about a specific set of skills, which is especially relevant for specialized hires who need to demonstrate domain-relevant expertise.
5. Personal story questions, which have you discuss situations in more detail to inform the interviewer about your skills and experiences on a deeper level and in a richer context, helping them to evaluate you based on actions and behaviors.

Let's look at those question types individually and go over the most common questions and strong answer examples for each.

[23] Do not fumble the introduction (icebreakers)

Introduction questions are used to break the ice at the beginning of the interview. Interviewers know that you are nervous and ask a couple of simple questions to make you feel more comfortable and at ease and to create a connection before diving into the real evaluation. Your answers to these questions will not make or break your application. In fact, they do not carry any weight in the interviewers' decision unless you behave strangely (e.g., overly nervous or stressed out, distant or avoidant), which would also be picked up throughout other parts of the interview. Consider that consultants are expected to be able to make small talk with clients. You do not need to prepare for this part of the interview. Typical questions you might expect are:

- ☑ *"How did you find out about this position?"*
- ☑ *"Do you know anyone who works for us?"*
- ☑ *"Did you find the office easily today?"*
- ☑ *"I see that you studied at <University of XYZ>. I took a couple of courses there. How did you like it?"*

[24] Know your resume

Resume questions are especially common at tier-2 firms while some MBB interviewers/top-tier firms do not touch upon them at all. Interviewers might ask about everything you have put on your resume. Therefore, you should be able to talk freely and naturally about all items, even the minor details if they happen to pique the interviewer's interest.

How can you introduce yourself and your resume?

Most commonly, you are asked to introduce yourself (often disguised as *"Talk about yourself"* or *"Please guide me through your resume"*). Simply lead the interviewer through the highlights of your resume in a top-down and structured manner. Pick three to four core experiences that are relevant for the role and describe how they have led you down the path of consulting, applying at that particular firm, implicitly showcasing why you are a strong candidate. Create an intriguing story instead of going line by line. For instance:

"Since starting university, three experiences made me pursue a career in management consulting. First, during my undergraduate years at XYZ, I enjoyed working in teams on several group projects. For instance, I was leading a team to do XYZ, which gained us broad recognition in the school. Second, during the summer of 2019, I was interning with an international bank. While I enjoyed the analytical and problem-solving aspects of the job, I was missing variety and new challenges. It was a job that contained quite a few routine tasks that had to be repeated every day. Third, in order to build on the teamwork aspect, the analytical aspect, and my desire for new challenges, I created the consulting club at my university in the fall of 2019 and have been working with three pro-bono clients since to help them shape their growth strategies and manage their finances. Throughout this time, I was juggling academic excellence, which you can see from my top five percent GPA, various work experiences that equipped me with relevant business and problem-solving skills, as well

as extracurricular engagements. It's the combination of these experiences and the positive feedback I received along the way that made me want to pursue a full-time career in consulting."

Consultants are natural storytellers. Rather than going one by one through every experience on your resume, using a *curated reading* process, create rich stories such as the one above to make your introduction more interesting and memorable. Add personal notes and touches throughout the story that might not be listed on your resume.

What are some more specific resume questions and how can you answer them?

Other common resume questions you should prepare for are:

- ☑ *"Why did you choose experience XYZ?"* (XYZ can be anything related to employment, university, or extracurricular activities)
- ☑ *"Discuss your educational/professional background."*
- ☑ *"What did you do at firm XYZ? What did you achieve?"*
- ☑ *"What did you do/learn in situation XYZ?"*
- ☑ *"What kind of work/part of your studies did you like best/worst?"*
- ☑ *"What were the biggest challenges in experience XYZ, how did you overcome them, what did you learn, how did you benefit?"*
- ☑ *"How did experience XYZ influence/change you?"*
- ☑ *"What three distinct skills did you develop during your years at university XYZ or at employer ABC?"*
- ☑ *"What did you learn at experience XYZ that would benefit us here at consulting firm ABC?"*
- ☑ *"What experience or combination of experiences made you want to join consulting?"*
- ☑ *"What achievement that you are proud of is not on your resume?"*
- ☑ *"What should I know about you that is not on your resume?"*

Answers to these questions are highly personal, hence, I am not a proponent of providing you with cookie-cutter answers for each. However, I want to show you how to approach such questions in general. When drafting your own answers, think about the following principles in order to stand out:

- ☑ Always keep your answers in a structured and top-down format with numbered points that are coherently tied together in a story as demonstrated above.
- ☑ Show authenticity with your answers and make them personal. Do not say things solely because you think they make you sound smart or look good. Answer in a way that is meaningful to you and that tells your story accurately in a memorable brief. Interviewers want to get to know the real you and understand your story and background. They can spot if you are putting on a show or discussing canned answers.
- ☑ Whenever you are asked about skills or about what you have learned, relate it back to areas that are relevant for the consulting job (e.g., *"..., which has helped me strengthen my analytical skills significantly."*)
- ☑ Do not hide your achievements. Consulting fit interviews are not the time for understatement. Have your achievements ready and ideally some figures to support them (e.g., *"Due to my initiative, the fund was able to raise 40% more donations the following year."*)
- ☑ Keep your answers focused on professional and academic experiences or extracurricular activities and leave out everything related to your personal life such as health, relationships, etc.
- ☑ Think deeply through every experience, skill, or interest you put on your resume and create a list of questions you might expect related to each point. Pay attention to the details as interviewers are sometimes matched based on common interests or backgrounds. For instance, do not put chess as a hobby of yours, then be startled when the interviewer asks you about your ELO score.

Some of these resume questions might be tied to more complex story questions. Adapt the depth of your answer as you see fit. More on these types of questions in **Chapter 27**.

[25] Make sure that you "fit"

With simple fit questions, interviewers try to elicit information about your motivation, personality, and behaviors, as well as your overall fit with the company. Answer these questions top-down, starting with a clear structure and the key piece of information, then providing supporting arguments.

How can you demonstrate your cultural fit?

Why consulting? Create a credible story arc about how your interest in and dedication to the consulting industry gradually increased over the last few years. List qualities of the job you like and link the answer to the most recent experiences from your resume. Show how you selected these experiences to help you prepare and develop the skills needed for a career in consulting. For instance:

"I chose consulting because it provides three unique benefits vis-a-vis other careers. First, the type of work you do, second, the way the work is conducted, third, the people you work with. My interest started to develop when I was taking mostly classes on strategic management and quantitative problem-solving. I enjoyed working through business cases, solving impactful problems for hypothetical clients during class. I then enrolled in the consulting club of my university and worked on a couple of pro-bono projects for local companies, becoming a project manager at the end of the year. During that time, I enjoyed the iterative nature of consulting work, the impact we had on our clients, as well as the high-calibre and motivated people you work with. It also provided me with the chance to further hone my problem-solving and communication skills. Last summer, I completed an internship with a <tier-2> consulting firm, where I also received a return offer, which further encouraged me to pursue this career."

Tailor the following common motivators for people entering consulting to your individual story: fun and smart colleagues, intellectually stimulating environment, high impact at a young age with top-tier clients, (sometimes) industry-changing projects, quick career progression, high-quality training, networking opportunities, tough challenges, steep learning curve, prestige and reputation, exit opportunities, and international exposure.

A different framing of this question for more confrontational interviewers is: *"Do you actually know what the job of a consultant is like? Do you want that?"* The *"why consulting"* is often asked in combination with "switching" questions that help the interviewer understand your motivation to change focus or jobs. If that is the case, you should expect questions such as: *"Up to now, you have shown a strong motivation to work on sustainability issues and worked in manufacturing companies. Why do you want to move to consulting now?"* or *"Why do you want to leave your current company and join a consulting firm?"*

When challenged, make sure to come up with a sensible story to justify your transition, again highlighting the qualities that you liked at your previous job, then talking about the things you were missing that you could only find in your new consulting role with that specific firm. Proper reasons for a switch to consulting or within consulting from one firm to another, on top of everything I have already listed above, are: greater exposure to more diverse topics, industries, geographies, and colleagues, the opportunity to become an expert on a specific topic quickly, a more challenging working environment with more responsibility, bigger impact, faster career growth, and better brand recognition.

Why our firm? Truth be told, this question can be answered in a similar manner for different firms and the interviewer would still be satisfied with your reply if you hit the right keywords and phrases. Still, you should try to tailor the answer based on your actual preferences. Points you could mention, which should be based on the research and networking you conduct before sending the application, are the following:

- ☑ the reputation and impact of the firm globally or within a specific region or functional area
- ☑ its values, culture and the people you have connected with and saw the best fit with (this should guide your decision about which offer to accept later). Attend recruiting events early on to learn about the culture and the people as both differ significantly across firms and countries. Drop names of current or former employees that you have met and talk about how the conversations impressed you

☑ the firm's client portfolio, unique specific industry, or functional expertise as well as firm-specific research that you have come across that intersects with your interests

☑ the firm's staffing model, for instance, more global such as McKinsey's or more local such as Bain's, depending on your preferences

☑ educational leave or other leave of absence programs offered

☑ specific time-out programs offered to manage work-life balance or other flexible working arrangements

☑ special training and development opportunities.

Summarize that such an environment can help you perform at your best and you would be motivated to bring your skills and energy to the table. You get bonus points for mentioning a previous connection to the firm such as a particular event you attended or someone within the firm you met and saying that the experience left you with a positive impression. Make it clear that you want to work at this firm because of its impact, the work, and reputation as well as its people and culture. When talking about values and culture, highlight that they resonate with you. **Always use specific examples for each talking point.** For instance, don't say *"I want to work for your firm because of its expertise in banking."* Rather say *"I believe that at your firm I could further develop my expertise in the South American banking sector. I have been an avid reader of the yearly regional banking reports that you publish and would love to contribute to this client base in the future."*

In general, you should have a broad knowledge about the consulting industry landscape in your region, the reputation of different firms, the type of work they do, the benefits, and their culture, amongst other things. You can learn about these talking points in conversations with peers, consultants, and HR as well as by browsing the firms' local websites. Come up with three bullet points that separate one firm from the others in your area (at least on paper).

Personal fit and culture. Direct questions about your cultural fit are similar to *"Why this firm?"* Every firm wants a successful applicant to fit into its distinct culture. Some firms – especially higher-tier – put great emphasis on, and interviewer efforts into, investigating a candidate's cultural fit. Sometimes, interviewers try to identify this subtly during the interview by reading between the lines. They might ask about your experiences with their firm that encouraged you to apply. At other times, they ask targeted cultural fit questions straight away. For instance, they could ask:

- ☑ *"Apart from your skills, why would you be a good fit for our firm?"*
- ☑ *"Do you think you could perform well in our culture?"*
- ☑ *"What do you know about our firm's culture?"*
- ☑ *"What would you bring to our firm to blend in and improve our culture?"*

To accurately and truthfully answer such questions, do your homework before the interviews. Ideally, you have already talked to consultants of the firm via email, LinkedIn, phone, or have even met them during events. You should be able to talk about what you have witnessed that has impressed you and further encouraged you to apply. Your observations might include the conduct of the consultants with each other or with other applicants, the way HR responded to your messages and questions, the stories you have heard from your peers that already work there, etc. It helps when you have colleagues or friends who are working there already and have encouraged you to apply because of their positive experiences and stories that resonate with your values and ambitions. You should mention such things during the interview. Again, highlight that in such an environment you can perform at your best and would be happy to contribute to the strong culture and social ties that you have heard about.

Do not underestimate these kinds of questions. Experienced hires often have trouble integrating into the specific and tight-knit company culture of top-tier consulting firms, leading to high turnover rates for that particular segment. Top-tier firms invest around USD 100,000 to hire and train a successful applicant (that figure has been floating around for a couple of years and confirmed by multiple HR sources I talked to). With such large upfront investments, firms want to keep new hires for a while and make sure that they can integrate easily.

How should you answer more specific fit questions?

Interviewers want evidence that you would perform well in the tough environment that is consulting. Demonstrate that you can work in fast-paced environments, enjoy solving complex problems in an ambiguous context and can handle steep learning curves. You want to showcase that you have the necessary stamina and resilience to work long hours and unpredictable schedules and thrive while working under pressure. Interviewers also want to see that you are a confident communicator, as well as a self-reflective and self-standing team player.

Strengths and weaknesses. This question might come up in several different variations. Find humble strengths, which are relevant for the work of a consultant, such as creativity, structured problem-solving, communication skills, etc., essentially all the skills I discuss in the case interview section. Strengthen your answers with short stories in which you exhibited the desired qualities. Every character trait you mention needs proof and support in the form of a story to be more memorable and more believable.

- ☑ Bad example: *"I am very strong at communicating results and deriving actions."*
- ☑ Strong example: *"I am very strong at communicating results and deriving actions. At my previous employer, I presented our department's year end results to the board in a way that helped to increase our budget by more than 20% by figuring out what motivates the board to take action."*

Be prepared to be queried more about such answers. Common variations of the strengths-question are *"Why you?"* or *"Why should we hire you?"* or *"What separates you from other candidates?"* or *"What does your boss/professor think about you?"*, where you would discuss a couple of strengths, including particular experience(s) that support each strength, linking them to the qualities needed for the job in the same manner as demonstrated above. You might briefly also talk about cultural aspects as discussed above as well. In any case, when giving answers try to be as structured and organized as possible, e.g., *"There are five reasons why I would be a great fit. First..."*

As regards **weaknesses**, find a true weakness of yours that is not a showstopper for consulting and discuss how you have learned about it the hard way and what you have done since then to overcome it. Do not sweat it; provided you demonstrate that you are actively working on your weaknesses and are otherwise a strong applicant, that is not an issue. You are expected to have some flaws.

Strong example: *"One weakness I am currently working on is communicating results effectively. I noticed this when I was asked to prepare a presentation for the board about my department's year end results. Back then, I structured my presentations pretty much bottom-up, starting with a problem diagnostic, then presenting the results and the actions that should follow. I noticed during the meeting that I lost some of the audience's attention. I have since read the Pyramid Principle by Minto and watched a couple of YouTube videos to work on my top-down communication skills and incorporated these principles in all documents and presentations I have worked on. Being 100% top-down is not something that always comes fully naturally to me and I have to remind myself when working on cases and presentations to implement it properly, but I have been making huge improvements over the last year already."*

Alternatively, the weaknesses question could also be framed as any of the following:

☑ *"What is one thing your former employer would like you to improve on?"*

☑ *"What negative feedback did you receive from a former manager or colleague?"*

☑ *"Tell me about a time when you received tough feedback."*

☑ *"What constructive development feedback would your current team share with you?"*

Rough experiences and crises. These types of questions are often asked in the following ways:

☑ *"What experiences or crises have shaped you?"*

☑ *"What hardships did you overcome?"*

☑ *"Tell me about a time where you have failed."*

☑ *"Tell me about a time you made a mistake."*

☑ *"Tell me about a rough experience and how you would approach it differently now?"*

☑ *"What makes you uncomfortable?"*

Some firms or interviewers put more emphasis on such questions (I am looking at you, BCG). Consulting engagements often enter crisis mode and interviewers are curious about what adverse events you have faced and how you have handled them.

Talk about what happened, your role, and the impact it had on you, your actions to overcome the situation, and what you have learned from it. You want to demonstrate authenticity and resilience when dealing with a crisis. While you can discuss your mistakes and failures that stem from it, highlight how you have come out of it stronger and how it has made you better in certain areas. Prepare answers that are related to your professional and educational endeavors. In some cases, it might also be okay to talk about something that has affected you personally (e.g., during the pursuit of a passion or hobby).

Personal satisfaction. Consulting interviewers want to understand where you take your energy from to evaluate if the consulting world would energize or drain you.

Commonly asked questions are:

- ☑ *"What drives you?"*
- ☑ *"What gives you personal satisfaction and energy?"*
- ☑ *"What are you passionate about?"*

For a strong answer, you want to talk about how you are driven by a certain set of values that made you overcome a challenge in an area that is relatable for the interviewer. Answers should be aligned with the type of work and the mission of a consulting firm as well as the role you are applying for.

For instance, the challenge you talk about might be placed in a team setting, where you were putting the team's success above all, pursuing a common goal. If not in a team setting, this question is also a good opportunity to show how ambitious and dedicated you were when you were working on a personal initiative and passion or pursuing a professional goal, overcoming a couple of obstacles and setbacks along the way. As above, you want to discuss situations where you demonstrated certain skills and resilience in a challenging environment.

An unusual variation of this question could be: *"Where do you see yourself in five years? And 10 years?"* You cannot talk about the past here. Values and personal preferences influence your long-term career plans. You do not need to mention that you will be in the same job or firm five years from now, but the type of work you mention for your future and skills needed for it should match the role you are currently applying for. Otherwise, interviewers might challenge your motivation and value-match with the consulting industry and the job. For instance, if you are applying for a sustainability consultant position, it would be perfectly appropriate to discuss how in five years' time you would implement the skills you have learned during your consulting stint with a leading NGO in the sector. I once worked with a medical doctor who wanted to join MBB to influence the public health policy of his home country both during his time in consulting and by switching to a public management position afterwards. Great story!

Biggest challenge. As above, interviewers might want to hear about your biggest challenges and achievements to match them with the expectations that are placed on you once you start in your new role. Potential questions could be:

- ☑ *"What was your biggest challenge so far?"*
- ☑ *"What did you do to overcome a big challenge?"*
- ☑ *"What is your biggest achievement?"*
- ☑ *"Tell me about an accomplishment you are most proud of."*

What you have achieved says a lot about your values, grit, skills, and capabilities. Again, this is no time to downplay any of your achievements or successes. Briefly introduce the context, discuss your motivation, then focus on your actions, which should be the core part of your answer. Lastly, discuss the outcome, talk about what you have learned from it, and how it has benefited you already.

Other options. Some interviewers might ask, *"What other career options do you have?"* or *"What other interviews or offers do you have lined up?"* Generally, such questions are anything but professional and your answer should have no impact on your success. If you are asked about it, make it clear that you actually have a plan lined up for yourself. You are eager to work for the firm you are interviewing with, but you have other offers on the table in case you fail. You are not expected to list any names or competing salaries.

Concerns. Another way to evaluate how you would perform in the stressful environment that is top-tier consulting is to ask about your concerns:

- ☑ *"What concerns would you have when working for a consultancy?"*
- ☑ *"What would you like the most and the least about working in this industry?"*
- ☑ *"How would you handle the tough environment or difficult clients?"*

When answering such questions, find a balance between staying true to yourself, being authentic, and highlighting that you do not expect this to be a problem. The concerns you mention could be ethical such as dealing with certain industries you do not want to work with or related to work on a higher level such as not getting enough exposure to different challenges, etc. I would stay away from mentioning long hours, difficult clients or the like if you are not asked about it explicitly.

If you are asked about such touchy subjects, an alternative framing would be to compare a tough and exhausting past experience (one concrete example) with the future expected workload, showing that you are used to working hard within challenging environments, with difficult people, solving complex problems. Discuss the motivation you get when working toward rewarding and impactful goals and highlight your appreciation for the support of your colleagues that you will work with once hired.

Passions and interests. Sometimes interviewers want to know what you are passionate about outside of work. Everything goes as long as it is communicated in a structured way, authentic, and somewhat of an interesting hobby or passion, essentially the same things you would say if you were on a Tinder date (hint: meeting friends is not an interesting conversation piece). Do not put interests on your resume that you have no idea about just to look cool, smart, or interesting (remember the chess example from before?). Rather, describe your hobbies in a meaningful and interesting way when drafting your resume. For instance:

- ☑ playing guitar → Playing electric and acoustic guitar for eight years, playing multiple concerts per year solo and with a band
- ☑ traveling → Traveled to 34 countries in Europe, Asia, and South America over the last five years
- ☑ opera → Fan of Italian opera from the late 19th century.

Questions might be phrased as:

- ☑ *"How do you recharge?"*
- ☑ *"What do you do for fun?"*
- ☑ *"What do you do besides work?"*
- ☑ *"I saw from your resume that you are an avid traveler and traveled to 34 countries over the last five years. Which one was your favorite trip?"*

[26] Demonstrate your skills, industry, or functional expertise

Depending on the size of the firm and its business activity or the role you are applying for, you might expect some questions about a very particular set of skills, your familiarity with certain tools and programs, or dedicated knowledge and expertise in certain areas. These questions can range from general queries about your familiarity with MS Office and skills that are needed in the day-to-day life of a consultant to more specific questions about data analysis tools or even expert knowledge about a specific industry or function.

If you apply for the generalist consulting track at larger top-tier firms, usually, you should not expect any of these questions. Rather, your skills are evaluated through story questions and during the resume screening. In any case, these firms put you through intense training programs to get you up to speed with basic tools such as Excel and have experts and specialists ready in the background to support you when you are dealing with unfamiliar environments, industries, and topics. Nevertheless, it does not hurt to think about potential answers in case it comes up. On the other hand, if you are applying for specialized roles or for generalist roles in smaller firms, you should definitely prepare for these types of questions. Let's look at a couple of examples.

What are general consulting skills questions?

To gauge your general aptitude, you might receive the question: *"What skills do you think are most important for this role?"* In this case, come up with a top-down answer and select a couple of the following skills and traits: Ability to work with complex data, problem-solving skills, strong analytics, creativity, strong communication skills, strong leadership and people skills, empathy, good business sense and intuition, strong quantitative reasoning and numerical skills, maturity, and confidence.

Follow the same communication approach that I have already discussed in earlier sections of the fit part and prepare answers that are concise, structured, and top-down, as well as supported with actual experiences. Go through each and bring a practical example of why it is important on the job and highlight how you were displaying this skill in a previous role or situation. The answer might be similar to the one you would give to the *"What are your strengths?"* question I discussed earlier. For instance: *"I believe there are five core traits of a successful consultant* (numbered and signposted). *First, strong communication skills. The most impactful recommendation is worthless if clients are not willing to implement it, which is largely driven by how the recommendation is framed and communicated. I noticed this when working on a pro-bono consulting project and had to tailor the message of our final presentation to meet the communication style of our client. Second..."*

The question might also be reversed: *"What skills are important that you do not have?"* Like the weakness question I discuss above, bring one example of an experience (focusing on a skill) that did not go so well. Discuss how you have worked on improving it by learning more about it and by exposing yourself to similar situations.

What are IT-related questions?

IT-related questions are not common for the reasons I describe above. They might be asked in smaller firms and in-house consultancies. The main tools that consultants work with nowadays are the following, ranked in their order of importance:

- ☑ **Analysis:** Excel, Alteryx, Access
- ☑ **Visualization:** PowerPoint, Tableau
- ☑ **Writing:** Word (used for research documents and client proposals mainly).

While you are not expected to be an expert in any of those, you should at least be somewhat familiar with the Microsoft Office Suite and should have used it before, either at university or work. Be prepared to discuss an example about how you were using a particular software in a specific situation. You want to convey that you are at least an intermediate user and can navigate your way around Excel, PowerPoint, and Word.

What are industry and functional knowledge questions?

Should you apply for a specialist role or the expert consulting track, expect questions common for your field or job description, and prepare accordingly. You should be able to talk about domain-relevant knowledge, relevant educational experiences and coursework, a collection of previous projects in that area, software tools that are commonly used, and current industry trends. You need to display knowledge and an opinion on the outlook and future of the area.

For instance, if you are applying for a corporate finance consultant role, you should be able to discuss corporate finance concepts, both basics, such as a P&Ls, and more advanced ones, such as company valuations, etc. You should also be able to refer to corporate finance courses you took, a finance degree you received, or other finance credentials you hold (e.g., the CFA), university projects on financial topics, or work experience in (corporate) finance, as well as Excel and PowerPoint skills, including the most common formulas and visualization techniques/formats. In addition, be prepared to describe regulatory changes that you are currently observing and your opinion on how the role of (corporate) finance will change in the future, what challenges you might expect, etc.

If this applies to you, think about these things before going into the interview for any specialized position. Generalists do not need to focus on these types of questions.

What are technical questions?

If you are applying for very technical roles (e.g., data analysts, programmers), you should expect technical questions similar to the IT questions above, just more specialized in nature. Think about questions such as:

- ☑ *"What technical skills do you have that are relevant for the role?"*
- ☑ *"What programs and software tools are you familiar with that we are using?"*
- ☑ *"Tell me about a project you worked on and how you have used a specific software to help you along the way?"*

☑ *"If given the chance to work with Program A or Program B, which one do you prefer and why?"*

Learn more about how to answer such questions by reading the part below on the McKinsey Technical Experience Interview. While the format is specific to McKinsey, the way you can prepare and communicate your answers to technical questions is the same as for any other firm.

What is the McKinsey Technical Experience Interview?

A specific technical interview is the McKinsey Technical Experience Interview (TEI). This interview format is used during the recruiting of experts such as analytics staff, designers, product engineers, agile coaches, programmers, etc. The TEI focuses on specific areas of technical or domain knowledge to evaluate a candidate's expertise in a given field.

McKinsey – like every other large consulting firm – has grown significantly and diversified its offering to clients over the last couple of years, hiring for new non-traditional consulting roles apart from the generalist consulting roles. With the variety of its job roles and the diversity of its new hires increasing, McKinsey changed parts of their interview format with the introduction of the TEI. The TEI can be different for different roles as it assesses specific skills needed for each. It spans a wide range of potential evaluations such as coding tests and project discussions with product engineers, portfolio reviews with designers, or discussions about coaching and agile methodologies with agile coaches, to name a few.

The technical interview gauges a candidate's abilities in a certain field with the interviewers discussing specific situations in detail. For instance, you might be asked about a specific problem that you have solved. Your interviewer wants to understand the nature of the problem, how you approached it (the core of the story), what tools you used to work on it (e.g., Python, R for analytical roles, graphic design programs for graphic designers). The focus is on you overcoming challenges to reach a certain outcome. To really understand the situation, your interviewers go very deep by asking probing questions such as:

☑ *"What did you think in that situation?"*
☑ *"What did you do next? Why?"*
☑ *"Why did you choose X over Y?"*
☑ *"What was the outcome?"*
☑ *"What did you learn?"*

In this interview, you are not expected to be 100% familiar or proficient with all the tools available for the job but rather demonstrate a deep understanding of the area, essential concepts, potential approaches, and solution spaces. Interviewers want to see how you think and approach problems and projects. It is not so much about correct solutions but the capability to discuss and evaluate different ideas and options.

Preparing for the TEI is similar to preparing for the Personal Experience Interview (see **Part 12**). Pick two projects in the relevant domain from your resume that you can talk about in detail. Make sure that at least one of the stories is set in a business context. For each story, think about the context and problem statement, highlighting that it was a critical problem for you to solve and the challenges you faced that made you step out of your comfort zone. Outline the innovative process, approach, and tools you chose and potentially changed along the way (be ready to defend your choices), the successful outcome, your key learnings, and how they influenced your future projects. Be prepared to go deeper into each of those buckets when prompted and expect a lot of *"why?"* questions.

[27] Tell personal stories

The last category of personal fit questions is a common part of interviews at McKinsey, BCG, and Bain. Interviewers sometimes refrain from asking direct questions about specific skills, personality traits, or personal values. Rather, they want you to tell stories about specific situations you faced. Through your stories, they get insights into your personality linked to areas that are important for the daily life of a consultant in a more indirect way.

A specific twist to it is the McKinsey Personal Experience Interview, which is a standardized interview format that revolves around four (at the time of writing) specific character traits. It is so unique that I cover it in an individual part of this book (**Part 12**). Back to your stories...

The stories you need to tell should convey one or more of your specific character traits or skills. Interviewers want to understand how you behaved in past events to make assumptions about how you would handle daily situations as a consultant in the future. If you are getting intimidated by this part of the interview, rest assured! You do not need to be superhuman. You can display attractive and fitting character traits in almost any professional situation; what is most important is to focus on specific and concrete actions that support what you want to display. A couple of ground rules:

- ☑ Illustrate how you acted in a specific situation from the more recent past (a maximum of three to four years back; for experienced hires, stories that date back longer are appropriate as well).
- ☑ Use stories from a professional environment (e.g., a previous work engagement or internship), a university experience, or from extracurricular activities.
- ☑ Keep the context brief and focus on your own actions that demonstrate the specific skill(s) or trait(s) the interviewer is asking about.
- ☑ Prepare stories by going through your resume, thinking about the most impactful experiences and most interesting situations

(see below for examples) and do not pick all stories from the same context or background.

What are personal stories that matter?

Below are a couple of specific skills and traits that you need to convey through stories. Learn about them and prepare accordingly. For each, I present elements that make the story stand out. Use the examples as inspiration for your own memorable stories and tailor them based on your own experiences.

Leadership

Questions that gauge your leadership potential:

- ☑ *"Tell me about a time when you were leading a team."*
- ☑ *"Tell me about a situation where you took on a leadership role."*
- ☑ *"Describe a situation in which you had to motivate a team."*
- ☑ *"Give me an example when you had to step up to lead a team out of a crisis."*
- ☑ *"Discuss a time when you were mentoring someone."*
- ☑ *"Discuss how you solved a conflict within a team."*
- ☑ *"Discuss how you were creating an inclusive work environment for a team."*

Content elements you include should demonstrate the following:

- ☑ You can handle a group that accepts you as their leader, with each member looking up to you.
- ☑ You can tailor your leadership style for different groups and people.
- ☑ You understand the different strengths, needs, and concerns of every team member.
- ☑ You can structure, divide, and delegate tasks.
- ☑ You can motivate your team and improve the team spirit and the working environment.
- ☑ You can coach team members in their areas of weakness, develop their talents, and increase their responsibilities.

☑ You mediate conflicts between team members, team members and outsiders, and team members and conflicting goals by aligning opposing parties.

☑ Your team can meet their individual (development) goals as well as the goal for the team as a whole.

☑ You are a trustworthy authority that people can learn from.

When telling such stories, always focus on your leadership role and the interpersonal interactions with each individual team member. If diversity and inclusion aspects are the focus of the story, pay attention to the following details:

☑ Consider how your team was diverse (e.g., culture, gender, background, expertise, experience, needs, opinions).

☑ Discuss how you created an inclusive work environment.

☑ Showcase that you paid attention to different needs of people.

☑ Highlight how you made every voice on the team heard.

☑ Demonstrate how you championed certain team members.

☑ Discuss how – due to your intervention – you ended up with a strong team and with diversity of opinion.

Summing up, show that your leadership had a positive impact on the team and every member, as well as that you led the team to a strong outcome of a particular task.

Ambition, drive, and achievement

Questions that gauge your drive, ambition, and initiative:

☑ *"Tell me about a goal you set for yourself and achieved."*

☑ *"Tell me about a situation when you had to be adaptable."*

☑ *"Tell me about a situation when you showed initiative."*

☑ *"Tell me about a tough problem you had and how you solved it."*

☑ *"Discuss a situation where you had to manage a lot of things at once. How did you manage?"*

☑ *"Discuss a situation when you collected and analyzed data to reach your goal."*

☑ *"Discuss a situation when you engaged other people to help you achieve a goal."*

☑ *"Tell me how you solved a challenging problem in a creative way."*

☑ *"Did you ever face a problem without having full information on how to solve it?"*

☑ *"Discuss a time where you had to change your plans or course of action in order to solve a problem."*

☑ *"Tell me about your biggest failure or mistake? How did you bounce back from it?"*

☑ *"Tell me about a setback you experienced and how you dealt with it."*

Content elements you include should demonstrate the following:

☑ *You are ambitious and dedicated to achieving a certain goal.*

☑ *You can pursue several goals at the same time, or you can handle multiple priorities in parallel.*

☑ *You are intrinsically motivated and not pushed by external factors.*

☑ *To achieve your desired outcome, you overcome obstacles, face headwinds, or setbacks.*

☑ *You are adaptable to changing situations or circumstances.*

☑ *You follow goals with energy and passion under time pressure.*

☑ *You surpass even your own expectations in the end.*

☑ *You come up with ingenious solutions and ideas that help you achieve your goals.*

☑ *You engage other people to support you along the way.*

If taking the initiative is the focus of the story:

☑ Discuss how you started something from scratch, either because you saw potential for impact or because of your passion for the topic.

☑ Describe how you participated in something that already exists, furthering its cause by adding value and creating impact.

☑ Talk about why you wanted to do it (e.g., *"I felt the need for something but there was no supply of it so far."*).

☑ Talk about how you overcame various obstacles and setbacks.

Personal impact and convincing

Questions that gauge your interpersonal skills:

☑ *"Describe a situation when you had a disagreement or conflict with a teammate."*

☑ *"Discuss a situation where you had to persuade or influence someone."*

☑ *"Tell me about a time when you disagreed with your manager or boss."*

☑ *"Was there ever a situation where you did not get along with a manager, colleague, or client and, if yes, how did you resolve it?"*

Content elements you include should demonstrate:

☑ how you persuade a group or individual to adopt a certain idea or plan of yours (this does not imply that they like you); the idea can be unpopular but lead to a necessary decision, recommendation, or collaboration

☑ how you get everyone on board and create a sustainable way of working, a constructive working environment, or even a definite solution to a difficult problem

☑ how you are able to understand different personalities, needs, concerns, incentives, and motivations, and based on that, tailor your arguments to make people change their mind

☑ how you had to change your approach after a setback. Including a setback or several setbacks makes your story more interesting.

Team player

Questions that gauge your team player attitude:

☑ *"When working in a team, what role do you usually play?"*

☑ *"Tell me about your last teamwork experience."*

☑ *"Discuss a situation where you prioritized the needs of the team over yours."*

☑ *"What makes effective teams, and how do you contribute to that?"*

☑ *"What do you do if your team is facing a crisis?"*

☑ *"Tell me about a situation where not everyone was contributing equally on a team project. How did you handle it?"*

Content elements you should include:

☑ As a team player, show that you rank your own goals below the team's goals.

☑ Show that you are willing to make sacrifices for the greater good of the team.

☑ Highlight that you are an integral part of a team and well respected.

☑ Discuss how your contributions are highly valued by all members of the team and the leadership (if you are not the leader in this situation) as well as potential outsiders you are dealing with.

When asked about your team participation, this does not necessarily have to be in an official leadership role. Similar characteristics and story items might work as described above for the leadership skill since consultants are natural leaders (on a micro or macro scale depending on their role and the project). You should not be the silent team member who takes no initiative. Clarify with the interviewer if they are interested in your leadership or team player skills and adapt your presentation accordingly.

Integrity and work ethic

Questions that gauge your integrity and work ethic:

☑ *"Did you ever work on a project or goal that went against your convictions?"*

☑ *"Tell me about a situation where it was difficult for you to be honest and transparent."*

☑ *"Did you ever find a colleague doing something wrong and, if yes, how did you react?"*

☑ *"Did you ever work with a manager or team you disagreed with?"*

☑ *"Tell me about a situation where you prioritized your client or customer over your firm or team."* (For instance, by making the team work one extra day to improve the analysis or recommendation.)

Content elements you should include:

☑ Demonstrate that you follow a very clear and distinct code of ethics and values, just like top-tier consulting firms do.

☑ Discuss situations where you needed to demonstrate your adherence to the highest personal and professional standards.

☑ Highlight how you stood by your values in the given situation.

- ☑ Emphasize that you always play by the rules and conduct yourself ethically all the time.
- ☑ Potentially discuss elements relating to convincing and teamplay (see above).

Resilience and working under pressure

Questions that gauge your resilience:

- ☑ *"Tell me about a time when you had to work with a difficult client, customer, or team member."*
- ☑ *"Tell me about a decision you or the team made that was not received well."*
- ☑ *"How do you deal with stress, pressure, and long working hours?"*
- ☑ *"Tell me about a project where you worked overtime. How did you go about it?"*
- ☑ *"Guide me through your decision-making logic based on a challenging example."*
- ☑ *"Tell me about a tough situation when you had to decide immediately on a difficult subject."*
- ☑ *"Did you ever make a wrong decision and, if yes, what was the impact?"*

Content elements you should include:

- ☑ Show that you can deal with difficult situations and decisions as well as long working hours similar to what consultants face on a daily basis.
- ☑ Discuss how you can prioritize what is right, even in difficult situations.
- ☑ Highlight that, if you make a mistake, you are quick to course-correct and treasure what you have learned from the situation.
- ☑ Elaborate on how you have handled tough situations in the past and how resilience made you come out of it stronger.
- ☑ Potentially add some elements I discuss for convincing and ambition (see above).

Communication

Questions that gauge your communication skills:

- ☑ *"What type of communicator are you?"*

- ☑ *"Do you prefer top-down or bottom-up communication?"*
- ☑ *"Is it easy for you to talk to people or present to people?"*
- ☑ *"Did you ever present on the spot without any preparation. How did it go?"*
- ☑ *"Tell me about a situation in which you had to communicate top-down/bottom-up."*
- ☑ *"Did you ever encounter any challenge bringing your message across?"*
- ☑ *"Tell me about a situation where you had a difficult conversation with a teammate, your manager, or a client/customer."*
- ☑ *"Provide one example about a time you prepared a speech or presentation for a private event or your job."*

Content elements you should include:

- ☑ Show that you are an expert communicator and facilitator by adjusting your message to the occasion, e.g., presenting bottom-up when explaining something or presenting top-down when discussing action items.
- ☑ Highlight that you can provide insights and lead discussion on the spot without too much preparation.
- ☑ Discuss how you tailor your message to the audience and different personalities, making sure to convey your message in the most effective manner.

Now that we have covered some important personal fit traits and skills packaged into stories, let's look at important characteristics that are the same for every story.

What are the characteristics of a good story?

Even if your stories do not need to portray you as superhuman, you still want them to make you shine in the best possible light and, more importantly, in a light that appeals to consulting interviewers. To achieve that, here are a few pointers that can make your stories more interesting, more engaging, and stronger overall:

- ☑ Every story needs to be concise and to the point as well as communicated in a top-down manner. You do not have a lot of time to talk, so focus on the core part that makes you stand out.

☑ Every story follows a clear story arc, including a brief context, then a focus on your actions to display certain traits and skills, followed by a successful outcome.

☑ You should be able to answer questions about the story without thinking for too long. If people start to think about the answers, I can usually tell that the stories are made up.

☑ You want your stories to take place in challenging environments.

    a. You might have encountered several obstacles or problems, which you decided to overcome with persistence, creativity, or hard work

    b. You might have encountered some resistance from people involved

    c. The odds were not in your favor, but you came out as a winner in the end.

☑ For behavioral stories, setbacks that you overcame improve the impression the interview has about you, and your stories are automatically considered stronger and more memorable.

☑ Talk about experiences from different contexts. Do not take all your stories from a single experience or role as consultancies are interested in candidates that show consistency in achievements and successes across different life stages.

☑ When talking about the context, keep it short. Of course, interviewers need to understand the context, which can usually be discussed in a couple of sentences. However, they are more interested in what you did in a situation to properly evaluate your actions and draw conclusions about your skills and character traits. Hence, focus on actions you took to overcome challenges.

☑ Have at least two stories per character trait or skill at hand, as sometimes you must talk about a particular trait or skill in several interviews in a row. Duplicates are usually not allowed. Sometimes, you might even have to tell two stories about the same trait in one interview. This is usually the case when the interviewer was not particularly satisfied with your first story.

[28] Ask the interviewer the right questions at the end

As the interview wraps up, you usually get a chance to ask the interviewer a few questions. While the questions you ask have no bearing on your interview outcome – outliers excluded – you should not neglect them. Think about what you would like to know beforehand and come prepared to the interviews.

Why should you make the most of this opportunity?

Now that the tables have turned and you are in the interviewer role, use this opportunity to your advantage. Get to know more about the firm, even after all the research you have done so far and all the personal connections you have made to get to this stage.

If you ask similar questions to all interviewers within and across firms, you should get a good range of answers to help you assess in greater detail the different companies and your fit with their culture and their people.

If you consider the advice provided in this book, employ the habits and techniques I teach, and prepare effectively, you should be able to choose from several high-quality top-tier offers. If you get a bunch of offers, you want to make sure to select the firm with the best fit. In the long term, this influences your satisfaction with the job as well as your performance and career progression the most. You must make sure to choose the place where you would like to work long hours day-in, day-out over a couple of years. For that matter, pay attention to the softer factors during the recruiting process and pick up all information and details necessary to make an informed decision.

The goal of your questions should be to get a benefit and real value out of the answers. One way to achieve this is to ask the interviewer personal questions, e.g. how they like the job, instead of generic questions that could be answered within one minute of browsing the company's website. Avoid asking questions that you might think sound smart only to impress the interviewers. They can smell that a mile away and the answers might not help you decide or help get you smarter about your fit with the company and its people. Focus on asking questions where you are genuinely interested in the answer.

What questions could you ask the interviewer?

In general, most questions are okay to ask if they are not too personal. If it is related to their journey to consulting and their life in the industry, ask everything you want to know more about. For instance:

- ☑ Ask about the case, e.g., *"Was the case you have given me based on a real-life assignment? If yes, how did it end, what did you recommend, and was the client satisfied? How did the implementation turn out?"*
- ☑ Ask something about their area of expertise, which is usually related to the case that you have discussed (e.g., recent trends, disruptions, news). You will see the resume of your interviewers before the interview, so you should know about their focus areas and expertise.
- ☑ Ask about their journey in the company. How did they progress through the ranks? Did they switch offices? Were they staffed globally, locally, or regionally?
- ☑ Ask about their own recruiting journey and what they did before joining the firm.
- ☑ Ask questions about the firm's strategy and areas which are not available on public sources, yet not confidential (e.g., office expansion plan, geographic changes, industry or functional focus areas, recent changes, outlook).
- ☑ Ask about staffing, the review process, and training opportunities available for new hires or experienced hires.
- ☑ Ask about the work-life balance and how they are handling it. Many candidates stay away from this question, yet it is worthwhile to ask and get different opinions on that important matter.
- ☑ *"How has the work and travel situation changed with the pandemic?"* What is their outlook on working at the client site vs. remotely from the firm's office for the next years?

- ☑ Ask what they are passionate about outside of work or how they use their time off to recharge.
- ☑ Ask about what they enjoy the most about the company culture.
- ☑ Ask about what they think are some of the toughest aspects of the job.

PART 11

Storytelling with the SCORE Framework: Give Your Most Impactful Answers

In this section I cover the following two questions:

- ☑ How can you set up and draft your stories in a structured manner?
- ☑ How should you communicate those stories to your interviewers most effectively?

Storytelling is one of the most important aspects in consulting. When preparing your longer-form stories for the personal fit part, I would recommend you approach it in two steps. First, create an interesting summary for your story that captures the attention of the interviewer. Second, draft the details of your story using the SCORE framework that I have developed and present in this part. You can use the summary and the SCORE framework to help you select and draft the right stories, as well as remember and structure them when talking to the interviewer.

[29] Tease your story with a brief summary

When asked to talk about a situation where you have demonstrated a character trait or skill, start out by summarizing the story in a headline and three key sentences. Every sentence in this part of the interview should add value to your story. Stay away from empty words, phrases, or filler sentences. Give each story a poignant headline (see an example below), so both you and the interviewer can remember it easily and the interviewer gets a memorable anchor to link to your face. Then, convey the key message in three sentences:

- ☑ **Situation:** what was the situation like?
- ☑ **Complication:** what issues did you face?
- ☑ **Resolution:** how did you overcome them?

When you provide a concise overview of your story, you convey the key message without rambling and allow the interviewer to state preferences regarding your story early on. They might want to dig deeper into your story or not. This is important because some stories might not fit the question, or the interviewer thinks that they are not interesting or impactful enough. In such cases, they can ask you about a different story without wasting too much time.

This brief introduction provides a background and sets the tone and stage for deeper discussions. You work both for yourself and the interviewer as you make it easier for you to talk about the individual sections of your story and easier for them to ask you targeted questions. Depending on the questions, you can highlight certain parts of a story or focus more on the specific traits and elements the interviewer wants to hear about.

[30] Dive into your story using the SCORE framework

If the interviewer is okay with your short summary and wants to hear more, they might ask you more specific questions or ask you to elaborate, usually starting with the context. At this point, use the SCORE framework as the backbone for your storytelling. I developed the SCORE approach, and I recommend it to all my clients. It is especially useful when you want to prepare and think deeply about all aspects of a situation to make sure not to forget anything while at the same time focusing on all the points the interviewer wants to hear. Also, the SCORE framework provides an anchor for a natural flow of explanation and thought during the interview.

Situation	Complication	Outcome expectation	Remedial action	End result
• What situation did you find yourself in? • Describe the context and your role	• What complication(s) did you face? • Explain the problem you had to deal with	• What would have been the outcome? • Discuss the consequences if no action taken	• What did you do to resolve the situation? • Explain your actions and your rationale	• How did the situation eventually end? • Discuss your impact and the success

■ The SCORE framework for personal fit stories

- ☑ **Situation:** Start with a brief description of the situation, focusing on your role and the context.
- ☑ **Complication:** Briefly highlight the issues you faced and discuss why the situation was challenging.
- ☑ **Outcome expectation:** Build suspense by highlighting the worst possible outcome if you had not intervened and acted.
- ☑ **Remedial action:** Discuss – in detail – your actions and behaviors to overcome all challenges; this is the core part of every story where you should spend the most time and include the most details and examples.

☑ **End result:** Briefly discuss the successful outcome of the situation.

Let's look at one example: Jane is asked by her interviewer to talk about a specific situation where she demonstrated leadership skills.

She answers: *"In my role as a product manager with my previous employer, I stepped up to lead a team of five people to prepare and hold a board presentation when my manager was on sick leave* **(HEADLINE)**. *My team had to present a strategy document in front of the board* **(SITUATION)**. *My boss got sick the day before and was not able to direct and structure the work for us, which could have resulted in a bad situation for my department* **(COMPLICATION)**. *I stepped up to guide the team to prepare a stellar presentation for the board on the next day* **(RESOLUTION)."**

The interviewer is intrigued by this short prompt and asks for details. Now Jane can go into the SCORE framework. The focus should be on her role and what she did to solve the situation, the *remedial action*!

She says: *"We had an important bi-annual board meeting scheduled, which my boss was driving. I had one work stream to prepare, as did all five other product managers on the team* **(SITUATION)**.

"On the crucial day before the meeting, my boss got sick, which initially brought our work to a grinding halt. She structured and coordinated our work, helped with problem-solving, and integrated all our work streams into a final presentation **(COMPLICATION)**.

"If we had stopped at this stage, we would have presented a non-aligned 80% version, leaving out crucial details of our progress and success stories. This would have reflected negatively on our team and each of us individually. The result would have been potential budget cuts in our department for next year **(OUTCOME EXPECTED)**.

"So, I had to step in and fill the role of my boss. I performed five key tasks to remedy the situation: First, I had to calm the team down, specifically Mark, a junior product manager, who freaked out. I held a short pep talk to improve everyone's mood and motivate the team. I grabbed Mark to get a coffee and discuss his concerns. I reassured him that everything would be fine.

"Second, I took 30 minutes in private to devise a strategy on how we could continue. I met the team to redelegate tasks, with me basically taking over the role of my boss and distributing the final tasks of my

workstream to two other colleagues. I knew that those two colleagues, Angela and Sam, were the most senior and could handle the additional pressure. I also scheduled two problem-solving sessions to align during the day and on the next morning. At this point, the team was happy that someone had taken the lead and stepped up.

"The third point is that one colleague was kind of confrontational, so I had to pull him in a one-on-one to discuss his concerns and mediate a conflict with another teammate. After telling him in a friendly but firm manner that now was not the time for disagreements, John agreed, apologized, and went back to work.

"Fourth, I integrated all aspects of the presentation throughout the day as I was receiving everyone's input and wrote speaker notes for each of them.

"The fifth point is that at the end of the day, I had to coach one colleague on my model so he could get the right output. It was Mark, who struggled with a specific part of the analysis since he had never done anything similar before. He was very happy with my help and was able to continue on his own after a bit of time and targeted advice **(REMEDIAL ACTION)**.

"The next day, due to my guidance and their hard work, my team had a stellar presentation in front of the board and was able to answer all the questions and challenges we received. The budget for next year was increased. We were all super happy and I took the team out for drinks in the evening **(END RESULT)."**

The interviewer will tell you quite soon in which direction your story should go and what parts you should focus on in the interest of time. The SCORE framework is extremely useful in this case.

Be aware that at firms such as McKinsey, interviewers might go very deep into each situation and ask specific questions such as, *"What did this person say?"*, *"How did this make you feel?"*, etc. Be prepared to talk about all aspects of a specific situation on a deeper level. For instance, based on the story above, the interviewer could ask: *"You said you had a confrontational colleague. Why was he confrontational and how did you approach this situation specifically? What did he say and what did you tell him? How was it resolved?"* If prompted to go into more depth, answer the question in a concise and top-down manner. If the interviewers want more details, they'll steer you in the right direction.

Remember exactly what happened in each situation. By asking

targeted questions, experienced interviewers can smell made up stories and overly crafted answers a mile away. If you have prepared just a few sentences or bullet points per SCORE letter (instead of writing full stories in long-form text), you are well prepared. You know what to say at the right time without sounding rehearsed.

I don't recommend writing down long-form stories but sticking to the most important bullet points for each letter of the SCORE framework. Create a table to prepare your individual stories in an organized manner. Finally, rehearse your answers with friends and peers. Let them play an active role and ask tricky questions to simulate a real-life interview situation.

<Character trait>	Job	Job	University	University	Extracurricular	Extracurricular
<Headline>						
Situation						
Complication						
Resolution						
Situation						
Complication						
Outcome Expectation						
Remedial Action						
End Result						

■ Consulting fit interview story template

PART 12

The McKinsey Personal Experience Interview: Prepare Deep and Impactful Stories

The McKinsey Personal Experience Interview (PEI) is one of the most talked-about aspects in consulting applications. It differs significantly from the personal fit interview conducted by other consulting firms. While the content of the interview has not changed in many years, most candidates are still a bit lost when it comes to preparing for it.

If you research via Google, most results present myths or half-truths that unnerve you in the best case and have you prepare irrelevant answers to non-existing questions, missing the actual point of these interviews in the worst case. There are even McKinsey case coaches out there that prey on people's limited knowledge about the PEI and talk about *"the 25 questions that cover 95% of the PEI."* There are not 25 questions. **There are four dimensions of the PEI and that is it.**

In this part of the book, I want to demystify the PEI and provide you with my insights from hearing well over 1,000 PEI stories in my career. I want to highlight what it really is about, how you can prepare most effectively for it, and how to answer the questions in the most impactful way possible.

[31] Understand how McKinsey employs the PEI

Only one percent of McKinsey applicants receive an offer from the firm. While the case interviews play an important part in the evaluation, the PEI is equally important. You can ace five cases in a row, but if you fail to demonstrate your leadership skills or your ability to influence senior leaders, you will not receive the offer.

I have noticed that many candidates focus ninety-five percent of their preparation efforts on the case and completely neglect their PEI stories. This is unfortunate since this is the part of the interview that is easy to prepare for and ace if you know what you are doing. During the interview, you do not want to remember a specific situation for the first time or make up stories on the spot, but rather remind yourself of your prepared answers. You want to make sure that these answers are structured, to the point, and exactly hit the dimensions that the questions try to assess. In the following I use *dimensions* and *traits* interchangeably.

McKinsey interviews are highly standardized across the globe to ensure objectivity and reduce bias. That is why they consist of the same two main components in each office, the Problem Solving Interview (what other firms call the case interview), and the Personal Experience Interview.

At its core, the McKinsey Personal Experience Interview is a behavioral interview, yet it comes with a twist. Instead of asking many rapid-fire questions like in a typical personal fit interview (e.g., *"What are your strengths? Weaknesses? Why consulting? Why McKinsey?"*) it revolves around three specific character traits that are discussed in great detail. Each Personal Experience Interview focuses on one specific trait at a time and can last up to 20 minutes. In the interviewing process, you must talk about three different traits, one per interview. Since for full-time positions you usually have at least five interviews, some traits might appear twice. More specifically, the dimensions covered are:

- ☑ Entrepreneurial Drive or Courageous Change
- ☑ Inclusive Leadership
- ☑ Personal Impact.

For that matter, PEIs always start with one question related to one of the desired traits. For instance, the interviewer might ask a very specific question such as *"Tell me about a time where you had to influence someone."* Based on this question, you need to present your story. The PEI is highly standardized to help interviewers understand how you behaved in past events to make assumptions about how you would handle daily situations as a McKinsey consultant in the future. The format helps to evaluate and compare candidates on a few objective metrics in the same manner as the McKinsey case interview. Now that you understand what the PEI is and how it is conducted, let's look at the perfect stories.

[32] Tell the perfect stories

A common misconception is that you need to be superhuman or present superhuman success stories in the PEI to make the cut. This is far from the truth. You need to present authentic situations that demonstrate how you achieved your goals, led teams, and influenced people in somewhat challenging circumstances. The stories need to show how you acted in a specific situation, set in a professional environment (e.g., a previous work engagement or internship), a university experience, or during an extracurricular activity. To succeed, your role is to tell the right stories within the right context. You should highlight only the most relevant content of the situation, convey how you displayed a specific trait in the best possible way, support your story with tangible examples of your actions and interactions with other people, and use the most effective communication and storytelling techniques. The closer the stories are to the consultant's typical challenges, the better.

What are the right stories for the PEI?

As briefly touched upon above, the PEI revolves around four different types of stories. Below, let's look at each dimension and potential content ideas that make for a strong story. One word of caution before I go into more detail. Use these as examples to inspire your own storytelling. *These are just examples*. While the format is standardized and the evaluation criteria are the same across the globe, your stories still need to show authenticity and a large portion of "uniqueness". Having overly prepared and rehearsed stories is as bad as having no prepared stories at all. Interviewers are trained to spot crafted stories. Not every story needs to contain every element I discuss below. Pick stories that contain a couple of relevant elements, discuss them in detail with concrete examples, and you're good to go. Also, there are multiple ways to demonstrate the different content elements. Tailor it to your situation. Now, let's get to it.

1. Inclusive Leadership

The interviewer asks you about a situation where you led a team through a challenging time to achieve a certain goal. For this dimension, you need to show that you

- ☑ can handle a diverse group that accepts you as their leader, with diversity being the result of different backgrounds, cultures, hierarchy levels, etc.
- ☑ make an effort to understand each team members strengths, weaknesses, needs, and concerns
- ☑ tailor your leadership style to different groups and group members
- ☑ have the ability to make the team succeed by helping to structure, divide, and delegate tasks and providing them with work plans, deadlines, and effective communication tools (including, for example, setting meeting agendas)
- ☑ motivate your team, improve the team spirit and the working environment for everyone involved
- ☑ are interested in the well-being of the team and their own individual development
- ☑ deal with potential conflicts between teammates effectively
- ☑ create an inclusive atmosphere that caters to individual needs, champions diversity, and inspires the best contribution from all team members.

Overall, showcase that your presence as a team leader has a positive impact on the team and leads to a strong outcome of a project or task. You do not need to be the formal leader of a team. You can also be an unofficial leader of a group or someone who steps up in the face of a challenge to coordinate and manage a team. This is not a story about problem-solving but about creating an environment that allows your team to solve a problem.

2. Entrepreneurial drive

For this dimension, the interviewer asks you about a situation where you set a goal for yourself and achieved it against all odds. You need to demonstrate

- ☑ ambition and dedication by pursuing the goal on top of other commitments you have at the same time

☑ an intrinsic desire and motivation to achieve this goal

☑ that you can quickly adjust to a new environment, task, and challenge

☑ how you overcome obstacles or face headwinds along the way by coming up with creative and new ideas or approaches

☑ that you are effective at engaging others to help you along the way

☑ how you follow your goals with energy and passion until you reach the outcome by managing your time while at the same time balancing tasks and energy

☑ that you are a self-starter who is able to generate large benefits, value, and positive change and impact for yourself and others.

3. Personal impact

For this dimension, you are asked to discuss how you influenced or persuaded an individual. This can either be about them adopting a certain idea or plan of yours, helping you with your plans, driving something together, etc. after they initially declined or rejected your perspective. Focus on stories that showcase how you

☑ work with challenging individuals, ideally in a more senior position compared to you

☑ are able to read and understand people as well as their personalities

☑ show interest in understanding people's concerns and reservations

☑ are able to convince them by using a mix of arguments tailored to their personality and stance as well as by employing effective communication and persuasion tools tailored to the situation

☑ create a sustainable way of working together, making them agree with your plan of action, or even finding a solution to a difficult problem.

4. Courageous Change

At the time of writing, McKinsey has started to replace the Entrepreneurial Drive dimension with a new dimension called

Courageous Change in a couple of countries. What they want you to talk about is a situation where you faced and maneuvered a significant change or an ambiguous situation, adapting to new circumstances and a setback. You need to demonstrate that you

- ☑ are able to quickly adjust to new situations and change your course of action if needed
- ☑ have the needed self-awareness and resilience to deal with setbacks and stressful environments
- ☑ use challenging situations as a learning and step-up opportunity
- ☑ can act based on the limited or ambiguous information that is available to you
- ☑ overcome obstacles or face headwinds along the way by coming up with creative and new ideas or approaches
- ☑ remain positive throughout the whole experience.

The new dimension is very similar to *Entrepreneurial Drive* and many of your content elements might overlap.

What makes a PEI story stand out?

Besides showcasing the relevant traits for each dimension through real-life examples, other characteristics enhance every story universally. To make your strong stories stand out, include the following elements:

- ☑ Think about situations set in challenging environments. You might have encountered several obstacles, which you decided to overcome with persistence, grit, and hard work. Ideally, you have encountered resistance and setbacks. The odds were not in your favor, but you came out as a winner in the end, whether this happened while pursuing your own set goal, dealing with changing circumstances while working with a team, or persuading someone.
- ☑ Provide a brief but exhaustive context for every story, then focus on how you worked through all challenges. One to two minutes are enough to cover the situation and the context. Eighty to ninety percent of the content should be about your own actions that resolved the situation and led to a positive outcome.

☑ Introduce all characters of a story. For instance, if you describe how you influenced a senior leader, first introduce them, and discuss their character and your relationship with them in a couple of sentences. Introduce your team in a leadership story. Add names to make it more tangible and personal.

☑ Focus on your own actions all the time. The interviewer is almost exclusively interested in how your contributions, actions, and behaviors changed the outcome. Everything needs to start and end with you and your own actions. Avoid extensive use of *"we"* and *"us"*; rather build sentences with *"I"* and *"my."*

☑ Do not go too deep into any technicalities. The focus is on your actions and interactions as well as your relationships with other people, not on extensive problem-solving, especially for *Personal Impact* and *Inclusive Leadership*. For the latter, you don't want to discuss how you solved the problem but how you created an environment for the team that allowed them to work on the problem effectively.

☑ Add personal statements and direct quotes from yourself and others involved in the situations. Think about what was said during your interactions, how people reacted, etc.

☑ Create a convincing headline or three-sentence summary that conveys the core message to instantly capture the attention of the interviewer and to make sure that the story won't be rejected right from the start. Your headline sentence should summarize the core part of the story. For instance, when talking about a leadership story a bad headline would be: *"I helped my employer define a new sales strategy."* A strong headline must include that you were leading a diverse team, consisting of at least a couple of people. The project you are working on is important to mention for the context but less relevant for the actual evaluation of your *Inclusive Leadership* skills: *"In my role as sales coordinator with employer X, I stepped up to lead a diverse team of seven sales managers to create and implement a new sales strategy."*

Now that you know what content is desirable for the PEI, let's look at how you can select the right stories from your resume.

How should you select your own personal stories?

When you go through your resume to select your PEI stories, you need to think about three aspects in the following order of importance:

1. **Fit with the actual dimension.** The stories need to fit the criteria set out by McKinsey to match with *Entrepreneurial Drive*, *Courageous Change*, *Inclusive Leadership*, and *Personal Impact*. See above for potential content ideas that are fitting.
2. **Diversity of experience.** Select stories from different areas of your life, e.g., jobs and career highlights, university experiences, and extracurricular engagements. Do not take all stories from one experience or a single situation and context.
3. **Recency.** In general, the more recent the better. Unless you interview for an experienced hire or more senior position, your stories should not date back more than two to three years.

Select and develop six stories based on the criteria and content elements mentioned above as you should have at least two stories per character trait at hand, because sometimes you must talk about a particular trait in several subsequent interviews. Duplicates are not allowed in most offices, meaning you cannot tell the same story twice to different interviewers. In some cases, you must tell two stories about the same trait in one interview. This is usually the case when the interviewer is not particularly satisfied with your first story, which should not happen if you follow the advice here. Your HR contact will tell you whether you need to prepare for *Entrepreneurial Drive* or *Courageous Change* in advance.

How detailed should your stories be?

When going through one story, you should highlight all the important aspects of the story by yourself. As a rule of thumb, interviewers usually ask more questions if:

- ☑ some elements of the story are unclear or confusing, e.g., when you are talking about someone without introducing them properly
- ☑ you do not volunteer important aspects and crucial parts of your story, e.g., by touching only the surface of the actions

you took and not discussing individual situations or examples on a deep enough level

☑ you do not hit relevant talking points that McKinsey wants to hear for a specific dimension, e.g., by focusing too much on how you were solving a problem from a conceptual angle instead of discussing your interactions with the team.

The more details you leave out, the less relevant your talking points, and the less structured your story is, the more questions you should expect.

When you introduce the story, keep the context brief, and focus 80% to 90% of your talking points on your actions and behaviors. Interviewers want to understand what YOU did to remedy the situation and how YOUR actions led to a successful outcome. Focus on a few specific pivotal moments that were crucial to reach a conclusion or outcome. The PEI is all about the depth of a story – two to four concrete actions discussed in detail – and not about being broad, talking a lot about the context and touching many small actions on a surface level. For these pivotal moments, go deep, remember your actions, the interactions, the discussions, your thoughts, etc. Add statements of people involved to enhance your stories and make them more tangible. The depth of your experience has a much stronger positive impact on your evaluation than listing a variety of different talking points, only scratching the broad surface.

Should you create stories that can be used for every dimension?

You should prepare unique stories for each dimension and not create summary stories that you can use for all dimensions with a few tweaks. I see this often. Before our coaching sessions, some of my clients prepare stories that could be used for each dimension of the PEI by highlighting different elements of the story. What they end up with might be a strong story overall if told to a friend or a different firm but an average story for each dimension McKinsey investigates, not showing the interviewer any performance spike. Craft individual and exclusive stories for each dimension to be considered distinctive.

[33] Set up and communicate your stories the right way

Apart from drafting the right stories with the right content, you need to tell each story in the most impactful manner. Storytelling is one of the key tools for successful management consultants to bring their messages across and increase buy-in within the team and in the organization they are consulting. Stories are used to convert analyses and recommendations into powerful messages to drive change. That is why for the PEI it is essential to communicate your stories effectively.

A tool you can use for this is the SCORE framework I have developed and already introduced earlier (in **Part 11**). I want to repeat it here with a concrete example for candidates who only read this section. Additionally, since PEI stories are usually longer compared to story questions in other consulting firms, I use a slightly different and extended version of the same story. The SCORE framework enables you to best prepare and present compelling top-down stories to your audience and consists of two parts, the introduction and the deep dive.

How should you introduce your PEI story?

In a McKinsey PEI interview, the interviewer asks you to introduce the story to make sure that it covers the right dimension before prompting you to dive deeper into it. Therefore, it is important to start with a punchy headline to create a memorable anchor and already convey the core of the story within one sentence. For instance, when asked about *Inclusive Leadership*, do not start with something like this: *"I was working for a company last year and we had a project to increase the sales of our online platform by 10%. My boss asked me to be part of this effort..."*

The first sentence needs to make clear that the story is appropriate for the relevant dimension in the most top-down and concise way.

Hence, say something along the lines of: *"In my role as Y at Company X, I stepped up to lead a team of seven people last year to increase online sales by 10%."*

If you want to add more details, add three sentences, each answering one of the following questions:

☑ **Situation:** what was the situation like?
☑ **Complication:** what issues did you face?
☑ **Resolution:** how did you overcome them?

Every sentence should add value. Refrain from empty words, phrases, or sentences. This short introduction provides a background and sets the tone and stage for deeper discussions. You work both for yourself and for the interviewer.

Now that you have introduced your story, the interviewer asks you to provide some context and dive deeper. If your summary is appropriate for the dimension, the story will not be rejected.

How should you discuss your story in the most impactful way?

Use the letters of the SCORE framework to discuss your story in more detail. The SCORE framework is especially useful when you want to prepare and think deeply about all aspects of a situation. It provides an anchor for a natural flow of explanation and thought during an interview. I created it after reviewing hundreds of PEI stories. Since then, I have implemented it with hundreds more with great success.

Situation	Complication	Outcome expectation	Remedial action	End result
• What situation did you find yourself in? • Describe the context and your role	• What complication(s) did you face? • Explain the problem you had to deal with	• What would have been the outcome? • Discuss the consequences if no action taken	• What did you do to resolve the situation? • Explain your actions and your rationale	• How did the situation eventually end? • Discuss your impact and the success

■ The SCORE framework for McKinsey PEI stories

The focus of each PEI story should be on the R, the remedial actions. Situation, complication, outcome expectation, and end result should only make up around 10 to 20% of your story. **What the interviewer cares about is how you solved the situation through your actions targeted at the different challenges you faced.**

Let's look at an example covering the introduction and the SCORE letters. Richard is asked by his McKinsey interviewer to talk about a specific situation where he demonstrated inclusive leadership skills.

He answers: *"I led a diverse team of five through a crisis in a last-minute effort to create and hold a board-level presentation when my boss got sick, with the team not knowing what to do in this situation* **(HEADLINE)**. *At my previous employer, we had to present a strategy document in front of the board* **(SITUATION)**. *My boss got sick the day before and was not able to direct and structure the work for us, which could have resulted in a bad situation for my department* **(COMPLICATION)**. *I took over from her, guided the team, and prepared a stellar presentation for the board the next day* **(RESOLUTION)**.*"*

The interviewer is intrigued by this short prompt and asks for more details. Now, Richard can go into the letters of the SCORE framework. The focus is on his role and what he did to solve the situation and overcome the challenges, the *remedial action*!

He says: *"We had an important bi-annual board meeting scheduled, which my boss was driving. I had one workstream to prepare, as did all five other country managers from five different countries on the team* **(SITUATION)**.

"The crucial day before the meeting, my boss got sick, which initially brought our work to a grinding halt. She structured and coordinated our work, helped with problem-solving, and integrated all our work streams into a final presentation **(COMPLICATION)**. *If we had stopped at this stage, we would have presented a non-aligned 80% version, leaving out crucial details of our progress and successes. This would have reflected negatively on our team and each of us individually. The result could have been potential budget cuts in our department for next year* **(OUTCOME EXPECTED)**.

"So, I had to step in and fill the role of my boss. In this situation, I had to overcome six crucial challenges. First, I had to calm the team down and understand everyone's state, specifically Martin, a 27-year-old junior country manager, who freaked out. I remember how he was saying that this would have a bad impact on all of us if it didn't go well.

I wanted to quickly resolve this negative energy and held a short pep talk to improve everyone's mood and motivate the team. I highlighted how in the past our team rose to every challenge, and it always worked out in our favor. I reminded them that we were known in the company as the team that could get everything done.

"I took Martin for a quick coffee and asked him what was bothering him. He told me something along the lines of: 'I am new to this department, and I want to make a good impression. I'm scared that if we fail, it will affect how I'm perceived by the higher-ups, and this might negatively impact my career progression in the future.' I asked him why he thought this would be the case to understand the way he was thinking about the situation. It became clear that he had faced a similar situation in his previous job, which eventually made him leave. I reassured him that this would not be the case here, but I was still expecting him to put in the crucial work for now. As for the rest, I would take care of that with the others. That seemed to alleviate his fear, and I could see his face light up.

"For the rest of the team, I had a group chat to understand what they were working on currently and what was still missing. Once I understood what was going on, I specifically asked if there were any concerns, but everyone seemed less agitated at that point since I'd told them that I would get back to them with a plan.

"Second, I took 30 minutes in private to devise a strategy. I met the team to redelegate tasks with me basically taking over the role of my boss. I distributed the final tasks of my workstream to two other colleagues and provided deadlines. I kept checking with them that the new task distribution made sense, and they agreed with their workloads. I specifically selected those two colleagues since I knew they were the most senior and the most experienced, so they had the capacity to add this to their plate. It was Deepti and Steve, who had both been with the company for a couple of years and were genuinely motivated team players, always trying to get the best outcome for the team. They had done some amazing work over the last couple of months, and I wanted them to shine in front of the board.

"Third, during the day, I was the single go-to person for each team member. Specifically, Armin, an older colleague who has been with the company for 15 years, struggled a bit with his tasks since he was not used to working under pressure. He was very diligent with his work but did not really show any ambition to take on more responsibilities than

what his current role entailed. I sat down with him and broke his work into more manageable smaller chunks to give him some more direction and guidance. I could see that it helped him and left, telling him to give me a call should he get stuck or need anything else. He never called, and he delivered on his promises.

"Fourth, as the team progressed, I scheduled two problem-solving sessions to align during the day and the next morning. They were definitely happy that someone took the lead and stepped up in this situation. During the first session, I redistributed some tasks from Martin to Steve as he was much more comfortable with quantitative analyses. He enjoyed working on this topic and thrived during this difficult time. I also think he enjoyed getting more responsibility and impact on the project outcome because he told me in a private conversation: 'You know, I didn't want to say it in front of the others, but I actually enjoy working on last minute deadlines and I enjoy the work you've asked me to do.' I couldn't help but smile at this statement.

"Fifth, it was not all smooth sailing as one colleague, Bella, was kind of confrontational. She had been with the company for more than 10 years and disagreed with Martin on several content points in the presentation. When I found out, I had to pull her in a one-on-one to discuss her concerns. I found out that the reason was more personal animosity between the two rather than valid content-related points. She felt more senior and, thus, thought that her opinion should count more than that of a new joiner. I asked them both in a room to highlight the fact that, at this stage, there was no space for any kind of fighting on the team and that I'd be happy to sort this out over dinner with them later this week once this was all sorted. That fixed the problem since they both understood the urgency of the situation. I made sure that Martin felt welcome on the team and not pushed too much into a corner because of this since he was new to the company and I'd noticed that he was not experienced in dealing with such kinds of conflicts. I reassured him that he was doing great work and these things could happen in stressful situations.

"Sixth, I integrated all aspects of the presentation throughout the day as I was receiving everyone's input and wrote speaker notes for each of them. I made sure to incorporate and keep the diversity of opinion, meaning I considered some of Bella's and some of Martin's ideas in the final presentation, while streamlining the overall message and visualization **(REMEDIAL ACTION)**.

"The next day, my team and I made a stellar presentation in front of the board and due to the speaker notes I wrote, they were able to answer all questions and challenges we received. The board praised the work and the budget for next year was increased. My team was super happy, and I took them out for drinks in the evening. When my boss returned from her sick leave, she congratulated me on my efforts and the result. She said she knew I had it in me but had hoped that I would have been able to demonstrate it in a less stressful situation. My boss increased my responsibility going forward, and soon after, I was actually promoted, in part due to the short-term firefighting abilities I displayed during these two days **(END RESULT)***."*

The story above is an end-to-end monologue. In a real interview, you won't get far without the interviewer trying to interrupt and steering the story in a particular direction. While you should be able to discuss the story without any directional hints or questions, be flexible enough to highlight certain elements or go deeper into certain aspects if needed. As mentioned earlier, McKinsey interviewers might go very deep into each situation and ask specific questions such as *"What did this person say?"*, *"How did this make you feel?"*, etc. Be prepared to talk about all aspects of a situation.

The story above is strong and more than enough to impress your interviewer. However, it does not contain all the potential content elements of an *Inclusive Leadership* story I discussed earlier; you do not need to cover everything. At the end of the day, you need to craft your own authentic stories based on your experiences that cover some of my talking points, including even more direct quotes and statements than above.

Prepare your stories accordingly, using just a few sentences or bullet points per item of the SCORE framework. This helps you have a clear structure and focused content yet enables you to be flexible enough to move through the story without sounding rehearsed or robot-like.

How should you practice your answers?

Finally, rehearse your answers with friends and peers. Let them play an active role and ask tricky questions to simulate a real-life McKinsey interview situation. Common questions you should prepare for and have your practice partners ask could be:

- ☑️ *"Can you describe this conversation in a bit more detail?"*
- ☑️ *"What happened next?"* or *"What did you do (next) in this situation?"*
- ☑️ *"How did you/he/she/they react?"* or *"What did you/he/she/they say?"*
- ☑️ *"How did this make you feel?"*
- ☑️ *"How was it perceived?"*
- ☑️ *"How did you perceive it?"*
- ☑️ *"What do you think he/she/they felt in this moment?"*
- ☑️ *"Why did you think/act that way?"*
- ☑️ *"Why was this important?"*
- ☑️ *"Why do you think he/she/they said that/acted like that/felt like that?"*

Other than those questions, there are a couple of interviewer best practice questions to ask to get the right information from interviewees. The questions differ for every dimension and are aimed at eliciting relevant and targeted answers from you for their scoring sheet. If you prepare the stories as discussed, you should be able to answer them with ease or won't even receive them since your stories fit the dimensions so well.

Final word: There are no clear guidelines on how interviewers ask about each dimension initially. Usually, it is very clear from their prompt what they want to discuss. However, if you are uncertain, just clarify along the lines of: *"Am I correct in assuming that you want me to talk about a story set in the context of Personal Impact?"*

[34] What is the McKinsey values and purpose interview?

At the time of writing, some McKinsey offices are experimenting with a values and purpose interview. The interview is a conversation about McKinsey's values catalog where you are expected to discuss your most important values – that are in line with McKinsey's – and how you have lived them in a certain situation. McKinsey will let you know in advance if this new assessment is part of your interviews. If it comes up, use the SCORE framework to prepare stories on some of the values, which can be found here: www.mckinsey.com/about-us/overview/our-purpose-mission-and-values

PART 13

Habits, Mindset, and Appearance: Win the Game Before You Get There

A candidate's mindset plays an important role in their performance. I want to share my observations of what separates excellent candidates from poor performers in that regard, as well as provide you with insights into the appropriate dress code. Adopting the right attitude and dressing well can help you tackle the challenge with confidence and ease. In this effort, I answer four questions:

☑ What are the mindset and character traits of successful applicants?
☑ How can you connect with the interviewer?
☑ How should you deal with a stress interview?
☑ How should you dress for your interviews and what else should you bring?

[35] Work on the right mindset

What are the character traits of successful applicants?

Besides strong problem-solving and storytelling skills, successful interviewees share a certain attitude and mindset. The following criteria are not always directly evaluated by the scoring cards of consulting interviewers, yet they play an important role in your performance and how you are perceived, which in turn impacts the hiring decision.

Confidence. Case interviews are a stressful endeavor. You might have invested five years into your degree and worked through several tough internships just so you can get your dream job at McKinsey. Now you put an enormous amount of pressure on yourself to pass the interviews. While everyone feels that pressure and interviewers are very aware of this (they have gone through the same process and see it with every candidate), a sure-fire way to bomb your interview is to appear overly nervous or stressed. Interviewers test if they can put you in front of a senior client, who might not be as nice as they are, without you having a public freak-out.

All successful candidates I have seen meet a minimum threshold of confidence in their abilities. They are markedly calmer as they listen, communicate, and move through the case. You might be the smartest person in the room, yet if your voice is trembling or you are constantly asking the interviewer if they are fine with your approach, you are hurting your performance and impression big time.

Owning your mistakes. The fastest way to get rejected during a case interview is not owning your mistakes. Interviewers want you to succeed, hence, intervene and provide hints if needed to bring you back on track early on. The worst thing that I still see often in coaching sessions is when interviewees become defensive about a mistake. They might play it down, urging that what I was saying is what they meant in the first place, or that it is what they have on their paper, yet they just communicated it the wrong way. Sometimes they highlight that they were about to get to that specific point (coincidentally after five minutes of rambling about something else).

Even worse is when the interviewer gives feedback and the candidate pushes back, arguing about who is right or wrong. Such candidates are instantly rejected in the interviewer's mind and likely will never be invited again, even with significant improvements to their resume. Strong candidates who get an offer are not flawless. They make mistakes too. The difference is that they own them, thank the interviewer for the clarification, adopt the help, and move on with confidence as if nothing had happened.

Authenticity. It is okay not to know everything. In fact, during case interviews you are required to clarify if something is unclear, just as you would in a real-world problem-solving session or conversation with a client or your team. Great candidates have no problem admitting that they do not know something. They are fine with asking and having the interviewers explain a concept in detail. Based on their newly appreciated understanding they are able to work on the case and develop sound recommendations. The opposite are candidates who are too afraid to ask, fearing that not-knowing something might make them look bad. They try to solve the case based on their limited understanding and fail considerably more often than their more authentic peers.

Humbleness. Great candidates solve the case in a down-to-earth manner. They are curious about the problem and how they can solve it, displaying an inquisitive nature. They are humble in the process. The opposite are candidates, usually from a highly prestigious school or program, who have prepared well with the best resources available and believe that they have seen every case there is and they know it all. Apart from solving the case, they engage in impression management to make their effort seem easy and flawless, up to extremes saying constantly how easy they think the case is. Get rid of the entitlement, attitude, and focus on solving the problem. Great problem solvers are often rejected if they attend case interviews with such an attitude, most often by partners who do not tolerate such behaviors on their teams.

Can-do attitude and proactivity. Excellent interviewees are usually excited to get going on the case. They have an investigative mindset and enjoy solving problems. For them, the case is more of a joint discussion than a one-sided evaluation. They communicate in an open manner, sharing their thinking along the way, as well as thinking ahead about where to move next. Such candidates are much less intimidated by the process since they enjoy working on it. Those that enjoy working through case interviews and solving business problems also find enjoyment on the job later on.

If you think that case interviews are tedious, boring, or just painful, you might want to reconsider your career aspirations. Similarly, proactive candidates develop their own solutions. There is a significant difference in the performance and in offer rates between candidates who learn how to think like a consultant and who develop their logical reasoning skills, and interviewees, who solely rely on memorized frameworks and apply them to cases in a reactive manner. There are no shortcuts to success.

How can you connect with the interviewer?

While consulting firms strive to conduct objective interviews, subjectivity and personal liking still play a role in candidate evaluation. Hence, it is important to connect with interviewers on a personal level as this makes you more likable in their eyes and eases some of the stress of the situation for you. I remember my third interview with McKinsey, where the interviewer and I laughed together and made jokes while working toward a case solution. It did not even feel like a real interview but collaborative problem-solving, and we both enjoyed it. While this is not the standard experience (my other five McKinsey interviews were more formal), it still showed me the importance of connecting with an interviewer very early on in my career, something I have spotted many times since from the other side of the table. To connect with the interviewer, you can actively pay attention to the following things.

Focus on commonalities. Interviewers are often paired with candidates based on certain commonalities (e.g., same university, same previous employer, same interests). Read through their resume before the interview and touch upon your shared experience or interests. (*"I saw you also graduated from XYZ. How did you like it, and did you also take the crazy class with professor ABC? I have some fun memories of that"*). Such conversation pieces are great for breaking the ice.

Appear friendly and open. Smile and keep your body language open, i.e., do not cross your arms in front of your body. Listen attentively and mirror your interviewer's posture, gestures, and expressions. Keep a healthy level of eye contact. Speak slowly and with passion, avoiding a monotonous voice. You may want to record yourself during case practice to identify flaws in your presentation.

Ask engaging questions. At the end of the interview, ask engaging questions. More on that in **Chapter 28**.

How can you deal with a stress interview?

What happens if the interviewer tries to stress or challenge you on purpose?

See it as a game. When interviewers try to stress you during the interview or are not friendly, ninety-five percent of the time, it is a pressure test to see how you react to it. Play along, just as you would in a daily life situation when dealing with a difficult person. Remember to stay confident and calm, stick to your case habits, stand your ground (unless you really made a mistake and they are pointing it out), and keep your friendly attitude. Trying to please them or trying to increase your likability will not have any impact on their interviewing style.

The remaining five percent who behave this way are just unprofessional and conduct the interview badly because they had a bad day or it's just their personality. What should you do about this?

Follow the same approach. Focus on what you can do to solve the case in a confident, calm, and constructive manner. If the interview experience is really bad (e.g., insulting, poor setting with bad connection), I would definitely raise it with HR.

[36] Dress to impress

Appearance is an important aspect for management consultants. Next time you walk around the airport, look around. You can usually spot them a mile away with their tailored outfits and Rimowa or Tumi carry-ons, usually rushing through the airports like there is no tomorrow. Once hired, you represent the legacy of your firm at the client site. Hence, it is important to look the part when you go through the interview process. When walking into top-tier consulting interviews, you do not want anything be left to chance.

How should you dress for your interviews?

Consulting firms are still relatively conservative organizations dealing with serious matters of large client organizations. Just fifteen years ago, it was frowned upon for a male consultant to wear dark brown leather shoes, a partner once told me; only black leather shoes were considered appropriate. Luckily, times are changing, and formal rules and attitudes have become more relaxed. Still, it's best to overdress for the occasion. The table below summarizes your options.

	Men	Women
Key piece	• Suit (neutral: black, navy blue, gray)	• Skirt or trouser suit (neutral: black, navy blue, gray) • Longer skirt or dress pants with blazer or jacket (same colors as above)
Shirt	• Shirt (white or light blue) with a classy tie with a simple knot complementing your outfit	• Blouse (white or light blue)
Shoes	• Leather dress shoes (black or dark brown)	• Flat or with a slight heel, closed toe (matching the colors of the outfit)
Accessories	• Leather belt matching the shoe color • Watch	• Leather belt (if it fits the outfit) • Watch • Jewelry you want to wear

■ Dress code options for your consulting case interview

Whatever you decide to wear, follow these four principles:

1. **You want to feel comfortable.** Some live interview rounds last from 9 a.m. to 5 p.m. Choose something you feel comfortable in looks-wise but also fit-wise.
2. **Keep it subtle and classy**. Keep your statement pieces at home. Stick to classic darker colors for suits, and brighter white or light blue colors for shirts and blouses. Avoid complex patterns. Choose a classic tie and a limited number of subtle accessories.
3. **Wear clothes in the right size.** You do not need to get a tailored piece but avoid clothes which are either too big or too small for you.
4. **If in doubt, overdress rather than underdress.**

If you are unsure about the dress code, reach out to HR to clarify. Often, the dress code is also specified in the email invite to the interviews.

What else is important for your appearance?

Apart from your dress code, what else is important for your appearance? Make sure that you arrive at the interviews in perfect shape, i.e.:

☑ Have a clean haircut (also if your hair is longer) and a trimmed beard or no beard for men.

☑ Wear make-up if you want but do not go overboard for women.

☑ Wear your hair open or in whatever form suits you for women.

☑ Brush your teeth, take a mint, take a shower, and use deodorant beforehand. You will sweat a lot during the interviews.

☑ Avoid strong perfumes or scents as they might not be to everyone's liking.

☑ Avoid chewing gum during the interview.

☑ If the interview is in person, have a firm handshake when introducing yourself to the interviewer.

What else should you bring for the interviews?

For on-site interviews you don't need to bring anything. Some candidates arrive at the office with their application portfolio including their cover letter, resume, references, as well as pens and paper. You don't need any of this. Interviewers have your resume and cover letter printed by HR. They do not care about references at this point. Any paper and pens you need for the interviews are provided by the firm. Most of the time you get a neat recruiting folder, containing a notebook, pens, the resumes of your interviewers, a time plan for the day, as well as some candy or other snacks. Your notes must be handed to the interviewers after each interview as they are destroyed. They don't look at them or analyze them.

To sum this section up, arrive at the interviews in a relatively conservative business professional attire that you feel comfortable in. The interviews are not the time for fashion experiments or bad outfit choices as a flashy appearance might reflect badly on your taste and interpersonal skills, which are relevant in a client-facing role. Ideally, your outfit does not attract any attention, neither positive nor negative. Your interviewers focus on your problem-solving skills, storytelling, and the fit with the company culture.

If you are taking the interviews in the office, arrive early to avoid rushing, adding to the stressful experience. If you are taking the interviews from home via Zoom or similar, you should still dress appropriately as outlined above. Some interviewers might tell you that you can get rid of the suit jacket and the tie during the interview. At home, make sure to have the following items ready as well as your environment primed: a notebook, a couple of extra sheets of paper, a couple of pens, a charged headset or wired headphones, a stable internet connection, and a quiet background. You could also consider placing a couple of cheat sheet printouts strategically in front of you as webcams usually do not record what is on your desk (e.g., my approach to structuring, charts, and math; a fraction table).

On the day before the interview, go to bed early to be fully rested the next day. Make sure you are hydrated and are not interviewing on an empty stomach. Eat something small before the interview, and if you have multiple interviews in succession, have some snacks ready for in-between. For professional hires, try not to schedule any other meetings on the day of the interview.

PART 14

Further Resources and Final Words: Practice What You Have Learned

[37] Further preparation materials

In this section I'll cover additional training materials that should help you on your journey to becoming a top-tier consultant.

StrategyCase.com and personal coaching offering

With the purchase of this book, you are eligible for a 15% discount on all products offered on StrategyCase.com (Code: THE1PERCENT2023).

Resume and cover letter

▶ Resume and cover letter guide and best practice templates:
  strategycase.com/consulting-cover-letter-and-resume-guide/
▶ Personalized application document screening:
  strategycase.com/consulting-cover-letter-and-resume-guide/

Aptitude tests

▶ McKinsey (Imbellus) Solve Game Guide: strategycase.com/
  mckinsey-imbellus-digital-assessment-guide/
▶ BCG Online Case (Casey) Guide: strategycase.com/bcg-online-
  case-chatbot-pymetrics-sparkhire/
▶ Bain Online Test (SOVA) Guide:
  strategycase.com/bain-aptitude-tests-sova-pymetrics-hirevue/
▶ Kearney Recruitment Test Guide:
  strategycase.com/kearney-recruitment-test-guide

Case interview and personal fit interview

▶ **Personal Case and Fit Coaching:**
strategycase.com/florian-coaching
▶ Case Structuring and Brainstorming Drills:
strategycase.com/consulting-structuring-drills/
▶ Case Exhibit Interpretation Drills:
strategycase.com/consulting-chart-drills/
▶ Case interview Math Mastery Course and Drills:
strategycase.com/case-interview-math/
▶ McKinsey Interview Video Academy:
strategycase.com/mckinsey-interviews/
▶ Case Interview Industry Overviews:
strategycase.com/case-interview-industry-cheat-sheets/

Free practice case interview resources

The cases can be used for individual case practice, individual drills (by focusing on the specific elements of the case), and partner mock interview practice.

Firm specific cases

▶ Case collections including real McKinsey, BCG, Bain, Deloitte, Accenture, Kearney, Roland Berger, Oliver Wyman, LEK, OC&C, Capital One and others (I link to StrategyCase.com since the directory of firm-specific cases is updated periodically as the links sometimes change): strategycase.com/practice-cases
▶ Case collection mostly for tier-2, tier-3, boutique, and in-house consultancies (avoid user-generated cases as they are mostly low-quality):
www.preplounge.com/en/management-consulting-cases

Case libraries and university consulting club case collection

Do not pay for existing case libraries. They rehash freely available cases, sometimes of bad quality.
▶ Consulting club case collection (link via StrategyCase.com as I am continuously updating and expanding the library): strategycase.com/practice-cases

Chart interpretation resources

A quick Google search for *"Chart of the day"* yields thousands of results that you can use to practice and hone your chart interpretation skills. To check your insights, compare them with the text of the articles accompanying the charts. Two specific examples:
- www.economist.com/graphic-detail
- www.cnbc.com/chart-of-the-day/

Math preparation apps

Math apps can help you improve your mental math as well as pen-and-paper math skills. For math logic, look at case examples or my math program discussed above.

Apple
- Magoosh Mental Math
- Mental Math Cards Challenge
- Coolmath Games: Fun Mini-Games

Android
- Magoosh Mental Math
- Matix Mental Math Games
- Math Games and Mental Arithmetic

Case interview feedback sheet

Use this for peer practice as directed in **Chapters 5 and 19.**
- strategycase.com/case-interview-feedback-sheet

Free sources to work on business sense and intuition
- Economist: www.economist.com
- Financial Times: www.ft.com
- Bloomberg Business News: www.bloomberg.com
- Your local business news outlets
- McKinsey Global Institute: www.mckinsey.com/mgi/our-research/all-research
- McKinsey Insights: www.mckinsey.com/featured-insights
- BCG Insights: www.bcg.com/featured-insights/thought-leadership-ideas
- Bain Insights: www.bain.com/insights/

▶ Kearney Insights:
www.kearney.com/why-were-different/insights-and-media
▶ Roland Berger Insights: www.rolandberger.com/en/Insights/
▶ Oliver Wyman Insights:
www.oliverwyman.com/our-expertise/insights.html
▶ LEK Insights: www.lek.com/insights
▶ Strategy& Insights:
www.strategyand.pwc.com/gx/en/insights/report-search.html
▶ Accenture Strategy Insights:
newsroom.accenture.com/subjects/strategy/
▶ Accenture Research Blog:
www.accenture.com/us-en/blogs/accenture-research
▶ EY Insights: www.ey.com/en_us/insights
▶ Deloitte Insights: www2.deloitte.com/us/en/insights.html
▶ KPMG Insights: home.kpmg/xx/en/home/insights.html

[38] Final words and contact details

I hope that with this book you've learned both the core concepts and nuanced details to stand out from the millions of applicants that try to enter the top-tier consulting industry every year. Now it is up to you to translate my recommendations and guidance into action and practice to build your case interview skills and prepare fit stories about your best self. Scoring an offer with top-tier consulting firms is no easy feat and demands significant attention, time, and effort, but it is all worthwhile in the end.

I have written this book with the mindset of a practitioner, having gone through more than 1,000 case and fit interviews, as well as answering thousands of questions in direct coaching sessions, via emails, forums, PrepLounge, Quora and other mediums. Based on these experiences, I've covered everything I know about consulting interviews and everything that I know is relevant for your journey. Make it your own and do it your way! I hope my dedication and sincere interest in your success shows.

I started the book with a quote from a McKinsey partner and one of my mentors. I want to end it with a quote from one of my clients in a review that he wrote on PrepLounge recently:

> *"You have to put in the groundwork for him to assist you, and if you do your bit well, Florian will take you the distance."*

Let this book and the advice contained in it take you the distance.

For feedback, personal support, or clarification of concepts discussed in the book, please reach out to florian@strategycase.com or visit StrategyCase.com.

Made in the USA
Las Vegas, NV
18 December 2023

83029547R00193